Cosmetics Marketing Strategy in the Era of the Digital Ecosystem

Young Won Park · Paul Hong

Cosmetics Marketing Strategy in the Era of the Digital Ecosystem

Revolutionizing Beauty in the New Market Frontier

Springer

Young Won Park
Graduate School of Humanities and Social Sciences
Saitama University
Shinjuku City, Tokyo, Japan

University of Tokyo
Tokyo, Japan

Paul Hong
John B. and Lillian E. Neff College of Business and Innovation
The University of Toledo
Toledo, OH, USA

ISBN 978-981-97-3673-7 ISBN 978-981-97-3674-4 (eBook)
https://doi.org/10.1007/978-981-97-3674-4

This Springer imprint is published by the registered company Springer Nature Singapore Pte Ltd.
The registered company address is: 152 Beach Road, #21-01/04 Gateway East, Singapore 189721, Singapore

Executive Summary

In the ever-evolving cosmetics industry, maintaining a competitive edge is not just a choice; it's a necessity. This executive summary distills the essential insights gathered from an exhaustive exploration of cosmetics marketing strategies in the era of digital transformation (DX). Drawing from the wealth of knowledge accumulated in preceding chapters, this summary offers a forward-looking perspective poised to guide cosmetics companies into the future.

At the core of this journey lies Chap. 1, which lays the foundation by illuminating the overarching trends shaping cosmetics marketing strategies. From the burgeoning demand for natural and organic cosmetics to the global phenomenon of clean beauty, these trends underscore a profound shift toward purity, sustainability, and transparency. Consumers now seek products that resonate with their values, setting the stage for a new paradigm in marketing strategies.

Chapters 2–10 constitute the heart of this exploration, offering a comprehensive analysis and real-world case studies that delve into various facets of cosmetics marketing. Topics span the gamut from digital marketing strategies and e-commerce platforms to word-of-mouth marketing and compelling case studies of industry giants like Cosmax, Shiseido, LG Chemical, and Amore Pacific. These chapters provide invaluable insights, illustrating the dynamic and adaptive nature required in the cosmetics industry to thrive in a rapidly changing landscape.

Chapters 11 and 12 emerge as the zenith of this executive summary, synthesizing the collective knowledge gleaned from the preceding chapters. It accentuates the industry's inherent dynamism and the absolute necessity for companies to acclimatize to evolving consumer values and expectations. The outlook for cosmetics marketing strategies in the DX era embodies the industry's commitment to inclusivity, innovation, and sustainability. As the cosmetics industry continues its transformation, the key to success lies in harmonizing strategies with the ever-shifting dynamics of consumer preferences.

In conclusion, the cosmetics industry stands at a pivotal crossroads, characterized by an array of trends and innovative strategies. By embracing these transformative changes and aligning with the evolving values of consumers, cosmetics companies can confidently navigate the era of digital transformation. In doing so, they will not only endure but also thrive with resilience and sustainable growth in this dynamic landscape.

Shinjuku City/Tokyo, Japan Young Won Park, Ph.D.
Toledo, USA Paul Hong, Ph.D., CMA

Contents

About the Authors

Young Won Park is a Professor of the Faculty of Economics, Graduate School of Humanities and Social Sciences at Saitama University and an Endowed Chair Professor of the Management Education and Research Center at the University of Tokyo, Japan. He holds a Ph.D. degree in the Department of Advanced Social and International Studies from the University of Tokyo, Japan. His articles have been published in journals including *Management Decision, International Journal of Production Economics, International Journal of Technology Management, International Journal of Information Management, Business Horizons, Journal of Business Research, Journal of Purchasing and Supply Management, Benchmarking: An International Journal, International Journal of Services and Operations Management, International Journal of Logistics Systems and Management, International Journal of Business Excellence, International Journal of Procurement Management, Akamon Management Review, Japan Academy of International Business Studies, Japanese Society for Science and Technology Studies, and the Japan Society of Information and Communication Research.* He has received research awards including a Certificate for Highly Cited Research in Business Horizons, Dissertation Paper Awards from the Japan Association for Social Informatics (JASI), Best Paper Awards from The Japan Society of Information and Communication Research (JSICR), Research Awards of the Social Science Field from The Telecommunications Advancement Foundation (TAF), and Research Students Awards of the Social Science Field from The Telecommunications Advancement Foundation (TAF). His research interests are in technology management, global strategy and IT strategy, and global supply chain management.

Paul Hong is a Distinguished University Professor and Department Chair of Information Systems and Supply Chain Management at the John B. and Lillian E. Neff College of Business and Innovation, University of Toledo, USA. He is a graduate of Yonsei University, Korea, with a BA in Economics. Additionally, he holds an MBA and an MA from Bowling Green State University, as well as a Ph.D. in Manufacturing Management and Engineering from the University of Toledo, USA. He is a certified management accountant (CMA).

He published papers in these prominent journals such as *Journal of Operations Management, Journal of Supply Chain Management, Journal of Business Logistics, Journal of Business Industrial Marketing, International Journal of Production Economics, Journal of Cleaner Production, IEEE Transactions on Engineering, Management, IEEE Access, Digital Policy, Regulation and Governance Journal of Systems, Information Technology, Journal of Information, Communication and Ethics in Society, Asia Pacific Business Review, Journal of Manufacturing Technology Management, Business Process Management Journal, International Journal of Quality and Service Sciences, Leadership and Organization Development Journal, Journal of Risk and Financial Management, and others.*

He released two books on *Development Network Capabilities in Turbulent Competitive Environments.* The first volume focused on *Practices of Global Firms from Korea and Japan* (2012, PRC; Taylor Francis) and the second volume on *Success Stories of Global Firms from the BRICs* (2014, PRC; Taylor Francis). His fourth book is on *Creative Innovative Firms from Japan: A Benchmark Inquiry into Firms from Three Rival Nations* (2019, Springer). His fifth book is *Rising Asia and American Hegemony: Case of Competitive Firms from Four Leading Nations* (Springer, 2020). He is Chair of the New Populism Conference and Editor-in-Chief of the New Populism Encyclopedia by Springer (2022). He is co-Editor-in-Chief of New Populism Encyclopedia (Springer, 2024). The encyclopedia includes contributions from all the major disciplines of the Social Sciences, making it a comprehensive source for examining new populism. As of February 20, 2024, it features 180 article entries. Several of his co-authored papers included in this encyclopedia address topics such as Future world of work, Globalization, and Corporate Social Responsibility. During 2020–2023, his insights on global supply chain issues have been featured in esteemed publications such as The Hill, Fortune, Wall Street Journal, Forbes, Business Insider, International Business Times, Columbus Dispatch, Toledo Blade, ABC TV, and PBS.

Chapter 1
Timeless Elegance: Tracing the Dynamic Evolution of Cosmetics Through History

Abstract The evolution of the cosmetics industry traces a fascinating journey from its inception in ancient civilizations to its current sophisticated state. This narrative explores the intricate mosaic of beauty rituals throughout history, showcasing how cosmetics have consistently played a pivotal role in societal and cultural expressions. From the kohl-lined eyes of the ancient Egyptians to the powdered faces of Renaissance aristocracy, beauty practices across different eras reflect a myriad of influences—geographical, technological, social, and political. This chapter chronicles not only the historical advancements in cosmetic formulations and applications but also the societal implications and personal stories interwoven with these beauty rituals, mirroring humanity's evolving ideals, scientific progress, and shifting cultural norms. In stark contrast, the modern era has witnessed a dramatic transformation in the cosmetics industry, characterized by large-scale industrial production and innovative marketing strategies. Global events, such as wars and the evolving role of women, have significantly influenced the industry, prompting adaptations in product formulation and marketing. The rise of iconic beauty brands and the advent of mass advertising have turned cosmetics into symbols of lifestyle and personal identity, making them accessible to a wider audience and an essential part of daily life. The chapter concludes by reflecting on how the historical context of cosmetics enriches our understanding of contemporary marketing strategies, underscoring the importance of authenticity and adaptability in the cosmetics industry's ever-evolving digital landscape.

1 Beginnings of Beauty: Cosmetics in Ancient Civilizations

From the banks of the Nile to the fertile crescent of Mesopotamia, the dusty plateaus of China, and the lush valleys of India, the story of cosmetics weaves through time and geography, a narrative as old as civilization itself. This chapter journeys back to where it all began, uncovering the earliest uses of cosmetics in ancient societies. We will explore the mystical substances used to adorn and protect, the rituals that defined cultural ethos, and the nascent trade that marked the dawn of a new global

Y. W. Park and P. Hong, *Cosmetics Marketing Strategy in the Era of the Digital Ecosystem*, https://doi.org/10.1007/978-981-97-3674-4_1

industry. Here, in the crucible of ancient wisdom and practice, lies the genesis of the cosmetics industry.

1.1 Ancient Egyptian Elegance

The ancient Egyptians were not just architectural pioneers but also one of the earliest cultures to extensively use cosmetics as a daily ritual. Kohl, with its mystical allure, served not only to beautify but also to protect against the harsh glare of the sun and ward off evil spirits. Red ochre gave cheeks and lips a flush of vitality, a testament to health and status. The application of these substances was more than a mere vanity affair; it was a profound expression of spirituality and societal order (Scott, 2016). The complex recipes and sacred rituals surrounding Egyptian cosmetics offer a glimpse into a society where beauty was interwoven with the divine.

Ancient Egyptian Kohl Containers and Applicators: An image depicting a set of ancient Egyptian cosmetic tools, including a kohl container and an applicator. The container could be made of carved stone or wood and adorned with hieroglyphics, illustrating the craftsmanship and cultural significance of such items. The applicator, possibly a thin stick made from a reed or metal, might also be decorated with semi-precious stones or motifs indicative of its importance in daily beauty rituals.

Surrounding the kohl container are various items including a shallow dish, possibly used for mixing and grinding pigments or for holding ground minerals before application. The presence of colorful stone inlays and gemstones suggests these tools belonged to someone of high status, as they display a level of craftsmanship and material value that would not have been accessible to all. Each piece is meticulously crafted, not just as a functional item, but as an object of art, demonstrating the ancient Egyptians' commitment to beauty and the high cultural value they placed on cosmetic practices. Their makeup routines were an integral part of their identity and daily life, as evidenced by the lasting impressions these tools have left on history.

The significance of makeup in ancient Egypt transcended the boundaries of class and gender. Pharaohs and commoners, priests, and laymen alike embellished their eyes with kohl, creating an iconic look that has endured through millennia as a symbol of Egyptian culture. Intricate containers and applicators, often buried with the dead, underscore the belief that beauty was as important in the afterlife as it was in the mortal realm. The meticulous care Egyptians applied to their appearance reflects a deep-rooted belief in the power of aesthetics and the integral role of cosmetics in daily life. A reproduction of an ancient Egyptian wall painting or mural showing a scene of individuals applying cosmetics—kohl on their eyes and red ochre on cheeks and lips—highlights the communal and ritualistic aspects of cosmetic application.

1.2 Mesopotamian Innovations

In Mesopotamia, often hailed as the cradle of civilization, we find some of the earliest documented cosmetic recipes. These ancient concoctions reveal a sophisticated use of natural resources, transforming minerals like malachite and lapis lazuli into coveted cosmetic powders. The Mesopotamians pioneered the trade of these precious materials, which would find their way across continents, influencing beauty standards far beyond their borders. This early exchange of cosmetic goods hints at a rudimentary global market, a precursor to today's interconnected economies.

The cultural impact of Mesopotamian cosmetics extended into the realms of both adornment and medicine. Recipes etched into clay tablets included ingredients for color and preservation, reflecting an early understanding of the properties of materials they used. These practices were not just about aesthetics; they were imbued with purpose and meaning, with ointments and creams serving to soothe skin in the dry Mesopotamian climate and to prepare the noble and the divine for ceremonial events. Through these early innovations, Mesopotamia contributed significantly to the cosmetic rituals that shaped human interaction with beauty.

In ancient Mesopotamia, the use of cosmetics went beyond mere vanity and was integrated into daily life and ritual. People utilized these recipes and materials for personal grooming, religious ceremonies, and medicinal purposes. The application of makeup was a deliberate and skillful act, with both men and women partaking in the practice. They would enhance their facial features for aesthetic appeal and social status, as well as to protect their skin from the sun and wind. Their methods were advanced, incorporating techniques such as mixing and setting to achieve the desired consistency and longevity of the cosmetics, reflecting an early understanding of the principles of chemistry.

The sophistication of Mesopotamian cosmetic recipes and materials suggests a civilization deeply invested in personal care, the science of aesthetics, and the complexities of social dynamics. The meticulous recording of recipes indicates a high value placed on knowledge and tradition, with practices likely passed down through generations. The attention to detail in both the creation and application of these materials illustrates a society where appearance and ritual were intertwined, and where advances in science were utilized to enhance human beauty and health. This legacy provides insight into the innovative spirit of the Mesopotamian civilization and its lasting influence on modern cosmetic and medicinal practices.

Note: The Metropolitan Museum of Art in New York, the British Museum in London, and the Egyptian Museum in Cairo are excellent starting points for such searches, as they hold significant collections of Egyptian artifacts. Additionally, the Griffith Institute at Oxford University has a large collection of materials related to Egyptology, including photographs of wall paintings and reliefs from tombs and other monuments.

1.3 Ancient Chinese Cosmetic Traditions

Venturing east, the ancient civilizations of Asia—China, India, Korea and Japan—brought their own distinctive contributions to the evolution of cosmetics.

In China, rice powder was used to create a smooth, pale complexion, a look highly valued and indicative of societal status. Chinese nobility viewed cosmetics as a necessary enhancement to one's persona, an extension of the inner virtues of propriety and refinement. In India, the Ayurvedic tradition harnessed the natural world for beauty treatments, blending herbs, and other organic materials into pastes and powders that nurtured the body while adhering to the principles of holistic well-being. The meticulous care in preparation and application of cosmetics in these cultures was a testament to their understanding of beauty as a holistic endeavor, encompassing physical, spiritual, and societal health.

Ancient Chinese Cosmetic Tools and Powders: A representation of ancient Chinese cosmetic tools might include a finely decorated porcelain bowl containing white rice powder, alongside a delicate bamboo brush used for application. The bowl could be adorned with traditional Chinese motifs, such as dragons or lotus flowers, symbolizing nobility and purity. This image reflects the elite status of cosmetic use in ancient China and the cultural appreciation for a pale, refined complexion.

In addition to rice powder, ancient Chinese cosmetics also incorporated ingredients like vermilion and cinnabar to create red pigments for the lips and cheeks, embodying the aesthetic ideals of the time. These materials were not only chosen for their vibrant colors but also for their supposed medicinal properties, aligning with traditional Chinese medicine's emphasis on harmony between beauty and health. Mirrors, often made of polished bronze, were essential tools, reflecting both literal images and the philosophical idea of self-reflection and awareness. The art of makeup application was considered a skilled and thoughtful process, with each step—from powdering the face to staining the lips—carried out with precision and care, symbolizing a cultured and dignified life.

1.4 Ancient Indian Cosmetic Traditions

In ancient India, beauty and cosmetics were deeply entwined with the holistic wellness system of Ayurveda, reflecting a culture that viewed external beauty as a reflection of internal health. The Ayurvedic tradition utilized a wealth of natural ingredients, such as herbs, flowers, and minerals, to create an array of beauty treatments that were both therapeutic and beautifying. Women and men alike used these natural concoctions for skincare, haircare, and overall body wellness. Turmeric, for instance, was popular for its purifying and antibacterial properties, often used in face packs for a radiant complexion. Sandalwood, revered for its cooling properties, was used in pastes to soothe and nourish the skin. The use of henna for intricate body art not only served as a decorative element but was also known for its cooling effects. This deep-rooted beauty culture in ancient India was more than just about aesthetics; it was a holistic approach that married the physical, spiritual, and natural worlds in a seamless blend, making beauty care an integral part of daily life and well-being.

In India, beauty practices were deeply intertwined with Ayurvedic principles, which stressed the balance of the mind, body, and spirit. Ingredients like turmeric, sandalwood, and neem were staples in cosmetic preparations, revered not only for their beautifying effects but also for their therapeutic properties. Turmeric, for example, was used in face masks to impart a natural glow while offering antiseptic benefits. The application of kohl, derived from natural substances, to outline the eyes was more than a cosmetic practice; it was believed to protect the eyes from the sun's glare and ward off evil spirits. The holistic approach of Ayurveda meant that beauty treatments were part of a larger lifestyle, one that valued wellness and harmony with nature, making the ritualistic aspect of their application as important as their aesthetic benefits.

Within this serene depiction of ancient Indian life, the meticulous attention to wellness rituals extends beyond the frame. The setting likely includes a tranquil outdoor space, perhaps a courtyard or garden, where the natural elements contribute to the healing practices. The sound of water from a nearby fountain or the rustle of leaves in a gentle breeze would complement the meditative process of self-care. Here, the communal aspect of beauty rituals fosters a shared cultural experience, allowing knowledge and techniques to be passed down through generations. It is not uncommon to see a guru or elder guiding these practices, emphasizing the importance of maintaining a regimen that nurtures both the external and internal self. This practice of communal self-care is ingrained in the fabric of society, reinforcing the idea that beauty and health are collective responsibilities.

These ancient rituals underscore the broader cultural and spiritual life of India, where every action, including the practice of beauty, is imbued with deeper meaning. The Ayurvedic texts often inscribed on palm leaves or carved into temple walls and provided a framework for these practices. They explained how aligning the individual's constitution with the rhythms of nature leads to optimal health and, by extension, radiant beauty. Seasonal and diurnal rhythms were considered when selecting ingredients for treatments, ensuring that each person's unique balance of the elemental energies, or doshas, was addressed. This ancient wisdom reveals a society that viewed the pursuit of beauty as a holistic endeavor, seamlessly woven into the spiritual tapestry of life and the eternal quest for harmony.

1.5 Beauty in Ancient Greece and Rome

In ancient Greece and Rome, the ever-evolving cosmopolitan contexts played a pivotal role in shaping the beauty standards and practices. As these civilizations expanded their territories and influence, they encountered a variety of cultures, each with its own unique beauty rituals. The introduction of luxury goods, cultural products, and perfumes from distant lands such as Egypt and Persia, became symbols of status and refinement. These imports, often carried along the Silk Road and other trade routes, were highly coveted and used by the elite to distinguish themselves. Perfumes, in particular, became an essential part of the grooming routine, used not just for their fragrant appeal but also for their supposed health benefits and divine connections, as aromatic offerings to the gods (Hawley, 2002).

The Mediterranean climate, characterized by its warm, sun-kissed fair weather, played a significant role in the Greco-Roman conception of beauty. The abundance of natural light contributed to a cultural appreciation for outdoor life, which in turn influenced beauty ideals—tanned skin from the Greek Isles, for example, was associated with labor and therefore less desirable, while the Romans valued the paleness that suggested a life of leisure indoors. This environment also provided a wealth of natural ingredients that were incorporated into beauty regimens, such as olive oil, which was used not only in food but also as a skin conditioner, and honey, celebrated for its healing properties (Hawley, 2002).

Cosmetics and beauty played a significant role in the development of the arts in ancient Greece and Rome. On stage, makeup was essential for performers to convey the characters they played, with stark contrasts and exaggerated features that could be seen from afar. In the realm of fine art, the ideals of beauty were perpetually enshrined in sculpture and paintings, capturing society's admiration for symmetry and proportion. Cosmetics were also a mainstay in social engagements, where appearances were crafted to reflect social status and to adhere to societal expectations. Banquets, public gatherings, and religious ceremonies all presented opportunities for individuals to display their wealth and sophistication through their beauty choices (Hawley, 2002).

The influx of wealth through international trade and military conquests led to an era of unprecedented prosperity in certain strata of Greek and Roman society. With newfound riches, the demand for luxury goods, including cosmetics, surged. The spoils of conquests and the wealth from trade meant that more people could afford such indulgences. Cosmetics, once the preserve of the aristocracy, began to find their way into the homes of the burgeoning middle class. This period saw the proliferation of beauty salons and barber shops, where men and women alike could go to have their hair styled, perfumed, and dyed, reflecting the infusion of new wealth into the cultural fabric of the time.

In these ancient societies, while men were often engaged in wars and political endeavors, women of certain classes found themselves with time for leisure and self-care. This leisure class of women, particularly in Rome, had the means to indulge in an array of cosmetic products. With their husbands or fathers away, these women had the autonomy to explore and indulge in luxury items, including exotic makeup and skincare concoctions. This era saw a flourishing of beauty culture, with women exchanging tips and secrets, contributing to a sophisticated understanding of aesthetics and personal care that would influence generations to come.

1.6 Ancient Korean Cosmetic Traditions

Korean Traditional Cosmetic Boxes (Najeon Chilgi): A traditional Korean cosmetic box, known as 'Najeon Chilgi', intricately inlaid with mother-of-pearl, demonstrates the importance of beauty routines in Korean culture. These boxes, often containing multiple compartments, would store various pigments and brushes. The elaborate exterior designs reflect the value placed on the art of self-adornment and the meticulous attention to detail that characterized Korean cosmetic practices (Jhin, 2011).

Ancient Korean cosmetic traditions reflect a deep-rooted history of beauty and self-care, integral to the cultural identity of Korea. The use of natural ingredients was a hallmark of these traditions. Women in ancient Korea often made their own cosmetics, using locally sourced materials like rice water, mung beans, and gourd stems. These ingredients were not only used for their beautifying effects but also for their beneficial properties to the skin. Rice water, for instance, was known for its brightening and cleansing qualities, making it a popular choice for face wash. Mung beans were ground into a fine powder and used as a gentle exfoliant, believed to refresh and rejuvenate the skin.

Another significant aspect of ancient Korean cosmetic practices was the emphasis on skincare routines. The philosophy was not merely about applying makeup but more about maintaining healthy, clear skin. The skincare regimen included several steps, each with its specific purpose. This would typically start with cleansing, followed by applying herbal tonics to balance the skin's health. The idea was to create a natural, radiant complexion that required minimal makeup. The emphasis on skincare over makeup is a tradition that has endured over centuries and remains a prominent feature of Korean beauty culture today. This holistic approach to beauty underscores the belief that true beauty stems from wellness and harmony within.

The holistic beauty regimen in ancient Korea extended into the realm of personal wellness, where the lines between cosmetics, medicine, and self-care blurred harmoniously. This interconnection is evident in practices like facial steaming with decoctions made from beneficial herbs and flowers, which was believed to open pores, facilitate cleansing, and infuse the skin with therapeutic properties. This ritualistic steaming was often followed by a cooling period, during which thinly sliced, chilled cucumbers or ginseng were placed on the skin to tighten pores and invigorate the complexion. Nutrition also played a crucial role, with dietary choices being made to enhance skin health from the inside out, reflecting the Korean adage that 'your face is a reflection of what you eat.' This comprehensive approach to beauty, deeply embedded in the fabric of Korean culture, emphasizes a lifestyle that nurtures the body as a whole, exemplifying the ancient Korean pursuit of holistic harmony (Jhin, 2011).

1.7 Ancient Japanese Cosmetic Traditions

Japanese Cosmetics and Ukiyo-e Prints: An Ukiyo-e print illustrating a Japanese woman applying makeup could provide a vivid depiction of historical cosmetic practices. The print may show the use of '*oshiroi*' (white face powder) and '*beni*' (red coloring for lips and cheeks) with traditional makeup tools like '*hera*' (spatulas) and '*fude*' (brushes). The artistic representation in the print captures the elegance of the beauty standards of the time, highlighting the societal emphasis on aesthetics and the artistry involved in self-presentation.

In ancient Japan, the pursuit of beauty was a refined art, deeply influenced by the cultural aesthetics of the era. The traditional makeup routine involved a base layer of '*oshiroi*', a white rice powder that was meticulously applied to create a flawless, porcelain-like complexion, symbolizing purity and beauty. This look was not only a beauty standard but also a status symbol, often associated with the nobility and the sophisticated courtesan class of the Edo period. To achieve the iconic red lips, '*beni*', a rouge made from safflower petals, was delicately applied with precision. The process was an intricate one, using different shades to create a gradation effect known as '*beni-kaburaki*', a technique that added depth and dimension to the lips.

Beyond the face, the cosmetic practices extended to elaborate hairstyles adorned with ornate hairpins and combs, signifying both social status and personal style. Women would often visit the '*yoshiwara*', the pleasure quarters, to observe the latest trends in fashion and beauty from the '*oiran*' or high-ranking courtesans, who were the epitomes of elegance and style. The intricate designs of kimonos, often chosen to complement the seasons and personal aesthetics, were part of the holistic approach to beauty. Each element, from the silk fabric to the motif, played a role in the overall presentation of oneself.

The art of makeup was a ritualistic process, infused with a philosophy that saw the act of beautifying oneself as a disciplined form of self-expression and respect for social customs. Traditional tools like 'hera' and 'fude' were not mere implements but were crafted with as much artistry as the makeup itself. These items were often made from natural materials such as bamboo and animal hair, designed to work harmoniously with the natural ingredients used in the cosmetics. The entire process was a meditative practice, reflecting a deep appreciation for the transient beauty of the world, a concept central to Japanese aesthetics known as '*mono no aware*'. The Ukiyo-e prints that depict these practices serve as a timeless reminder of the elaborate and nuanced tradition of beauty in ancient Japan, capturing the transient world of fashion and elegance with a grace that continues to fascinate the world to this day.

2 From Alchemy to Acceptance: Cosmetics in the Middle Ages and Renaissance

In the tapestry of cosmetic history, the Middle Ages and the Renaissance represent a complex interplay of concealment and celebration. As the world transitioned from the ancient practices of openly celebrated beauty rituals to the more subdued Middle Ages, the use of cosmetics underwent a transformation. The church's growing influence cast a shadow over makeup, yet, beneath the surface, the tradition of personal adornment lived on through discreet practices. This period set the stage for the Renaissance, a time when Europe would witness a resurgence of cosmetic use, redefining beauty ideals once again. It was also an era marked by scientific inquiry, where the mystique of alchemy began to unfold into the beginnings of modern chemistry, refining the art and science of cosmetics.

2.1 *Medieval Modesty and Makeup*

During the medieval era, the church's moral authority cast a pall over the use of cosmetics, denouncing them as tools of deception and vanity. Despite such condemnations, women and men of various classes continued to employ subtle forms of beautification. Behind the closed doors of their chambers, women concocted homemade recipes, utilizing natural ingredients like herbs and berries to enhance their features. These clandestine beauty rituals often passed down through whispered advice, reflected a society grappling with the tension between piety and the human desire for personal adornment. The duality of cosmetics as both a symbol of modesty and a quiet rebellion against asceticism characterized the medieval approach to beauty.

2.2 *Renaissance of Beauty*

The Renaissance era heralded a renewed embrace of cosmetics, influenced by the flourishing arts and the revival of classical ideals (Ames-Lewis & Rogers, 2019). The courts of Europe became stages for opulent displays of personal beauty, where the use of cosmetics signified status and sophistication. Lead-based powders and creams, though hazardous by today's standards, were coveted for their ability to impart a fashionably pale visage, echoing the marble statues of antiquity. This period saw a blossoming of beauty ideals that celebrated human aesthetics, with cosmetics playing a pivotal role in societal rituals and the self-expression of the European elite.

Renaissance beauty rituals and standards were a departure from the medieval era, emphasizing a lavish and intricate approach to personal adornment. Portraits from this period, such as Fra Filippo Lippi's "Portrait of a Woman" (1445), depict women with rouged cheeks and lips, a fair complexion, and coiffed blonde hair, reflecting the era's beauty ideals influenced by figures like Petrarch's muse Laura. These standards were largely dictated by societal expectations and were considered a woman's duty to uphold (Hunt et al., 2011). Women used various methods to modify their appearance to align with these ideals, from plucking their hairlines to applying potentially harmful substances like lead oxide and mercury to whiten their skin.

The Renaissance era marked a vivid embrace of beauty, with art and philosophy intertwining to establish new standards of female beauty. Women aspired to have fine, oval faces with high foreheads, thin eyebrows, straight noses, small mouths, and pale yet flushed skin, which were all signs of youth, health, and wealth. Hair was to be honey blonde and curly, and hands were to display slender fingers with light-colored veins. These beauty standards were pervasive, with women employing various techniques to meet them, despite the potential health risks associated with some of the cosmetic preparations used.

The Renaissance era marked a pivotal moment in the history of portraiture, especially concerning the depiction of women and the use of cosmetics, which signified status and sophistication. The National Gallery of Art features "Virtue and Beauty: Leonardo's 'Ginevra de' Benci' and Renaissance Portraits of Women", showcasing the transformation in female portraiture during this period. The collection demonstrates a shift from profile to three-quarter or frontal views, making portraits more communicative and elaborate. Leonardo's portrait of Ginevra de' Benci, with her chalk-white skin and highlighted cheeks, is a quintessential example of the era's beauty ideals, emphasizing pale complexions and rosy cheeks as hallmarks of beauty and virtue.

2.3 *Scientific Advancements and Alchemy*

In the transformative era of the Renaissance, the mystical practices of alchemy began to merge with the nascent field of science. Alchemists, the precursors to modern chemists, sought to understand the properties of substances and their transformative powers. Their work laid important foundations for the cosmetic industry, as they developed methods to distill essences and create purer, more effective cosmetic preparations. This period of scientific exploration led to the identification of harmful practices, such as the use of lead in makeup, prompting a gradual reformation towards safer beauty products. The intellectual curiosity of the time fueled advancements that would ultimately enhance the quality and safety of cosmetics, shaping the industry's future trajectory.

However, during the Renaissance period, alchemy and the study of materials were prominent aspects of the scientific pursuit. Illustrations from historical alchemical texts often depicted intricate processes such as distillation, the transformation of substances, and the quest for the philosopher's stone, symbolizing the alchemical goal of transmutation. These images, some of which can be found in the Getty

Alchemy Collection or the digital archives of the Science History Institute, are rich with symbolic meaning and reflect the era's intersection of science, mysticism, and art. Furthermore, the Renaissance was a period of significant advancement in the development and use of scientific instruments. Distillation apparatuses, astrolabes, and other devices were crucial to the era's explorations in chemistry, astronomy, and physics. These instruments, often crafted with precision and artistry, can be seen in the collections of museums such as the Smithsonian or through educational resources focusing on the history of science. They exemplify the period's innovative spirit and the rise of empirical methods that would eventually lead to the modern scientific revolution (Smith & Findlen, 2013).

The convergence of alchemy, science, and the arts during the Renaissance also played a pivotal role in the evolution of cosmetics. Alchemists, with their mastery of substances and transformational techniques, laid the groundwork for modern chemistry, which includes the formulation of cosmetics (Kemp, 2000). The distillation processes depicted in alchemical texts were not only aimed at transmuting base metals into gold or finding the elixir of life but also in extracting essences and creating compounds that could be used for medicinal and beautification purposes (Riordan, 2004). These early experiments with materials led to the development of lotions, creams, and perfumes that have become the basis of today's cosmetic industry. Thus, the artistic representation of a woman adorned in the beauty standards of the Renaissance serves as a nod to the era's rich legacy in the cosmetic sciences—a legacy born from the alchemical experiments and the era's quest to understand and enhance human beauty through scientific means (Smith & Findlen, 2013).

3 Industrialization and Innovation: The Birth of Modern Cosmetics

The 19th and early twentieth centuries marked a revolutionary era in the history of cosmetics, characterized by the advent of industrialization and innovative breakthroughs. This period witnessed the transformation of cosmetics from artisanal concoctions to mass-produced products, ushering in the age of modern beauty. Advances in chemistry and manufacturing enabled the creation of a wide range of safe, standardized cosmetics, making them accessible to a broader public than ever before (Blanco-Dávila, 2000). The emergence of iconic beauty brands during this time revolutionized marketing and consumer culture, while the establishment of regulatory standards ensured product safety and quality. This era set the foundation for the cosmetics industry as we know it today, combining scientific progress with commercial savvy to meet the beauty needs of the burgeoning modern world.

3.1 Cosmetic Chemistry Breakthroughs

The industrial era brought about pivotal changes in cosmetic chemistry, significantly enhancing the safety and efficacy of beauty products. Key scientific discoveries, such as the synthesis of new dyes and preservatives, paved the way for the mass production of a diverse array of cosmetics (Dey & Dubey, 2023). Innovations in emulsification processes allowed for the creation of more stable and smoother creams and lotions, revolutionizing skincare products. These advancements were not just about aesthetics; they also meant that cosmetics could be produced on a large scale while maintaining consistent quality and safety standards. This shift laid the groundwork for the modern cosmetics industry, making beauty products more accessible and reliable for consumers.

During the industrial revolution, the field of cosmetic chemistry underwent significant breakthroughs that transformed the way beauty products were formulated and manufactured. The discovery and synthesis of aniline dyes, for instance, expanded the color palette available to cosmetic creators, allowing for the production of vibrant and previously unattainable hues in products like lipsticks and eyeshadows. The advent of preservatives extended the shelf life of these products, making them safer and more convenient for public use. Advances in emulsification, which is the process of mixing oil and water to create a homogeneous and stable product, led to the development of creams and lotions that were smoother, more hydrating, and easier to apply. These innovations were crucial in shifting cosmetics from artisanal concoctions to scientifically engineered products. The ability to produce cosmetics in large volumes, with rigorous quality control, meant that beauty products became a staple of everyday life, affordable and accessible to a broader audience. This era laid the foundation for the modern cosmetics industry, focusing on consumer safety, product performance, and standardized production. Consequently, the industrial revolution's legacy in cosmetics continues to resonate today, with ongoing research and development pushing the boundaries of science to meet the evolving demands of beauty and personal care.

The advancements in cosmetic chemistry during this period laid a robust foundation for the large-scale development of the cosmetic industry in the years to come. The industrialization of cosmetic production was made possible by the standardization of formulas and the adoption of manufacturing processes that ensured consistency and quality across batches. With the help of scientific research, ingredients could be synthesized and tested for specific properties, allowing for the creation of a wide range of products tailored to various skin types and beauty concerns. This scientific rigor also led to improved safety standards, ensuring that products were free of harmful substances and suitable for widespread consumer use (Khan and Alam, 2019).

Furthermore, the evolution of cosmetic chemistry into a full-fledged scientific discipline meant that the industry could innovate rapidly, responding to consumer demands with new textures, scents, and functions. The principles of mass production were applied, enabling cosmetics to be manufactured in quantities that had been previously unimaginable. As a result, beauty products, once the luxury of the elite, became accessible to the general public, revolutionizing the way people approached personal grooming. This democratization of beauty products was accompanied by marketing and branding efforts that made cosmetics desirable to a broad audience, ensuring the industry's exponential growth and enduring success.

3.2 *The Changing Role of Women and Societal Attitudes*

The evolving role of women in society, from gaining the right to vote to entering the workforce, influenced cosmetic companies' marketing and product offerings. It would delve into how these changes prompted a broader range of beauty products designed to meet the needs of the modern woman and how companies have continually adapted to reflect the progressive empowerment of their primary consumer base.

The evolving role of women in society had a profound impact on the cosmetic industry. As women gained greater social and political rights, including the right to vote, there was a corresponding shift in how they were portrayed and perceived in advertising and media. This change was reflected in the cosmetics industry through more diverse and empowering marketing strategies and product lines, recognizing women's evolving roles and needs.

- The early stages of women's societal advancement. This includes women gaining the right to vote and their initial forays into the workforce. It presents the essence of the past era symbolizing the beginning of the journey towards women's empowerment and the corresponding initial responses from the cosmetic industry.
- The evolving roles of women over time captures key moments of societal change and the cosmetic industry's adaptation. The transitions show the gradual shift in women's status, their increasing participation in various professional fields, and the changing perceptions of women in society.
- Modern and vibrant visuals reflect contemporary empowerment including depictions of women in diverse professional roles, highlighting their economic independence and social equality. The cosmetic industry's responses, such as the introduction of advanced, multi-functional beauty products and empowering marketing campaigns, highlight how cosmetic firms have evolved to meet the needs of the modern woman.

Overall, the journey of women's empowerment, along with the economic independence of Black Americans and women, from past to present has closely coincided with the cosmetic industry's evolving response to these societal changes (Bundles, 2002). The progression from muted, passive roles to vibrant, modern transitions emphasize the significant strides made in women's roles and the industry's continual adaptation to reflect and support these advancements. The massive increase in the women's workforce during and after the World Wars, and later during other societal shifts, led to significant changes in women's economic power and independence. This increase in income among women translated into greater spending power, which the cosmetic industry capitalized on by broadening its product range and marketing messages to appeal to the working woman.

As a result, cosmetic firms continually adapted their marketing strategies and product offerings. They introduced products that were convenient and practical for working women, such as long-wear makeup and multi-functional products. Marketing campaigns also evolved to resonate with the empowered woman, focusing on themes of independence, personal choice, and self-expression. Furthermore, this shift heralded a new era of inclusivity and diversity in beauty standards, with products and advertisements increasingly catering to a wider range of ethnicities, ages, and lifestyles. The cosmetic industry's evolution mirrors the broader societal journey towards gender equality, demonstrating how commercial entities can both influence and be influenced by cultural and social dynamics. In essence, the changing face of the cosmetic industry reflects the changing face of womanhood itself, marking an ongoing dialogue between consumer needs and industry innovation.

Here, the narrative would shift to how global events such as wars, economic depressions, and booms influenced these companies. This would include how they navigated resource scarcity, shifts in consumer behavior, and the changing role of women in society, reflecting how external events can pivot a company's trajectory. As we transition from the broader impact of socio-economic shifts to the specific challenges of war and resource allocation, it's crucial to recognize the resilience and adaptability of the cosmetics industry. In times of global upheaval, these companies had to swiftly adjust to new realities, often marked by shortages and changing consumer priorities. These challenges prompted cosmetic firms to rethink their strategies and product offerings, leading to innovative solutions that would have a lasting impact on their business models and product development.

The period between global upheavals and the focused response to war-induced resource scarcity was a time of significant transformation for cosmetic companies. They had to navigate not just the immediate challenges of material shortages but also the shifting landscape of consumer needs and societal roles, particularly those of women. As women's roles in society evolved, especially during war times when they entered the workforce in large numbers, cosmetic firms had to recalibrate their marketing and product development strategies to align with these changes, setting the stage for the detailed exploration of war and resource allocation.

3.3 Hollywood's Influence on Beauty

Hollywood's golden age cast a spotlight on the cosmetics industry, profoundly influencing beauty standards and product popularity. Cinema icons not only mesmerized audiences with their performances but also set new trends in beauty and fashion. Makeup artists like Max Factor and Helena Rubinstein became celebrities in their own right, their products and techniques coveted by both stars and fans (Dootson, 2016). The adoption of Technicolor film further emphasized the need for more sophisticated makeup, leading to innovations in product formulation and application. Celebrity endorsements became a powerful marketing tool, as the public sought to emulate the glamorous looks seen on the silver screen. Hollywood's influence extended beyond mere trends, shaping societal perceptions of beauty and elegance (Smith et al., 1999).

The growth of the movie industry, exemplified by Hollywood's golden age, had a profound impact on popularizing cosmetic products. As film became a dominant form of entertainment and cultural expression, the faces of actors and actresses on the big screen became the de facto trendsetters for beauty. Hollywood stars were idolized, and their carefully curated images, created with the help of makeup artists, set new beauty standards for the public to aspire to. With the advent of color films, there was an even greater emphasis on makeup, as the vibrant new medium required more pronounced and varied color palettes to stand out on screen.

This shift in filmmaking technology led to a demand for more diverse and sophisticated cosmetics, expanding the customer base from theater actors to the general populace who wanted to replicate the movie star look. The makeup industry responded by developing new formulas and products that could meet both the practical needs of film production and the aesthetic desires of the public. The visibility of these products, used by some of the most famous faces in the world, provided an unprecedented level of advertising and desirability (Dootson, 2016).

The widespread distribution of cosmetic products through diverse channels was largely propelled by the influence of the film industry. Retailers, from high-end department stores to local drugstores, began to stock beauty products that were associated with Hollywood glamour. This accessibility allowed consumers from various economic backgrounds to purchase items that were once considered luxury goods. Marketing strategies often highlighted the connection to Hollywood, with products bearing the names of movie stars or featuring images from popular films on the packaging, further solidifying the connection between the cosmetics industry and the allure of the silver screen (Smith et al., 1999).

3.4 Wartime Cosmetics

The world wars of the twentieth century had a significant impact on the cosmetics industry. During these times, resource scarcity necessitated the use of alternative ingredients and simpler beauty routines. The war effort also led to women entering the workforce in large numbers, prompting a shift towards more practical and resilient makeup products that could withstand the rigors of labor-intensive jobs. Brands like Elizabeth Arden even developed cosmetics specifically for women in the military. Despite rationing and economic hardships, the demand for cosmetics remained strong, symbolizing a form of morale-boosting normalcy and femininity in challenging times (Delano, 2000). The ingenuity and adaptability shown by the cosmetics industry during wartime demonstrated its resilience and the enduring importance of beauty in people's lives.

The impact of war on cosmetic manufacturing was significant. Wartime economies shifted the production priorities to support the war effort, leading to a scarcity of raw materials traditionally used in cosmetics. Ingredients like alcohol, oils, and fats were repurposed for military use, forcing cosmetic companies to innovate with alternative substances. Despite these challenges, the cosmetic industry continued to thrive, with many brands finding ways to maintain production, even under these strict constraints. This period saw the emergence of simpler, more resource-efficient products that reflected the need for practicality during times of rationing. The industry's innovative responses to resource scarcity were a testament to its resilience. Cosmetics companies began to use synthetic materials to replace natural ingredients that were no longer available. They also adapted their packaging, with some brands producing smaller, more durable containers that catered to the mobile lifestyle of women in service. Makeup items became multipurpose, with products like lipstick doubling as cheek tint, maximizing utility for women on the front lines or those contributing to the war effort at home.

The rise of practical beauty routines catered to a broad and growing customer segment, including women in active service and those working in factories and fields. These routines emphasized a quick, simple approach to beauty that was aligned with the austere conditions of wartime. The notion of "putting your best face forward" took on a patriotic tone, as maintaining one's appearance became a symbol of morale and a nod to normalcy. Post-war, these practical beauty routines would lay the foundation for a burgeoning consumer culture, with the cosmetics industry at its helm, expanding to meet the desires of women who had grown accustomed to the empowerment and independence of wartime life.

3.5 Adaptation to Wartime and Economic Fluctuations

Cosmetic industry's response to the resource limitations imposed by global conflicts. During wartime, the cosmetic industry faced significant resource limitations. The impact of the Great Depression on the cosmetic industry was profound. As economic hardship gripped the world, consumer spending power dwindled, leading to a shift in the cosmetic market. Companies were forced to reevaluate their strategies to cater to a more budget-conscious audience. This period saw a surge in affordable beauty products, as luxury cosmetics became inaccessible to the majority. The demand for versatile and long-lasting products rose, leading to innovations that are still influential in modern cosmetics. Additionally, the Great Depression underscored the importance of cosmetics in providing a sense of normalcy and self-care during tough times, a sentiment that carried over into subsequent conflicts.

World War II and the Cold War era, including the Korean War, further challenged the cosmetic industry. During World War II, the industry faced stringent resource rationing, with many ingredients being diverted for military use. This led to a surge in creativity, with companies developing new synthetic materials to replace natural ones. The wartime also saw the rise of multi-purpose products, such as lipsticks that doubled as cheek tints, aligning with the practical needs of women who were increasingly involved in the workforce and war efforts. The Cold War period continued this trend of innovation, as geopolitical tensions and the ongoing Korean War maintained resource pressures. Cosmetic firms not only adapted to these challenges but also played a pivotal role in uplifting morale. The era's cosmetics reflected a blend of practicality and escapism, offering a sense of normalcy and luxury amidst the uncertainties of the Cold War. These periods were instrumental in shaping the cosmetic industry's approach to product development, marketing strategies, and consumer engagement, leaving a lasting impact that resonates in the industry's contemporary practices.

The adage "necessity is the mother of invention" aptly encapsulates the cosmetic industry's response during these challenging times. Faced with unprecedented resource limitations, companies were compelled to rethink and reinvent. This period marked a significant shift towards continuous innovation, as the industry delved into the development of synthetic ingredients and multi-functional products. These innovations were not merely stopgap solutions but laid the foundation for a new era in cosmetic chemistry and product design. The exploration of synthetic materials opened up a world of possibilities, leading to more diverse and versatile products that could cater to a wider range of skin types and aesthetic preferences. This era of forced creativity not only helped the industry survive the immediate crises but also propelled it into a future where innovation became a constant, driving force, leading to advancements in product quality, safety, and sustainability.

During these tumultuous times, the cosmetic industry also recognized its role in boosting morale and providing a semblance of normalcy. Amidst the backdrop of war and economic hardship, the act of maintaining daily routines, including personal care, became a significant psychological anchor. Cosmetics played a key role in this aspect, offering a sense of control and self-expression when much of the world was in chaos. The ability to maintain one's appearance was not just about vanity but about preserving dignity and identity during times of upheaval. This understanding led cosmetic companies to focus not just on the functional aspects of their products but also on their emotional and psychological impact. Campaigns and product lines were developed with the intent of uplifting spirits and reinforcing resilience. This emphasis on the psychological benefits of cosmetics, born out of necessity during wartime, has since become a central tenet in the industry, influencing marketing strategies and product development to this day.

Overall, the cosmetic industry's resilience and ingenuity sustained the underlying processes of innovations in response to the constraints of wartime and economic downturns. Overall, the cosmetic industry's resilience and ingenuity sustained the underlying processes of innovations in response to the constraints of wartime and economic downturns. This period of adversity forged a new path for the industry, one where adaptability and creativity became core values. The legacy of this era is evident in today's cosmetic landscape, where the emphasis on versatile, inclusive, and sustainable products continues to echo the lessons learned from those challenging times. Ultimately, the industry's journey through these historical periods highlights the remarkable capacity of human ingenuity to not only adapt to changing circumstances but to thrive and innovate in the face of adversity.

4 The Cosmetics Industry Growth in the 20th Century

The twentieth century marked a golden era in the world of cosmetics, characterized by unprecedented growth and glamour. This period saw the industry flourish, driven by cultural shifts, technological advancements, and global events (Oumeish, 2001). The influence of Hollywood and the rise of the film industry played a pivotal role in shaping beauty ideals and popularizing cosmetic products, making stars out of makeup artists and their celebrity clients. Additionally, the challenges of wartime brought about innovative adaptations in cosmetic manufacturing and usage, reflecting the resilience and ingenuity of the era. Moreover, the burgeoning field of advertising transformed the way cosmetics were marketed, leveraging the power of print and, later, television media to reach a wider audience than ever before. This era of glamour and growth fundamentally reshaped the cosmetics industry, setting the stage for its modern incarnation as a pillar of both beauty and commerce.

Between the rise of Hollywood's glamorous influence and the direct marketing of beauty ideals, the mid-twentieth century also witnessed a significant democratization of beauty. The post-war era ushered in an economic boom, leading to increased consumer spending power and a burgeoning middle class eager to indulge in the luxuries once reserved for the elite. This newfound accessibility meant that cosmetics were no longer just the domain of movie stars and the wealthy; they became a staple in the everyday lives of women across various socioeconomic backgrounds. The expansion of retail infrastructure, with department stores and drugstores stocking a wide array of beauty products, facilitated this shift. The era was marked by the birth of many brands that became mainstays on vanities around the world. As beauty products became more accessible, they also became a form of self-expression and personal identity for the average consumer, further embedding the cosmetics industry into the fabric of daily life and culture.

4.1 Beauty Brand Concept

Cosmetic companies developed their brand identity and expanded their market reach. It would cover pivotal marketing campaigns, the evolution of their logos and packaging, and strategies for entering international markets. The focus would be on how these brands became household names and the role of advertising in this process. As the narrative transitions from the foundational aspects of cosmetic firms to the crafting of their brand identities, it's crucial to understand the strategic journey these companies embarked upon. This bridge between their original stories and the meticulous crafting of their public personas is where businesses become brands. It's a transformation that involves not just a logo or a unique packaging design, but the distillation of a company's ethos into a visual and experiential form that resonates with consumers (Tungate, 2011). These brands moved beyond mere products to become symbols of culture and identity, influencing lifestyles and aspirations.

Branding is a narrative of connection—between the brand and its audience, between products and the lives they become a part of, and between corporate visions and consumer realities (Tungate, 2011). As these companies expanded their reach, their brand identities needed to encapsulate the essence of their growth, adapting and evolving to maintain relevance in an ever-changing global market.

The contemporary design aesthetics emphasize minimalism and functionality, which are popular in current consumer trends. This image captures the dynamic journey of a cosmetic brand's identity, narrating a story of transformation from traditional methods to a contemporary ethos while maintaining a core connection to the brand's original mission and values. The illustration serves as a visual metaphor for a brand that honors its heritage while embracing the future, aiming to resonate with consumers across different eras. The evolution of brand identity often involves three key processes: rebranding to stay relevant in the modern market, redesigning to align with evolving consumer aesthetics, and repackaging to reflect environmental and ethical considerations. These processes are essential for brands to maintain a strong presence in the competitive cosmetics industry.

4.2 Advertising for Products

The age of advertising, particularly for the cosmetics industry, was defined by a shift from product-based to lifestyle-based marketing. Advertisers began to understand that they were not just selling a lipstick or a cream but an aspirational image, a promise of beauty, and a lifestyle choice. This approach was built on the creation of compelling narratives that were brought to life through the glamour of Hollywood and the persuasive powers of visual storytelling. The development of color printing technology enabled these narratives to be vividly captured in magazine spreads and billboards, captivating the imaginations of potential customers and imprinting brand identities in the public consciousness. The twentieth century also ushered in the age of advertising for the cosmetics industry.

The inclusion of color swatches and a range of cosmetic products indicates the diversity of choices available to consumers, highlighting the customization and personalization that became possible as the industry evolved. The economic success and profitability of the cosmetic industry represents the storied history and legacy of these cosmetic firms. Overall, it captures the essence of how these companies have engaged with their audiences and maintained their place in the competitive landscape of beauty and personal care. Campaign strategies in the cosmetics industry typically address three primary needs: connecting emotionally with consumers, differentiating the brand from competitors, and effectively communicating the product's unique selling propositions. Successful campaigns are those that effectively intertwine these elements to create a compelling narrative that appeals to the target market.

4.3 Emergence of Beauty Brands

During the industrial revolution, the cosmetics industry saw the rise of brands that would become household names. Entrepreneurs recognized the potential of branding and marketing in selling beauty products, leading to the birth of companies that are still influential today. These pioneering brands understood the power of a strong identity and targeted advertising, often using glamorous imagery and celebrity endorsements to appeal to their audiences (Findlay, 2019). This era marked the beginning of beauty as a major commercial enterprise, with branding emerging as a key tool in creating customer loyalty and differentiating products in a growing market. The success of these early beauty brands set a template for marketing and brand building that continues to shape the industry.

During the industrial revolution, the emergence of beauty brands transformed the landscape of personal care products. Pioneering entrepreneurs realized the importance of creating a unique image and narrative around their products, leading to the establishment of some of the earliest beauty brands. These brands often adopted names and logos that exuded elegance and grace, appealing to the aspirations of their customers. The strategy extended beyond the product itself, infusing every aspect of the experience with a sense of exclusivity and desirability. It was the dawn of a new era in consumer goods, where the brand's identity played a crucial role in capturing market share.

The rise of these beauty brands was characterized by innovative marketing strategies that included glamorous advertising, celebrity endorsements, and evocative packaging design. They tapped into the power of media, especially women's magazines, to reach a wider audience and create an emotional connection with consumers. This era saw the birth of beauty moguls who were as much celebrated for their entrepreneurial spirit as for their products. They crafted stories that resonated with the feminine ethos of the time, promoting ideals of beauty and sophistication that were coveted by women across different strata of society.

The success of these early beauty brands laid down the principles of brand building that remain influential to this day. Creating a strong visual identity, developing a narrative that resonates with consumers, and engaging through targeted advertising have become the pillars of brand strategy in the cosmetics industry. These tactics have evolved with time but the core objective remains the same—to create a loyal customer base and differentiate from competitor.

Product design and packaging are equally crucial in crafting a brand identity. One brand may have introduced eco-friendly packaging to align with its commitment to sustainability, while another might have redesigned its products to feature ergonomic shapes for better user experience. A third brand's journey could involve the integration of technology in packaging, like QR codes or augmented reality features, enhancing customer engagement and experience. Each story underscores how product design and packaging are instrumental in shaping a brand's identity and its relationship with consumers.

5 Conclusion

The historical journey of the cosmetics industry up to the 20th Century is a rich narrative that spans millennia, encapsulating the essence of human creativity and adaptation. From the ceremonial paints of ancient tribes to the digitally augmented beauty experiences of today, each chapter in the story of cosmetics underscores a deep-rooted human desire to enhance and express oneself. This expedition through time illustrates how beauty practices have evolved alongside civilizations, informed by the shifting sands of culture, science, and technology. It highlights how cosmetics have been perennially reinvented, serving as a mirror to the changing tides of societal values, economic conditions, and artistic expressions (Dos Santos et al., 2023). This panoramic overview is not just about tracing the lineage of beauty products; it's about understanding the complex relationship between human identity and the pursuit of beauty (Rasmussen, 2018).

This historical overview lays a robust foundation for examining diverse factors related to the book "Cosmetics Marketing Strategy in the Era of Digital Ecosystem" and specifically informs the content of Chapter 1. By retracing the steps of our ancestors in their use of cosmetics, we gain insights into the enduring power of beauty as a form of personal and cultural expression. The past narratives and practices provide valuable lessons for today's dynamic marketing strategies, emphasizing the need for authenticity, adaptability, and resonance with consumers' values (Mangtani et al., 2020). In the digital age, where the cosmetics industry grapples with rapid technological changes and a global marketplace, understanding the historical context enriches our perspective and strategy, allowing us to chart a course that is both innovative and deeply rooted in the rich soil of our shared human experience (Lee and Lee, 2020).

References

Ames-Lewis, F., & Rogers, M. (Eds.). (2019). *Concepts of beauty in Renaissance art*. Routledge.

Blanco-Dávila, F. (2000). Beauty and the body: The origins of cosmetics. *Plastic and Reconstructive Surgery, 105*(3), 1196–1204.

Bundles, A. L. (2002). *On her own ground: The life and times of Madam CJ Walker*. Scribner.

Delano, P. D. (2000). Making up for war: Sexuality and citizenship in wartime culture. *Feminist Studies, 26*(1), 33–68.

Dey, A., & Dubey, S. K. (2023). Cosmetics science and skin care: History and concepts. In *Nanocosmetics* (pp. 1–15). CRC Press.

Dootson, K. S. (2016). "The Hollywood Powder Puff War": Technicolor cosmetics in the 1930s. *Film History: An International Journal, 28*(1), 107–131.

Dos Santos, R. C., de Brito Silva, M. J., da Costa, M. F., & Batista, K. (2023). Go vegan! digital influence and social media use in the purchase intention of vegan products in the cosmetics industry. *Social Network Analysis and Mining, 13*(49), 1–13.

Findlay, R. (2019). "Trust us, we're you": Aspirational realness in the digital communication of contemporary fashion and beauty brands. *Communication, Culture & Critique, 12*(4), 553–569.

Hawley, R. (2002). The dynamics of beauty in Classical Greece. In *Changing bodies, changing meanings* (pp. 53–70). Routledge.

Hunt, K. A., Fate, J., & Dodds, B. (2011). Cultural and social influences on the perception of beauty: A case analysis of the cosmetics industry. *Journal of Business Case Studies (JBCS), 7*(1), 1–10.

Jhin, M. (2011). *Asian beauty secrets: Ancient and modern tips from the far east*. Bush Street Press.

Kemp, M. (2000). *Visualizations: The nature book of art and science*. University of California Press.

Khan, A. D., & Alam, M. N. (2019). Cosmetics and their associated adverse effects: A review. *Journal of Applied Pharmaceutical Sciences and Research, 2*(1), 1–6.

Lee, S. M., & Lee, D. (2020). "Untact": A new customer service strategy in the digital age. *Service Business, 14*(1), 1–22.

Mangtani, N., Bajpai, N., Sahasrabudhe, S., & Wasule, D. (2020). Importance of artificial intelligence and augmented reality in cosmetic and beauty industry post COVID 19. *World Journal of Pharmaceutical Research, 9*(8), 2296–2308.

Oumeish, O. Y. (2001). The cultural and philosophical concepts of cosmetics in beauty and art through the medical history of mankind. *Clinics in Dermatology, 19*(4), 375–386.

Rasmussen, L. (2018). Parasocial interaction in the digital age: An examination of relationship building and the effectiveness of YouTube celebrities. *The Journal of Social Media in Society, 7*(1), 280–294.

Riordan, T. (2004). *Inventing beauty: A history of the innovations that have made us beautiful*. Broadway.

Scott, D. A. (2016). A review of ancient Egyptian pigments and cosmetics. *Studies in Conservation, 61*(4), 185–202.

Smith, P., & Findlen, P. (Eds.). (2013). *Merchants and marvels: Commerce, science, and art in early modern Europe*. Routledge.

Smith, S. M., McIntosh, W. D., & Bazzini, D. G. (1999). Are the beautiful good in Hollywood? An investigation of the beauty-and-goodness stereotype on film. *Basic and Applied Social Psychology, 21*(1), 69–80.

Tungate, M. (2011). *Branded beauty: How marketing changed the way we look*. Kogan Page Publishers.

Chapter 2
Rising Titans: Unveiling the Enduring Foundations of Global Cosmetic Leaders

Abstract In this chapter, we embark on a historical journey through the evolution of major cosmetic companies, starting with their foundations and early innovations. This chapter delves into the personal stories of visionary founders like Helena Rubinstein, Max Factor, Madam C. J. Walker, and Eugène Schueller, whose pioneering efforts laid the groundwork for today's beauty industry. We explore their initial product offerings, which were groundbreaking for their time, and how these visionaries harnessed their unique socio-cultural backgrounds to fulfill the needs of their era. Their early innovations, combining scientific discoveries with emerging cosmetic raw materials, set the stage for enduring brand success. Further, the chapter shifts to technological advances in manufacturing, highlighting the transformation from small-scale, artisanal methods to modern, large-scale industrial production. This transition, driven by scientific breakthroughs like safer synthetic dyes and long-lasting formulations, enabled these companies to stay at the industry's forefront. The narrative also explores the critical role of research and technological advancements in developing safer, more sustainable, and innovative products. As we journey through the evolution of ingredients and safety standards, we witness the industry's shift towards natural and safe ingredients, responding to growing consumer demands for environmentally friendly and health-conscious products. The chapter concludes by examining the sustainable and inclusive beauty movement, which reflects a significant shift towards more responsible and empathetic industry practices. This evolution encompasses not only greener formulations and eco-friendly packaging but also a broader representation of beauty standards, acknowledging the diversity of skin types and needs. As we close this chapter, we gain a comprehensive understanding of how these cosmetic companies have not only shaped beauty standards and marketing strategies but also adapted to the ever-evolving relationship between society and self-image, solidifying their global influence in the beauty and cosmetics world.

Y. W. Park and P. Hong, *Cosmetics Marketing Strategy in the Era of the Digital Ecosystem*, https://doi.org/10.1007/978-981-97-3674-4_2

1 Foundations and Early Innovations

The origins of these cosmetic firms, focusing on their founders, the historical context of their creation, and the early products defined their brand. As we embark on the journey of "Foundations and Early Innovations," we enter the realm where ground-breaking ideas were nurtured into existence, where the seeds of what would become cosmetic empires were sown. This narrative bridge is where we connect the dots between the inception of an idea and the person who dared to dream it into reality. It is a tale of how raw ambition and acute observation of the cultural zeitgeist merged to create products that resonated with the desires and needs of an era. Before we delve into the personal stories of the visionaries, we pause to appreciate the confluence of timing, societal needs, and individual foresight that allowed these pioneers to craft not just products, but entire industries from the ground up. This segment sets the stage for understanding how original missions and foundational values were crucial in shaping the identities of brands that have stood the test of time (Jones, 2010).

1.1 Origins and Visionaries

This chapter focuses on the stories of the founders, their initial vision, and how their personal narratives and the socio-cultural environment of their time influenced the inception of their companies. It would shed light on the original mission and values that set the foundation for their brand's identity.

Max Factor, a Polish-Jewish businessman and visionary artist, established his brand by selling handmade creams, fragrances, and wigs in Russia before moving to the United States (Basten, 2011). His "Color Harmony" range of face powder and the decision to coin the term "make-up" significantly boosted his brand's prominence. Max Factor, a luminary, revolutionized makeup for the silver screen in the early twentieth century and extended his innovations to everyday makeup. Max Factor's early work at a local pharmacy and later at the Imperial Russian Grand Opera laid the foundation for his understanding of makeup's transformative power. His move to America and subsequent focus on film makeup led to the patented "Color Harmony" face powders, catering to the screen actors' specific needs and setting a new standard in the industry (Basten, 2011).

Madam C. J. Walker, born Sarah Breedlove, is emblematically positioned in the background to acknowledge her groundbreaking role in African American hair care and her status as one of the first African American female millionaires in the United States. Her entrepreneurial spirit led to the creation of a homemade line of hair care products specifically for Black women, effectively filling a void in the market and empowering others economically (Bundles, 2002). The backdrop, featuring a clock and vintage designs, sets the scene in the early twentieth century—a period marked by considerable advancements in the cosmetics industry. Walker's personal battle with hair loss spurred her to innovate, developing specialized products that fostered self-care and economic independence for African American women. Her story is a testament to the profound impact of personal experiences and cultural insights on innovation in the beauty sector.

Eugène Schueller's pioneering efforts in the cosmetic industry marked the birth of L'Oréal, one of the world's most renowned beauty and cosmetics companies. In 1909, Schueller, a young French chemist, introduced a groundbreaking hair dye formula named "Auréale." This innovation was a game-changer for the beauty industry, as it allowed individuals to alter their hair color effectively and safely. Recognizing the potential of his invention, Schueller began distributing his products to Parisian hairdressers during the early twentieth century, a strategic move that showcased his entrepreneurial spirit and laid the foundation for L'Oréal's future success. The success of "Auréale" marked the inception of a brand that would become synonymous with innovation and quality in the beauty world, with L'Oréal's expansion from a single hair dye product to a comprehensive range of cosmetics and skincare offerings over the years being a testament to Schueller's vision and dedication. His commitment to research and development set a precedent for the company's unwavering pursuit of excellence. L'Oréal's global reach and influence have reshaped beauty standards worldwide, making it a household name and an industry leader. The pioneering spirit of Eugène Schueller and the initial success of "Auréale" have left an indelible mark on the cosmetic industry, shaping its trajectory for generations to come (Jones, 2010, 2011).

Business success requires the scientific knowledge and materials available at the time. It would cover the earliest innovations that distinguished these brands and set the stage for future growth. Each pioneer's initial product offerings were innovative for their time, incorporating scientific discoveries and inventing new cosmetic raw materials. Their creations were not just products but were also accompanied by personal stories of overcoming challenges and leveraging their unique socio-cultural backgrounds to meet the needs of their times. These earliest innovations laid the groundwork for the enduring success of their brands. These narratives describe the initial challenges and opportunities the firms faced, such as competition, market demands, and the economic context of their time. It would examine how these early enterprises positioned themselves in the market and secured their first successes.

In conclusion, the personal sagas of Helena Rubinstein, Max Factor, Madam C. J. Walker, and Eugène Schueller are interwoven with the fabric of the modern cosmetic industry. Their foresight and innovations not only filled market gaps but also redefined societal norms and beauty standards. Their legacies illustrate how individual creativity, when harnessed with strategic acumen and an understanding of the socio-cultural zeitgeist, can engender brands that endure and evolve over time. As this chapter has demonstrated, the foundations laid by these visionaries were instrumental in building empires that transcended the boundaries of their initial product lines, allowing them to make a lasting imprint on the industry and the world at large. The subsequent chapters will delve into how these brands have navigated the evolving landscapes of business, culture, and technology to maintain their relevance and leadership in the dynamic world of beauty and cosmetics.

1.2 Technological Advances in Manufacturing

Cosmetic firms adopted advancements in science and technology to develop new products and enhance existing ones. It would highlight key scientific breakthroughs, such as the development of non-toxic dyes or long-lasting formulations, that allowed these companies to stay at the forefront of the industry. In discussing science and product development in the cosmetics industry, it is essential to recognize the pivotal role of research and technological advancements. Continuous investment in research and development has enabled these firms to pioneer new products, offering enhanced benefits and addressing a wide range of consumer needs. Advancements in fields like chemistry, dermatology, and biotechnology have been fundamental in driving innovation within the cosmetics industry. These scientific strides have enabled the development of advanced formulations that are not only effective but also safer and more sustainable.

The cosmetics industry has experienced a remarkable evolution from its historical roots to the modern era. In the period before the 1900s, cosmetics were predominantly crafted in small batches using artisanal methods, characterized by the use of locally available ingredients and traditional methods. This approach, highlighted by Martin (2009), resulted in limited product accessibility and variety, with cosmetics primarily used by the affluent and considered luxury items. The industry was not yet designed for the mass market, and products were generally unstandardized, focusing heavily on natural ingredients and simple formulations (Butler, 2000).

In stark contrast, the contemporary landscape of cosmetics production has undergone a significant transformation. This change has been primarily driven by technological and biotechnological advances, as well as an improved understanding of economies of scale. Innovations like nanoemulsions and lipid vesicles have allowed for more sophisticated and diverse products (Vuillemard, 1991; Yukuyama et al., 2016). The industrialization of production processes has also played a crucial role, increasing product volume while reducing costs. Gomes et al. (2020) emphasize the impact of biotechnological advancements in introducing novel ingredients and methods in formulation. Bennur and Malhotra (2023) further highlight how economies of scale enable companies to produce high-quality products more affordably, broadening consumer accessibility. This shift has democratized beauty products and transformed the cosmetics industry into a significant global economic player, marked by mass production, standardization, and a focus on continual innovation and marketing.

Moreover, the development of large-scale production in the cosmetics industry is closely tied to advancements in technology, such as automation and precision engineering. These technological improvements have enhanced quality control and consistency in mass production, meeting global demands more efficiently. Cosmetic manufacturing processes now embody precision, efficiency, customization, sustainability, and quality control. Automation, in particular, has revolutionized cosmetic manufacturing by improving production speed and accuracy, reducing waste, and minimizing human error. The incorporation of biotechnology and nanotechnology has led to the creation of innovative products with superior properties, while the integration of digital technologies like AI and machine learning optimizes production processes and predictive maintenance, paving the way for smarter manufacturing systems.

As the cosmetics industry grew, it became imperative to protect consumers from potential hazards associated with chemical ingredients and to ensure that the claims made by manufacturers were truthful and not misleading (Lintner, 2009). Government regulatory bodies set guidelines on the composition, labeling, and marketing of cosmetic products. These regulations helped to prevent the use of toxic substances, enforced good manufacturing practices, and provided a clear framework within which manufacturers could operate with integrity and accountability (Califf et al., 2017).

The rapid growth of the cosmetics industry underscored the need for regulation and standardization to ensure product safety and quality. Governments and industry bodies began to establish guidelines and standards to protect consumers from harmful ingredients and false advertising (Cornell et al., 2019). These regulations were critical in building consumer trust and credibility in the industry. Standardization also played a vital role in the industry's expansion, ensuring that products met consistent quality and safety criteria regardless of where they were produced. The establishment of these regulatory frameworks was a crucial step in the professionalization of the cosmetics industry, paving the way for its global expansion and enduring success.

Quality standards were crucial not only for maintaining safety but also for facilitating the scaling of production across different regions and markets. Consistent standards ensured that a product manufactured in one country would meet the same quality and safety criteria when produced in another, thus simplifying international trade and distribution. This uniformity allowed brands to scale up production while assuring consumers that products would perform consistently, regardless of where they were purchased. The professionalization of the cosmetics industry through regulation and standardization has been instrumental in its global expansion (Califf et al., 2017; Cornell et al., 2019; Lintner, 2009). It has instilled a level of consumer trust that is critical in an industry based on personal care and wellness. By adhering to these established guidelines, cosmetics companies can innovate and grow while ensuring the well-being of their customers and the reliability of their products. This foundation has enabled the cosmetics industry to evolve into a diverse and robust market, continuing to thrive and adapt to new scientific advancements and consumer expectations.

1.3 Innovations in Ingredients and Safety

The cosmetic industry has witnessed several key scientific breakthroughs, notably in the areas of ingredient safety, product performance, and environmental impact. These include the discovery of safer synthetic dyes to replace harmful coal tar derivatives, the use of natural and organic compounds for skin health, and advances in preserving agents to prolong shelf life without using harsh chemicals. Additionally, breakthroughs in nanotechnology have enabled more efficient delivery of active ingredients, and biotechnology has played a role in developing new materials and compounds for cosmetic use.

Historically, the cosmetics industry has utilized a range of compounds that, over time, have been identified as harmful. These include substances like lead, which was used in face powders and creams, and coal tar derivatives in hair dyes. The recognition of the adverse health effects of such ingredients prompted a reevaluation of cosmetic formulations. The development of new and safer ingredients has been a critical element in modern cosmetics. This involves extensive research into alternative compounds that are effective yet benign. Safety assessments, hypoallergenic testing, and ensuring non-toxicity have become central to this development process. This shift often requires balancing efficacy with safety, ensuring products deliver desired results without compromising health.

There was a steady shift towards safer, more natural product formulations (Seelig et al., 2021). The word "OILD" within a triangular hazard sign could be a creative play on the word "old," suggesting the outdated and potentially dangerous ingredients that are being phased out. Surrounding this sign are test tubes in a rack, each labeled differently, perhaps denoting new, safer alternatives that are replacing the old ingredients. A microscope and a laboratory setup, complete with beakers and scientific apparatus, denote rigorous research and testing protocols. The presence of greenery, leaves, and herbal elements emphasizes the use of natural components in modern cosmetics, reflecting a growing consumer demand for environmental brand identification (Seelig et al., 2021). There's also a timepiece, which might signify the ongoing progression and development in the industry over time. The inclusion of molecular structures, a DNA helix, and other scientific motifs illustrates the role of advanced research in the development of new cosmetic compounds.

There has been a significant push toward natural and safe ingredients in response to consumer demand for more environmentally friendly and health-conscious products. This has led to the innovation of ingredients derived from natural sources, such as plant extracts and minerals, which are perceived as safer and more sustainable. Companies are investing in green chemistry and ethical sourcing to meet these consumer expectations. Governmental regulatory changes have had a significant impact on the cosmetics industry. Regulatory bodies like the FDA and the European Union have established stricter guidelines on ingredient safety, banning or restricting the use of certain harmful substances. These regulations have compelled cosmetic firms to reformulate products and adopt more transparent labeling practices, enhancing consumer trust and industry accountability.

1.4 Sustainable and Inclusive Beauty

In recent years, the cosmetics industry has seen a growing demand for sustainability and inclusivity. Consumers are increasingly seeking products that are not only effective but also ethically produced, environmentally friendly, and inclusive in their representation. This shift has prompted brands to embrace greener formulations, eco-friendly packaging, and transparent supply chains, partly in response to the adverse effects traditionally associated with cosmetic products (Khan & Alam, 2019). Additionally, the industry is moving towards a more inclusive approach, with a broader range of shades and products designed for diverse skin types and needs. This evolution reflects a deeper societal change where beauty is being redefined to encompass a broader spectrum of humanity, respecting the planet and its diverse inhabitants. The movement towards sustainable and inclusive beauty marks a significant step towards a more responsible and empathetic industry.

The cosmetic industry's response to sustainable development requirements has been increasingly proactive. Brands are reformulating products to include natural, organic, and non-toxic ingredients, reducing their ecological footprint. Efforts in eco-friendly packaging, such as using recyclable materials or reducing plastic use, are becoming more common. Additionally, companies are more transparent about their supply chains, ensuring fair trade and ethical sourcing practices. This shift towards sustainability is in response to consumer awareness and the global call to protect the environment. In line with the global push for longevity and well-being, the cosmetics industry is contributing by developing products that support healthy living and aging gracefully. Skincare lines are increasingly focusing on not only aesthetics but also skin health, incorporating medical-grade ingredients and leveraging technological advancements. Anti-aging products with active ingredients that promote skin regeneration and protection are prevalent. The industry is aligning with the healthcare sector to create cosmetics that contribute to a sustainable lifestyle, aiming to enhance not just beauty but also the quality and longevity of life.

The concept of beauty within the industry is undergoing a significant transformation, moving beyond the traditional Western concept of white beauty. There is a growing recognition of diverse beauty standards, which is reflected in a wider range of product shades, models of different ethnicities in marketing campaigns, and products formulated for a variety of skin types. This inclusivity is not only a response to a diverse consumer base but also part of a broader cultural shift towards celebrating and respecting individual uniqueness and rejecting a one-size-fits-all beauty standard. The movement towards sustainable and inclusive beauty reflects societal changes that prioritize environmental consciousness and celebrate diversity. As the industry continues to evolve, it becomes clear that the future of cosmetics is not just about looking good but also about doing good—for people and the planet. This progressive outlook is redefining the role of the cosmetics industry in the twenty-first century, positioning it as a force for positive change in the world.

2 An Overview of Global Top Twenty Beauty Firms

The global beauty industry is a tapestry woven from the threads of tradition, innovation, and cultural influences. Standing tall within this intricate weave are the top 20 global cosmetic firms, each a titan, commanding substantial influence over beauty trends, consumer habits, and economic flows in the global market. These firms are not merely producers of beauty products; they are trendsetters, culture shapers, and economic powerhouses that drive the industry forward. Understanding the profiles of these leading companies is crucial in grasping the full picture of the global cosmetics industry. It reveals the interplay between brand heritage, innovation, and strategic market positioning that has enabled these companies to thrive in a competitive landscape.

The importance of studying these firms extends beyond mere rankings by sales revenue. Their stories are narratives of resilience, agility, and foresight. For industry observers, entrepreneurs, and consumers alike, there is much to learn from how these companies have adapted to the shifting sands of consumer demand, regulatory environments, and technological advancements. Before engaging in a detailed discussion of the broader issues facing the global cosmetics industry, it is imperative to explore the individual journeys of these industry leaders. Their successes and challenges provide invaluable insights into the dynamics of market dominance and the continuous push for relevance in a world where beauty ideals are as diverse as they are universal. The profiles of these top 20 firms serve as a prelude to understanding the complexities and driving forces behind the global beauty narrative,

Figure 1 shows the current landscape of the cosmetic industry's most influential top 20 global players, examining their market positioning, sales revenue, and strategic directions that keep them at the industry's apex. In the transition between analysing the current landscape of cosmetic industry leaders and delving into their market presence and revenue, it's important to recognize how these companies have maintained their positions at the apex of the industry. This involves a nuanced understanding of market dynamics, consumer preferences, and the ability to anticipate and adapt to industry trends. The strategies employed by these firms, ranging from innovative product development to effective global marketing campaigns, have been pivotal in securing their market dominance. Additionally, their ability to navigate the challenges and opportunities presented by the ever-evolving global market has been key to their sustained success.

2.1 Profiles of Global Top 20 Cosmetic Firms

This is an overview of the top global cosmetic firms by sales revenue, as shown in the provided figure. It would discuss the factors contributing to the financial success of these firms, including their product range, market strategies, and geographic footprint. Here are brief descriptions of

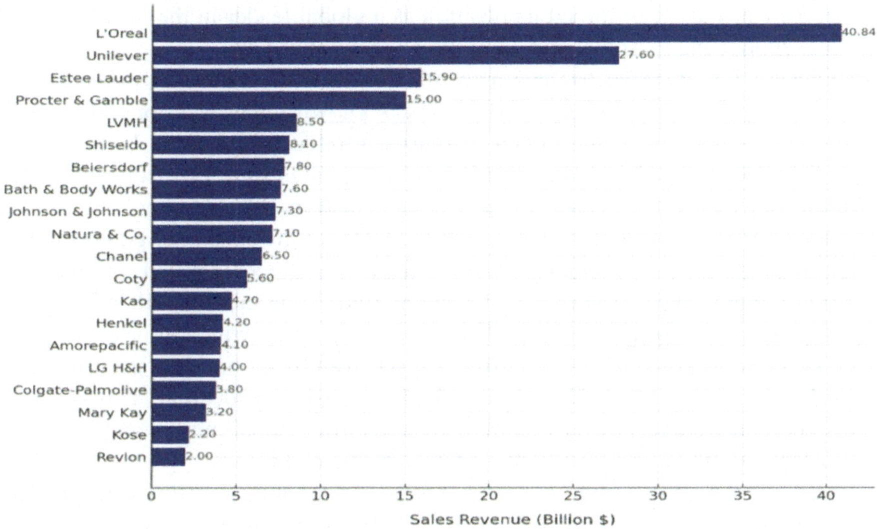

Fig. 1 2022 sales revenue of top 20 global cosmetic companies

- L'Oréal, one of the world's largest cosmetics and beauty companies, was founded in 1909 by Eugène Schueller, a young French chemist. Schueller developed a hair dye formula which he named "Auréale" and started selling his products to Parisian hairdressers. From this initial product, L'Oréal expanded its offerings significantly over the years. Today, L'Oréal's product range covers a broad spectrum of the beauty industry. The company is known for its hair care products, including shampoos, conditioners, hair colour, and styling products under various brands such as L'Oréal Paris and Kérastase. In skincare, L'Oréal offers moisturizers, cleansers, serums, and anti-aging products through brands like Lancôme, Biotherm, and La Roche-Posay.

  The company is also prominent in makeup, with a product line that includes foundations, lipsticks, eyeshadows, and mascaras, sold under brands such as Maybelline New York, NYX Professional Makeup, and Giorgio Armani Beauty. L'Oréal has also made significant strides in the development of sunscreen and sun protection products, particularly through its La Roche-Posay and Vichy brands, which are recommended by dermatologists worldwide. The company's historical commitment to research and innovation has kept it at the forefront of the beauty industry. L'Oréal also emphasizes sustainability and ethical practices in its business model, adapting to the changing demands of consumers and the global market. L'Oréal reported strong sales growth in 2022, with annual sales reaching 38.26 billion euros, marking an 18.5% increase as reported, and a 10.9% rise on a like-for-like basis. This performance indicates a considerable growth of 23.4% compared to 2019. Their success is attributed to innovation leadership, highly desirable brands, operational agility, and the commitment of their teams. The company has also reinforced its position as a global leader in the beauty market while supporting its social and environmental commitment.

- Unilever's history dates to the nineteenth century, with its origins in the merger of several companies. The company as it is known today was formed in 1930 through the merger of the Dutch margarine producer Margarine Unie and the British soap maker Lever Brothers. These companies were themselves founded in the late 1800s, with Lever Brothers established in 1885. Unilever has a wide range of products that span across several sectors of the consumer goods market, including food and beverages, cleaning agents, and personal care products. In terms of financial performance, Unilever reported strong sales growth in 2022. The company's underlying sales growth accelerated to 9.0%, with a turnover increase of 14.5% to €60.1 billion. This growth was driven by all business groups within Unilever, despite the challenges of inflation and volume decline. This financial data demonstrates Unilever's significant role in the global market and its ability to adapt and thrive even in challenging economic conditions.

  Unilever, with its rich history and expansive portfolio, is distinguished by two key aspects: Diverse Product Portfolio and Brand Strength. Unilever's product range spans various sectors, making it unique in the consumer goods market. From food and beverages to personal care and cleaning agents, Unilever manages a wide array of well-known brands like Dove, Lipton, Ben & Jerry's, and Axe/Lynx. This diversity allows Unilever to cater to a broad spectrum of consumer needs and preferences, contributing to its resilience and growth in the global market. The strength of its brands, recognized worldwide, is a testament to Unilever's marketing prowess and its ability to maintain relevance across different product categories. Another defining characteristic of Unilever is its commitment to sustainability and social responsibility. The company has been a leader in integrating sustainable practices into its business model, focusing on reducing environmental impact, promoting sustainable sourcing, and aiming for a positive social footprint. Unilever's initiatives in these areas are not just about compliance but are integral to its business strategy and brand ethos, resonating strongly with consumers who are increasingly conscious of the environmental and social impact of the products they purchase.

- The Estée Lauder Companies, founded in 1946 by Estée Lauder herself, has grown into one of the world's leading manufacturers of skincare, makeup, fragrance, and hair care products. In 2022, the company reported a 9% increase in full-year net sales, reaching $17.74 billion. The growth was driven by double-digit increases in the Americas and EMEA regions. Despite a challenging economic environment, Estée Lauder has continued to achieve significant growth over the past five years, demonstrating the strength of its brand portfolio and global reach. The Estée Lauder Companies, known for their growth and expansion in the beauty industry, can be characterized by two distinctive aspects: Brand Portfolio and Luxury Positioning: Estée Lauder owns a diverse and prestigious portfolio of beauty brands that cater to a wide range of consumer preferences and price points. This includes not only the flagship Estée Lauder brand but also other high-end names like Clinique, MAC, La Mer, and Tom Ford Beauty. The company's strategy has been to maintain a strong position in the luxury beauty market, offering high-quality, innovative products that appeal to discerning consumers. This diverse brand portfolio allows Estée Lauder to tap into various market segments and consumer trends effectively. Estée Lauder's significant growth, particularly in the Americas and EMEA regions, highlights its successful global expansion strategy. The company has adapted its products and marketing to resonate with local tastes and beauty standards in various international markets. This global reach, combined with a keen understanding of regional differences in beauty preferences, has been instrumental in driving its consistent sales growth. Additionally, Estée Lauder has shown a strong ability to navigate through various economic environments while maintaining its growth trajectory.

- Procter & Gamble (P&G) was founded in 1837 by William Procter and James Gamble. The company started by selling soap and candles and has since expanded into a multinational corporation with a diverse range of consumer goods. In 2022, P&G reported $15 billion. P&G's key products include household names like Tide laundry detergent, Pampers diapers, and Gillette razors. In addition to its rich history and diverse product portfolio, two distinctive aspects of P&G are Innovation and Brand Leadership. P&G is known for its strong emphasis on innovation and research, which has led to the development of many market-leading products and technologies. This focus on innovation has helped P&G's brands, like Tide, Pampers, and Gillette, become household names, often setting industry standards in their respective categories. P&G has a substantial global presence, operating in numerous countries worldwide. This extensive reach is complemented by the company's commitment to social responsibility and sustainability. P&G engages in various initiatives aimed at improving community health and hygiene, reducing environmental impact, and promoting diversity and inclusion both within the company and in its wider community engagements.
- LVMH, also known as Moët Hennessy Louis Vuitton, was formed in 1987 through the merger of the fashion house Louis Vuitton (founded in 1854) and Moët Hennessy, which itself came about from a 1971 merger between champagne producer Moët & Chandon (founded in 1743) and cognac manufacturer Hennessy (founded in 1765). LVMH is the world's largest luxury goods company, with a vast portfolio that includes over 75 prestigious brands across various segments such as fashion and leather goods, perfumes and cosmetics, watches and jewellery, wines and spirits, and selective retailing. In 2022, LVMH recorded a revenue of €79.2 billion, which was an increase of 23% from the previous year. This significant growth is attributed to strong demand across all business groups, with notable performances by Fashion & Leather Goods, which include iconic brands like Louis Vuitton and Christian Dior, among others. The United States, Europe, and Japan experienced sharp rises in business, benefiting from strong local demand and the recovery of international travel, while Asia remained stable despite health situation developments in China. Two distinct characteristics of LVMH are its emphasis on high-quality products and innovation, as well as a strong social and

economic footprint, particularly in France. The company is recognized for its commitment to sustainability and has been awarded a triple "A" rating by the CDP (Carbon Disclosure Project) for its efforts in protecting the climate, forests, and water.

- Shiseido was founded in 1872, making it one of the oldest cosmetics companies in the world. Over the years, Shiseido has become known for its wide range of beauty products, including skincare, makeup, fragrances, and hair care products. Some of its key premium brands include ELIXIR, which is renowned for being the number one skincare brand in Japan for consecutive years, ANESSA, known for its sunscreen products, and d program, which caters to sensitive skin. In 2022, Shiseido celebrated its 150th anniversary and reported net sales of ¥1,067.4 billion, marking a year-on-year increase of 5.7%. The company has a robust research and development philosophy termed "Dynamic Harmony," which reflects its commitment to beauty innovation. Two distinct characteristics that stand out for Shiseido are its long history of UV research, with the company having over 100 years of history in this field, and its dedication to inclusivity and diversity within its global workforce. Shiseido is also recognized for its significant social contributions, such as investing heavily in employee training and development, particularly in France, and for its focus on sustainability and ethical business practices.
- Beiersdorf, the company behind the globally recognized brand NIVEA, was founded in 1882 by pharmacist Paul C. Beiersdorf. The company has since grown to become a major player in the skin care industry. Among its key products, Beiersdorf is known for NIVEA, one of the world's leading skincare brands, as well as other notable brands such as Eucerin, La Prairie, and Hansaplast/Elastoplast. In 2022, Beiersdorf reported group sales of €8.8 billion, reflecting a nominal growth of 15.4% from the previous year, with a 10.2% organic sales growth. This performance marks a significant stride in the company's recent financial history, despite the volatile market environment. Two distinct characteristics that define Beiersdorf are its longstanding commitment to skin care and innovation, with over 140 years of history in the industry, and its dedication to sustainability and social responsibility. The company has made significant investments in digitalization and AI to enhance its product offerings and customer experience. Beiersdorf's focus on sustainability is also evident in its efforts to achieve fully circular resources and contribute to a climate-caring future.
- Bath & Body Works, a prominent retailer in the personal care and fragrance industry, was founded in 1990. It is known for its wide range of bath and body products, including fragrances, lotions, candles, and soaps. In 2022, the company generated net sales of approximately $7.56 billion. Two distinct characteristics of Bath & Body Works are its focus on creating a broad variety of fragrances and its strong presence in North America with over 1,800 stores. The company has become synonymous with accessible luxury in everyday personal care and home fragrance products.
- Johnson & Johnson, founded in 1886 by Robert Wood Johnson, James Wood Johnson, and Edward Mead Johnson, is a leading multinational corporation in pharmaceuticals and medical devices. In 2022, the company generated revenue of

$94.94 billion. Known for products like Band-Aid, Tylenol, and Johnson's Baby products, it has significantly influenced healthcare and consumer goods sectors. Two distinct characteristics of Johnson & Johnson are its long-standing reputation for innovation in healthcare and its global presence, with operations in multiple countries and a wide range of healthcare products. The company is also recognized for its commitment to ethical practices and sustainability in its operation.

- Chanel, the iconic French luxury fashion house, was founded in 1910 by Coco Chanel. Known for revolutionizing women's fashion by introducing more functional and comfortable yet elegant designs, Chanel has remained a prominent name in the fashion industry. The brand specializes in haute couture, ready-to-wear clothing, accessories, jewellery, and perfumes, with Chanel No. 5 being one of its most famous and enduring products. In 2022, Chanel reported revenue of $15.6 billion, indicating its substantial presence in the luxury goods market. Two distinct characteristics of Chanel are its long-standing reputation for elegance and luxury, and its ability to continuously innovate while maintaining the classic Chanel aesthetic. The company, which is still privately owned by the Wertheimer family, has been headquartered in London since 2018, though it was originally established in Paris.
- Coty Inc. is a notable player in the beauty and cosmetics industry. Here is an overview of Coty's history. Coty was founded in 1904 by François Coty in Paris, France. It started as a fragrance company and gradually expanded into one of the world's largest beauty companies. Sales of Coty Corporation in 2022 is 5.6 billion ($). Coty's product range primarily focused on fragrances, cosmetics, and skin and body care. They are known for their luxury perfume brands such as Calvin Klein, Marc Jacobs, and Chloé. In addition to fragrances, Coty also produces a wide array of colour cosmetics and skincare products, with brands like Rimmel and CoverGirl under their umbrella. Coty is recognized for its innovation in the beauty industry, especially in fragrances and cosmetics. The company has a history of developing unique and popular scents, as well as high-quality makeup products. Coty operates globally, with a significant presence across continents. They have a diverse portfolio that not only includes luxury brands but also mass-market products, catering to a wide range of consumer preferences and budgets.
- Kao Corporation is a major Japanese company known for its diverse range of products, particularly in the fields of beauty, healthcare, and chemicals. Kao Corporation was founded in 1887 by Tomiro Nagase as a manufacturer of quality facial soaps. Since then, it has expanded significantly and diversified into a broad array of products. Kao's product line is extensive, including beauty care products like skincare and haircare items, under famous brands like Bioré, Jergens, and John Frieda. They also produce home care products like laundry detergents and cleaning agents, as well as a range of chemicals used in various industrial applications. Sales of Kao Corporation in 2022 is 4.7 billion ($). Kao is known for its commitment to innovation and sustainability. The company invests heavily in research and development to create new products that meet the changing needs of consumers while also focusing on environmentally friendly practices. Kao also operates globally, with a significant presence in many countries. They are notable

for their sensitivity to local cultures and preferences, tailoring their products and marketing strategies to suit different regions effectively.

- Henkel AG & Co. KGaA is a renowned global company with a rich history and diverse product portfolio. Henkel was founded in 1876 by Fritz Henkel in Aachen, Germany. Initially, the company focused on laundry detergents, launching the first self-acting detergent, Persil, in 1907. Over the years, Henkel has grown into a global enterprise. Sales of Henkel Corporation in 2022 is 4.2 billion ($). Henkel is a world leader in adhesives, sealants, and functional coatings for both industrial and consumer applications. Beauty Care segment includes hair care, hair colorants, hair styling, body care, skin care, and oral care products, with well-known brands like Schwarzkopf, Dial, and Syoss. Laundry & Home Care segment is famous for its laundry detergents and household cleaners, with brands like Persil, Purex, and All.
- Amorepacific Corporation is a major South Korean beauty and cosmetics conglomerate. Amorepacific was founded in 1945 by Suh Sung-Whan. It started as a small family business under the name "Pacific Chemical Industries," and has since grown into one of South Korea's largest beauty companies, significantly influencing the global beauty industry. Sales of Amorepacific Corporation in 2022 is 4.1 billion ($). Amorepacific's product range is extensive and diverse, primarily focusing on skincare, makeup, and fragrances. The company owns several popular brands, including Sulwhasoo, Laneige, Mamonde, and Innisfree. These brands are known for their innovative skincare and cosmetic products, often incorporating unique natural ingredients and advanced technology. Amorepacific is known for its commitment to research and development in beauty technology. The company has been a pioneer in using natural ingredients and advanced technology to create high-quality beauty and skincare products. The company has played a significant role in popularizing Korean beauty standards and products worldwide. Known for its 'K-beauty' products, Amorepacific has successfully expanded globally, appealing to diverse consumer bases with its innovative products and cultural influence.
- LG Household & Health Care, often abbreviated as LG H&H, is a significant player in the South Korean and global market for beauty, health, and household goods. LG H&H was founded in 1947, initially as the Lak Hui Chemical Industrial Corp. (now known as LG Chem). It became part of the LG Group in 1958 and eventually evolved into LG Household & Health Care in 2001 after merging with LG Household & Health Care Ltd. LG H&H has a wide array of products across various segments. Beauty and Cosmetics segment is well-known for their beauty and skincare brands like The History of Whoo, belif, and CNP. These brands offer a range of high-quality skincare, makeup, and personal care products. Healthcare segment includes products like oral care and over-the-counter pharmaceuticals. Household Goods segment also manufactures a variety of household products, including laundry detergents, surface cleaners, and air fresheners. Sales of LG H&H in 2022 is 4.0 billion ($). LG H&H is known for its commitment to innovation, quality, and research in product development. This is

evident in their advanced skincare technologies and high-quality household products. While rooted in South Korea, LG H&H has expanded globally, adapting to, and embracing diverse cultural beauty and health practices. They are recognized for integrating traditional Korean beauty ingredients and practices with modern technology.

- Colgate-Palmolive is a global leader in the production and distribution of household, health care, and personal products. Colgate-Palmolive has its origins in the early nineteenth century. William Colgate founded a starch, soap, and candle business in New York City in 1806. The company later merged with the Palmolive-Peet Company, originally founded in 1864, and eventually became known as Colgate-Palmolive in 1953. Colgate-Palmolive's product portfolio is diverse, including Oral Care. The company is best known for its oral care products, including toothpaste, toothbrushes, and dental floss. Colgate is one of the most recognizable brands in this category globally. Personal Care includes soaps, shampoos, and body washes, with notable brands like Palmolive and Sanex. Home Care produces household cleaning products, as well as laundry detergents. Colgate-Palmolive also owns Hill's Pet Nutrition, a leading brand in pet food. Sales of Colgate-Palmolive in 2022 is 3.8 billion ($). Two Distinct Characteristics are Global Presence and Brand Recognition. Colgate-Palmolive is a household name with a strong global presence. Their products are sold in numerous countries worldwide, making them one of the most recognizable consumer goods companies. The company has a strong focus on sustainability and social responsibility. They have initiatives aimed at reducing environmental impact, promoting oral health education, and engaging in community programs around the world.
- Mary Kay Inc. is a well-known American multi-level marketing company specializing in beauty products. Mary Kay was founded in 1963 by Mary Kay Ash in Dallas, Texas. Ash started the company with a vision to provide rewarding opportunities for women and produce cosmetics that catered to a wide range of beauty needs. Mary Kay's product line primarily focuses on cosmetics and skincare. This includes a wide range of products like facial skincare treatments, makeup for eyes, lips, and face, sunscreens, fragrances, and even men's skincare products. The brand is known for its personalized skin care solutions and high-quality makeup products. Sales of Mary Kay Inc. in 2022 is 3.2 billion ($). Two Distinct Characteristics are Direct Sales and Independent Consultant Model. Mary Kay is notable for its use of a direct sales model, primarily through independent consultants. This approach not only allows for personalized customer service but also provides entrepreneurial opportunities for a large network of independent sales representatives. Mary Kay has a strong focus on empowering women, which is evident in its business model and corporate culture. The company also engages in various philanthropic activities, with a particular emphasis on causes related to women, such as ending domestic violence and supporting female entrepreneurship.

- Kose Corporation is a prominent Japanese cosmetics and skincare company with a rich history and a diverse range of products. Kose Corporation was founded in 1946 by Kozaburo Kobayashi. The company started with a focus on high-quality cosmetics and has grown to become one of Japan's leading beauty and skincare brands with international reach. Sales of Kose Corporation in 2022 is 2.2 billion ($). Kose's product range is extensive, covering a wide array of skincare, cosmetics, and beauty products. They are known for their skincare lines, including high-end products under the brand Decorté, and more affordable lines such as Sekkisei. Their products cater to a variety of skincare needs, from anti-aging treatments to whitening and moisturizing products. They also offer a range of makeup products. Two Distinct Characteristics are Innovation and Research in Skincare. Kose is renowned for its commitment to research and innovation in skincare. The company invests significantly in developing innovative technologies and formulations to improve the efficacy of its products and meet the evolving needs of consumers. While rooted in Japan, Kose has expanded its presence globally. The company is known for its ability to adapt to distinct cultural beauty standards and preferences, offering products that cater to a diverse customer base across various regions.
- Revlon is a well-known American multinational company in the cosmetics, skin care, fragrance, and personal care industry. Revlon was founded in 1932 by Charles Revson and his brother Joseph, along with a chemist, Charles Lachman, who contributed the "L" in the Revlon name. Starting with a specific product—a new type of nail enamel—the company grew rapidly and expanded into a wide range of beauty products. Sales of Revlon Corporation in 2022 is 2.0 billion ($). Revlon's product portfolio includes a wide variety of beauty and personal care products.

2.2 Common Characteristics of Top 20 Firms

The top twenty global cosmetic firms exhibit several common characteristics that not only define their success but also shape the industry at large. These traits are not mere coincidences but rather the result of strategic choices, innovative practices, and a deep-rooted understanding of the market and consumer behavior. They have managed to navigate the complex terrain of global commerce, adapting to and often anticipating changes in consumer preferences and global market trends. These companies serve as benchmarks for industry standards, and their business models offer invaluable insights into achieving longevity and sustaining power in a competitive landscape.

Firstly, longevity and sustaining power of global firms. their longevity and staying power are remarkable, with many boasting over a century of operations. For instance, L'Oréal, founded in 1909, has continued to grow through continuous innovation and adaptation to market changes. This durability in the marketplace speaks to a profound understanding of consumer needs and an ability to evolve with changing times, embodying the principles outlined by Cusumano (2010) for sustaining power in an uncertain world. Companies like Johnson & Johnson, with roots going back to 1886, have become household names by consistently delivering products that resonate with consumers across generations. Their ability to pivot and embrace innovation, whether through product development or entering new market segments, has been central to their enduring presence. Johnson & Johnson's longstanding reputation in healthcare has also enabled it to expand into a wide range of consumer goods, evidencing its strategic agility. Such firms stand as historical landmarks in the industry, their brands woven into the fabric of daily life, testifying to the trust and reliability they've cultivated over decades.

These firms are often at the forefront of socio-cultural changes, influencing and adapting to shifts in consumer behavior and societal values. Estée Lauder, for instance, is not only a significant player in luxury cosmetics but also actively adapts to regional beauty preferences and maintains a strong global market presence. Managing sustainability initiatives is a critical challenge for cosmetic companies because modern consumers are increasingly environmentally conscious. This consumer shift demands that companies adopt sustainable practices in sourcing materials, manufacturing products, and designing packaging. These initiatives are crucial for reducing environmental impact and aligning with consumers' values. For cosmetic companies, this means balancing business goals with ecological responsibility, which is vital for maintaining consumer trust and brand reputation in a market that values sustainability (Hart & Milstein, 2003). Moreover, the top firms' longevity can also be attributed to their ability to maintain relevance by aligning with socio-cultural trends and consumer ideologies. For example, Colgate-Palmolive, established in 1806, has demonstrated an ongoing commitment to sustainability and social responsibility, key concerns in today's market. Their global presence and brand recognition are not just the result of historical inertia but are actively maintained through initiatives that address current global challenges such as environmental sustainability and community health. By doing so, they not only secure their market position but also contribute positively to societal progress, reinforcing their image as responsible and forward-thinking leaders in the cosmetic industry.

Secondly, *innovativeness, adaptability and responsiveness.* These companies display tremendous innovative capabilities, seen in their new product developments and organizational renewal. For example, Shiseido, with its 150-year history, is recognized for its dedication to beauty innovation and R&D, particularly in UV research and sensitive skin products, demonstrating organizational adaptive capability (Akgün et al., 2012). Adapting to rapidly changing consumer preferences is essential for cosmetic firms to remain competitive and relevant, an agility that is crucial in the context of born-global firms (Efrat et al., 2017). This approach is critical because it directly affects a company's ability to attract and retain customers in a market where consumer preferences are increasingly driven by values and personalized experiences. Firms must be able to swiftly adjust their product offerings to align with these new preferences. This adaptability ensures they continue to meet their customers' needs and desires, which is vital for maintaining customer loyalty and market share in a dynamic industry landscape. This approach is critical because it directly affects a company's ability to attract and retain customers in a market where consumer preferences are increasingly driven by values and personalized experiences.

In essence, the evolving competitive landscape pushes all players in the industry to constantly improve and adapt, which ultimately benefits consumers with more diverse and advanced product offerings. The innovative spirit of these firms is not confined to product development alone; it extends into the very ethos of how they conduct business. Shiseido's investment in research and development is a testament to their commitment to pushing the boundaries of beauty science. By focusing on specialized areas such as UV protection and catering to sensitive skin, Shiseido demonstrates a keen sensitivity to the nuanced demands of its diverse customer base. This innovative approach is not just about responding to current trends but about anticipating future needs and driving the industry forward. It is this proactive stance in innovation that allows firms like Shiseido to not only adapt to the market but to lead it, setting new standards and expectations for beauty products. In addition to Shiseido, the innovative capabilities of these top firms are further exemplified by their organizational agility in responding to global market shifts. For example, companies like Estée Lauder continuously adapt their business strategies to harness technological advancements, digital marketing, and e-commerce platforms to engage with consumers in the digital age. They understand that innovation is a holistic process that involves not just the creation of new products but also the reinvention of marketing tactics and business models. By doing so, they maintain a competitive edge in an industry that is as dynamic as it is diverse, ensuring that their legacy of innovation remains relevant and resonant with the expectations of modern consumers.

The proactive response of the cosmetic industry to market shifts, as exemplified by L'Oréal's sustainability program, highlights the implementation of responsive supply chain strategies in global complexity (Roh et al., 2014). By leveraging advancements in green chemistry and sustainable sourcing, L'Oréal and others are not only minimizing their environmental footprint but also leading the way in corporate environmental responsibility. The move towards more sustainable practices is not only a response to consumer demand but also a reflection of a broader corporate consciousness that recognizes the importance of stewardship for our planet. These efforts are multifaceted, ranging from raw material procurement to the end-of-life cycle of products, demonstrating a holistic approach to sustainability. Moreover, such initiatives have become a critical aspect of brand storytelling, with companies like Unilever using their sustainability efforts as a core part of their corporate identity. By integrating their commitment to the environment into their marketing strategies, these firms are engaging with consumers on a deeper level, aligning brand values with consumer ideals. This strategic alignment not only enhances brand loyalty but also sets a precedent in the industry, prompting others to follow suit. As a result, sustainability is no longer a niche concern but a central tenet in the business models of the world's leading cosmetic firms. Their efforts to reduce their ecological impact go hand-in-hand with their pursuit of innovation, ultimately shaping a more sustainable future for the entire industry.

Thirdly, *global orientation with differentiation advantage*. These firms have a global orientation, with a diverse range of product offerings, yet they also demonstrate unique strengths through differentiation strategies. Beiersdorf, the creator of NIVEA, has established itself as a leader in skincare by combining a broad product line with a specific focus on skin health and a long-standing commitment to sustainability. The rise of competition in the cosmetics market, particularly from emerging indie brands and digital-first companies, presents a significant challenge for established firms. These newer companies often bring fresh perspectives and innovations, appealing to niche markets or rapidly adapting to digital trends (Kane et al., 2015). This increased competition compels established firms to continually innovate and reinvent their strategies to stay relevant. They must not only keep up with the latest trends and technological advancements but also differentiate themselves to maintain a unique appeal.

The global orientation of these firms is critical, even in times of market contraction like the COVID-19 pandemic, which saw many companies retreat from international markets. Yet, global firms often rely on diverse markets to generate substantial portions of their revenue, making a broad geographical presence not just an asset but a necessity (Ciravegna & Michailova, 2022). For instance, during the pandemic, companies that maintained a strong global orientation were better positioned to mitigate the risks of localized downturns. They could capitalize on the shifting dynamics of different regional markets, where the impact of the pandemic varied. This global perspective enabled them to swiftly adjust their strategies, whether by shifting sales channels, reallocating marketing resources, or adapting supply chains to ensure continuity of operations and product delivery (Hong et al., 2023). Furthermore, a global footprint provided these firms with a broader view of the pandemic's impact, allowing for more informed decision-making and resource distribution. By maintaining a global perspective, companies like L'Oréal and Unilever continued to engage with consumers worldwide, despite the challenges posed by the pandemic, reinforcing the importance of global markets for sustained business growth. Their resilience underscores the significance of a global orientation as not merely a strategy for expansion but as a fundamental component of corporate robustness in unpredictable times.

Fourth, *geographical concentration.* The geographical origins of the top global cosmetic firms, predominantly from the USA, UK, Germany, Japan, South Korea, and the Netherlands, reveal a significant concentration of cosmetic industry leaders in these countries (Goerzen & Geisler Asmussen, 2007). This clustering reflects the historical development of the beauty industry, economic prosperity, and market maturity, which have all played crucial roles in fostering the growth of major cosmetic firms. These countries have been at the forefront of technological advancements, research and development, and consumer market evolution, contributing to the sustainability of these global giants (Patel et al., 2018). The presence of a robust consumer base, supported by high disposable incomes and a culture that values personal grooming and beauty, has further contributed to the growth of these firms. Additionally, these countries often have a favorable business environment, with supportive government policies, strong intellectual property rights protection, and significant investment in innovation, all of which are critical for the growth and sustainability of these global giants (Clifford, 1999; Tungate, 2011).

The absence of top cosmetic firms from countries like China, India, Russia, or other BRICS nations indicates various market dynamics and industry development stages. While these countries have large consumer markets, they have historically lagged in terms of home-grown global cosmetic giants due to factors such as less investment in research and development, varying degrees of economic development, and different consumer preferences. However, the growing middle class and increasing disposable incomes in these countries present significant opportunities for growth and expansion. The evolving cosmetic market in these regions, with local brands gaining popularity and international firms expanding, suggests that we may soon see the rise of major players from these areas, as supported by research on born-global firms (Knight et al., 2004).

Lastly, *soft power and the cosmetic market.* The wealth generated through international trade and conquests has historically allowed these companies to flourish. The inflow of riches has facilitated the proliferation of beauty salons and barber shops, expanding the availability and accessibility of cosmetic products. This economic prosperity is mirrored today by the likes of LVMH, whose luxury goods appeal to affluent markets and capitalize on strong local demand. Meanwhile, companies like Procter & Gamble show how a diverse product range and brand strength, combined with a commitment to social responsibility, can sustain a firm's position at the top. These characteristics collectively ensure that these leading firms not only serve as pillars of the global cosmetics industry but also act as catalysts for its ongoing evolution, reflecting the soft power strategies of nations (Lee, 2009; Nye, 1990). Focusing on the Korean cosmetic industry, companies like Amorepacific and LG Household & Health Care have gained international recognition, particularly for popularizing the K-beauty concept. The success of these firms is rooted in their innovative product offerings, which often focus on natural ingredients and advanced skincare technologies. Unique beauty's emphasis on skincare routines, including the use of sheet masks, essences, and BB creams, has resonated globally, appealing to consumers seeking gentle yet effective skincare solutions. The growth potential for these Japanese and Korean firms is significant, as they continue to expand their global footprint, capitalizing on the growing demand for Asian beauty products worldwide (Tsutomu, 2015). Their strategies often involve tailoring products to meet local needs while maintaining the core principles of K-beauty, thus striking a balance between global appeal and local relevance (Chitty, 2016).

Within a foreseeable future, we expect brand firms from China, India, and other BRICS nations to join the list of top global cosmetic companies. Global prominence is a result of a combination of historical, economic, and market maturity factors, which are indicative of the soft power within national contexts (Nye, 1990). These countries, while having enormous potential consumer bases, have traditionally been more focused on other sectors for economic growth. Additionally, the cosmetic industry in these regions might have faced challenges such as lack of innovation, lower levels of disposable income, or different cultural attitudes towards beauty and personal care products. However, the landscape is changing rapidly. With increasing economic development, growing middle classes, and a surge in consumer spending power, these countries are becoming hotbeds for cosmetic market growth. Local brands are emerging and gaining popularity, and there is a growing interest from international companies looking to tap into these burgeoning markets. The future might see the rise of global cosmetic leaders from these regions, driven by local innovation, understanding of regional beauty standards, and the ability to cater to a diverse consumer base (Lee, 2009; Nye, 1990).

3 Conclusion

The continuous integration of science and technology in product development is a driving force in the evolution of the cosmetics industry. Leading cosmetic firms are at the forefront of this trend, leveraging advanced research to deliver innovative products that offer enhanced performance and cater to the specific needs of consumers. By investing in cutting-edge science, these firms are able to create sophisticated formulations that provide benefits such as improved skin care results, longer-lasting makeup, and more effective hair treatments. This scientific approach allows for the customization of products for different skin types, climates, and personal preferences, which is crucial in a market that values individuality and results.

The landscape of the top 20 global cosmetic firms reveals a rich tapestry of cultural heritage intertwined with expansive global reach. Each company's origins and national identity often influence its brand ethos, product design, and marketing strategies. These firms skillfully balance their cultural roots with a global perspective, allowing them to resonate with consumers across different socio-cultural backgrounds. By embracing their unique cultural backgrounds and combining them with a broad international outlook, these companies are able to create diverse product lines that appeal to a wide audience. They acknowledge and celebrate diversity, not only in beauty standards but also in consumer habits and expectations, leading to a more inclusive and understanding global market.

References

Akgün, A. E., Keskin, H., & Byrne, J. (2012). Antecedents and contingent effects of organizational adaptive capability on firm product innovativeness. *Journal of Product Innovation Management, 29*, 171–189.

Basten, F. E. (2011). *Max factor: The man who changed the faces of the world*. Skyhorse.

Bennur, S., & Malhotra, D. K. (2023). Scaling up beauty: An analysis of economies of scale in the cosmetics industry. *Journal of Applied Business & Economics, 25*(2), 243–251.

Bundles, A. L. (2002). *On her own ground: The life and times of Madam CJ Walker*. Scribner.

Butler, H. (2000). Cosmetics through the ages. *Poucher's perfumes, cosmetics and soaps* (pp. 13–63). Springer, Netherlands.

Califf, R. M., McCall, J., & Mark, D. B. (2017). Cosmetics, regulations, and the public health: Understanding the safety of medical and other products. *JAMA Internal Medicine, 177*(8), 1080–1082.

Chitty, N. (2016). Soft power, civic virtue and world politics (section overview). In *The Routledge handbook of soft power* (pp. 29–56). Routledge.

Clifford, M. J. (1999). *Brand name modernism: Helena Rubinstein's art collection, femininity, and the marketing of modern style, 1925–1940*. University of California.

Cornell, E. M., Janetos, T. M., & Xu, S. (2019). Time for a makeover-cosmetics regulation in the United States. *Journal of Cosmetic Dermatology, 18*(6), 2041–2047.

Ciravegna, L., & Michailova, S. (2022). Why the world economy needs, but will not get, more globalization in the post-COVID-19 decade. *Journal of International Business Studies, 53*, 1–15.

Cusumano, M. A. (2010). *Staying power: Six enduring principles for managing strategy and innovation in an uncertain world (lessons from Microsoft, Apple, Intel, Google, Toyota and more)*. Oxford University Press.

Efrat, K., Gilboa, S., & Yonatany, M. (2017). When marketing and innovation interact: The case of born-global firms. *International Business Review, 26*(2), 380–390.

Goerzen, A., & Geisler Asmussen, C. (2007). The geographic orientation of multinational enterprises and its implications for performance. In *Regional aspects of multinationality and performance* (pp. 65–83). Emerald Group Publishing Limited.

Gomes, C., Silva, A. C., Marques, A. C., Sousa Lobo, J., & Amaral, M. H. (2020). Biotechnology applied to cosmetics and aesthetic medicines. *Cosmetics, 7*(2), 33. https://doi.org/10.3390/cosmetics7020033

Hart, S. L., & Milstein, M. B. (2003). Creating sustainable value. *Academy of Management Perspectives, 17*(2), 56–67.

Hong, P., Jagani, S., Pham, P., & Jung, E. (2023). Globalization orientation, business practices and performance outcomes: An empirical investigation of B2B manufacturing firms. *Journal of Business & Industrial Marketing, 38*(10), 2259–2274.

Jones, G. (2011). Globalization and beauty: A historical and firm perspective. *EurAmerica, 41*(4), 885–916.

Jones, G. (2010). *Beauty imagined: A history of the global beauty industry*. Oxford University Press.

Kane, G. C., Palmer, D., Phillips, A. N., & Kiron, D. (2015). Is your business ready for a digital future? *MIT Sloan Management Review, 56*(4), 37–44.

Knight, G., Koed Madsen, T., & Servais, P. (2004). An inquiry into born-global firms in Europe and the USA. *International Marketing Review, 21*(6), 645–665.

Khan, A. D., & Alam, M. N. (2019). Cosmetics and their associated adverse effects: A review. *Journal of Applied Pharmaceutical Sciences and Research, 2*(1), 1–6.

Lee, G. (2009). A theory of soft power and Korea's soft power strategy. *The Korean Journal of Defense Analysis, 21*(2), 205–218.

Lintner, K. (2009). *Global regulatory issues for the cosmetics industry*. Elsevier.

Martin, M. (2009). *Selling Beauty: Cosmetics, Commerce, and French Society, 1750–1830* (Vol. 127). Johns Hopkins University Press.

Nye, J. S. (1990). Soft power. *Foreign Policy, 80*, 153–171.

Patel, P. C., Criaco, G., & Naldi, L. (2018). Geographic diversification and the survival of born-globals. *Journal of Management, 44*(5), 2008–2036.

Roh, J., Hong, P., & Min, H. (2014). Implementation of a responsive supply chain strategy in global complexity: The case of manufacturing firms. *International Journal of Production Economics, 147*, 198–210.

Seelig, M. I., Sun, R., Deng, H., & Pal, S. (2021). Is it all for show?: Environmental brand identification on skin care and cosmetic websites. *Journal of Marketing Communications, 27*(4), 436–456.

Tsutomu, S. (2015). Japan's creative industries: Culture as a source of soft power in the industrial sector. In *Soft power superpowers* (pp. 128–153). Routledge.

Tungate, M. (2011). *Branded beauty: How marketing changed the way we look*. Kogan Page Publishers.

Vuillemard, J. C. (1991). Recent advances in the large-scale production of lipid vesicles for use in food products: Microfluidization. *Journal of Microencapsulation, 8*(4), 547–562.

Yukuyama, M. N., Ghisleni, D. D. M., Pinto, T. D. J. A., & Bou-Chacra, N. A. (2016). Nanoemulsion: Process selection and application in cosmetics–a review. *International Journal of Cosmetic Science, 38*(1), 13–24.

Chapter 3
Beauty Reimagined: Navigating the Cosmetic Industry's Digital Transformation

Abstract In this chapter we delve into the dramatic digital transformation of the cosmetics industry, which has seen traditional business models upended by the rise of e-commerce, social media marketing, and digital innovation. This shift has been propelled by consumer demand for more accessible, personalized, and diverse shopping experiences. Cosmetic companies have leveraged technological advancements to meet these demands, transitioning from brick-and-mortar stores to online marketplaces and utilizing data analytics to tailor their marketing strategies and product offerings. The chapter underscores the significance of mobile commerce and the role of influencers in shaping modern consumer behaviors, reflecting the cosmetics industry's redefined landscape, where e-commerce has become an integral component of business strategy. This chapter also highlights the industry's response to COVID-19, with brands adapting by producing sanitizers and cleaners while navigating the decreased demand for traditional makeup. Despite these challenges, the market has shown resilience, with projections indicating continued growth fueled by an increasing preference for organic and sustainable products. The rise of "green labeling" and the move towards natural, non-toxic cosmetics are reshaping market dynamics, underscoring the importance of transparency and ethical manufacturing. As the industry continues to evolve, it becomes clear that success hinges on the seamless integration of quality, sustainability, and ethical practices into both product development and marketing strategies.

As we turn the pages of history, we see that the cosmetic industry, once anchored in the tactile charm of brick-and-mortar stores, has confidently entered the digital commerce space. This chapter aims to demystify the evolution of e-commerce in this sparkling sector, a shift from the sensory-rich experience of physical stores to the expansive reach of the online world. Traditional retail, with its hands-on approach allowing customers to touch, feel, and try products, offered instant gratification and personalized service. This created a deep connection between brands and their consumers and has long been a cornerstone of success for physical stores in the cosmetics industry, fostering an experience that seemed irreplaceable by digital channels.

Y. W. Park and P. Hong, *Cosmetics Marketing Strategy in the Era of the Digital Ecosystem*, https://doi.org/10.1007/978-981-97-3674-4_3

Yet, with the rise of the digital era, technological advancements have heralded a new epoch in consumerism, positioning e-commerce as a strong competitor to traditional retail (Park & Shintaku, 2022). This chapter will examine how mobile commerce, personalized digital experiences, and improved logistics have redefined shopping for beauty products. Convenience now enables customers to satisfy their beauty needs at any time and place. AI-driven personalization and data analytics offer bespoke shopping experiences that once seemed exclusive to in-person interactions. Moreover, efficiency in product delivery sets a new standard, optimizing the entire supply chain from production to home delivery to meet the sophisticated demands of today's consumer. These changes are not just altering consumer habits; they are reshaping the competitive landscape of the vast cosmetics industry.

1 The E-Commerce Emergence: Navigating the New Beauty Landscape

Cosmetic firms have transitioned from brick-and-mortar retail to online sales platforms. Brick-and-mortar retail is defined by three essential characteristics that have traditionally underpinned its success. Firstly, the tactile experience: customers have the ability to touch, feel, and try products, which is particularly vital in the cosmetics industry. Secondly, immediacy: physical stores offer instant gratification where customers can take home their purchases immediately. Lastly, personal service: the in-store experience often includes personalized advice and service from knowledgeable staff, which can forge strong customer relationships and loyalty.

Technological advancements have made e-commerce a viable and profitable sales channel, such as mobile commerce, personalized shopping experiences, and sophisticated logistics solutions. The drivers propelling e-commerce forward build upon its unique strengths, significantly transforming the way consumers interact with the cosmetic industry. The first driver is convenience, with the broad applications and availability of digital technologies, online shopping allowing consumers to purchase anytime, anywhere, from a variety of devices, including through mobile commerce (Westerman et al., 2014). The second is customization, where AI and data analytics provide personalized shopping experiences by recommending products tailored to individual preferences. The third driver is efficiency, with advanced logistics solutions streamlining the supply chain, from warehousing to last-mile delivery, ensuring timely and reliable product delivery to the customer's doorstep. These drivers are not just reshaping consumer expectations but also redefining the competitive landscape within the cosmetic sector.

We now delve into the profound metamorphosis the cosmetics industry has undergone in the digital era. This chapter illuminates how the advent of digital technology has not merely altered, but revolutionized the way cosmetic brands operate, interact with consumers, and innovate their products. The emergence of e-commerce platforms, digital marketing strategies, and social media engagement has dramatically shifted the landscape, turning digital prowess into a crucial component for success in the beauty sector. This chapter explores the origins of this digital transformation, tracing the initial steps cosmetic companies took to integrate digital technologies into their business models, and how these early adaptations set the stage for a complete overhaul of the industry.

The journey begins with a look at the initial forays into digital spaces by pioneering beauty brands. These trailblazers recognized the potential of the internet as a new frontier for marketing and customer engagement. The early adoption of digital tools and platforms signaled a significant departure from traditional marketing and retail methods. Brands began to experiment with online stores, digital advertising campaigns, and leveraging the nascent power of social media. This phase marked the beginning of a paradigm shift, where the rules of engagement between brands and consumers started to evolve. The chapter examines these initial steps, shedding light on how they laid the foundation for more advanced digital integrations, from augmented reality (AR) in product testing to leveraging big data for personalized customer experiences, which are now hallmarks of the modern cosmetics industry.

1.1 Beyond the Storefront: The Beauty Industry's Shift to Digital Domains

There was the initial shift of cosmetic brands from physical stores to the online marketplace. It would explore the strategic decisions involved in this transition, the challenges brands faced in moving to a digital platform, and how they adapted to the changing retail landscape. Key focus areas might include the logistics of setting up online stores, integrating supply chains, and the initial customer response to buying cosmetics online, which traditionally relied heavily on in-person experiences.

The e-commerce market is characterized by three distinctive features that have become the hallmark of modern retail. Firstly, there's the accessibility factor—e-commerce platforms provide consumers with 24/7 access to products and information, a significant departure from the traditional retail schedule. Secondly, e-commerce platforms offer a level of convenience unmatched by physical stores, as consumers can browse, compare, and purchase products from the comfort of their own homes. Lastly, the customization and personalization capabilities of online shopping—utilizing data analytics and AI—allow for a tailored shopping experience, where recommendations and searches are aligned with individual consumer preferences and past shopping behavior.

Despite the surge in online shopping, the continued relevance of traditional store networks cannot be overstressed. Brick-and-mortar stores offer sensory experiences that digital platforms cannot replicate, such as the ability to physically sample and assess products. They also fulfill the immediate gratification of on-the-spot purchases without the wait for delivery. Furthermore, in-person retail provides a social aspect to shopping, which can be an important draw for many customers. These stores also act as a physical touchpoint for brand-building and customer service excellence. As such, the synergy between online and offline channels is key; each supports the other, offering consumers a composite, omnichannel experience that leverages the strengths of both forms of commerce. This complementary relationship is critical for cosmetic firms that wish to maintain a broad and diverse customer base while capitalizing on the expansive reach and efficiency that e-commerce provides.

The increasing role of the supply chain and distribution network in the cosmetic industry is pivotal to its success in the e-commerce era. As consumer expectations for rapid delivery and real-time stock availability rise, the ability to manage and synchronize supply chains effectively becomes a competitive advantage. Advanced distribution networks are now central to operational efficiency, enabling cosmetic companies to scale up and meet demand across diverse markets (Yi et al., 2021). These networks must be agile and responsive, capable of adapting to market changes, seasonal demands, and consumer trends. The integration of global and local distribution hubs, supported by advanced forecasting and inventory management systems, ensures that products are delivered quickly and efficiently, minimizing delays and maximizing customer satisfaction.

The application of complex logistical platforms in supporting this sophisticated distribution network is multifaceted. They not only facilitate the smooth transition of goods from manufacturers to end consumers but also provide vital data that drives decision-making throughout the supply chain. By leveraging technologies such as the Internet of Things (IoT), artificial intelligence (AI), and machine learning, these platforms can optimize routes, predict maintenance, and manage resources effectively. They also play a crucial role in reverse logistics, managing returns in a way that is cost-effective for the company and convenient for the customer. These logistical platforms are the backbone of e-commerce operations, ensuring that the right products reach the right customers at the right time, creating a seamless link between the virtual and physical elements of the consumer experience.

Achieving a harmonious relationship between the physical and virtual markets hinges on three critical factors. The first is the customer experience; whether online or in-store, the consumer's journey must be seamless, consistent, and brand-aligned. Secondly, inventory transparency is paramount. Customers expect to see the same availability of products online as they would in-store, necessitating integrated inventory management systems. The third factor is the synergy between physical and online presence. Physical stores can serve as showrooms for online shoppers, while online platforms can act as gateways to in-store visits, each channel enhancing the other. Together, these elements foster a cohesive brand experience that maximizes customer engagement and loyalty across all touchpoints.

As the reach of e-commerce transcends borders, cosmetic brands have the opportunity to tap into a global customer base. This expansion is not without its challenges, such as the need to navigate diverse regulatory environments and cultural preferences. However, the potential for growth is enormous. Globalization facilitates the spread of beauty trends at an unprecedented pace, with social media and digital marketing playing critical roles in shaping consumer preferences worldwide. This global interconnectedness also demands that brands be more innovative and adaptive, ensuring their products meet the varied needs and expectations of a diverse international audience. As a result, the cosmetic industry is experiencing a flourishing exchange of ideas, trends, and products, which in turn fuels its continuous growth and evolution.

The transition of cosmetic firms from traditional retail to online platforms requires mobile commerce, and the role of data analytics in shaping marketing strategies. The shift to online sales has involved leveraging advanced technologies to create personalized shopping experiences and efficient logistic systems. Mobile commerce has further revolutionized how consumers engage with brands, making purchasing cosmetics more accessible and convenient. Data analytics plays a critical role in understanding consumer behavior, allowing firms to tailor their marketing strategies and product offerings to meet the specific needs and preferences of their diverse customer base. This digital transformation has redefined the landscape of the cosmetics industry, making e-commerce a vital component of business strategy.

1.2 The Future Unveiled: Projecting the Cosmetics Industry's Global Trajectory

Since the mid-2010s, the cosmetics industry has been at a major turning point. In addition to changes in the environment due to COVID-19, which is still having an impact as of 2023, the industry continues to be reorganized as global cosmetics companies seek to purchase powerful brands. Even in the European and North American markets, where the markets are already mature, the market stagnated briefly due to COVID-19, but is continuing to grow again, and growth in the South American, Asian, and African markets is particularly noticeable. Unlike other industrial products, cosmetics are not products that can be sold in large quantities cheaply. Because it is a product that realizes beauty, it requires qualitative beauty that cannot be captured in numbers such as culture, emotion, and image. For this reason, it is essential for cosmetics manufacturers to have a deep understanding of culture and emotions.

The COVID-19 pandemic had a significant impact on the cosmetics market owing to complete lockdown imposed across several countries that have temporarily halted the manufacturing process. Moreover, the specialty stores and brand outlets, where cosmetics are majorly sold, were closed to protect the spread of coronavirus, which greatly affected the cosmetics market demand. Furthermore, work from home regulations, compulsion on masks, and social distancing norms have made it less mandatory for the people to wear makeup. The majority of the people worked from home and due to travel restrictions, people found it less important to wear makeup. To cope up with the crisis and to help society in recovering from the pandemic, the cosmetic manufacturers have started manufacturing cleaners and hand sanitizers.

Figure 1 shows the annual growth rate of the global cosmetics market from 2004 to 2022. In 2022, the global cosmetics market grew by an estimated six percent compared to the previous sales year. According to the latest statistics, total revenues from the global cosmetics market are set to hit $104 billion in 2023. This represents a whopping 11.8% year-over-year increase, which is the second-largest annual growth expected in at least 11 years. From 2018 to 2028, the global cosmetics market is mostly set to follow a growth trend. With the exception of 2020, it's forecast to increase its revenues year after year. In 2020, the industry shrunk by 20% from $90 billion the year before, to $72 billion as a result of the COVID-19 pandemic. Not only was this the only and biggest year-on-year decrease, but it is also the lowest revenue expected in the period from 2018 to 2028. In addition, projected Growth of the Global Cosmetics Market (2021–2031) continuously shows market growth with a CAGR of 6.3% (Research Dive Analysis, 2022). This upward trajectory, with a compound annual growth rate (CAGR) of 6.3%, is indicative of the industry's resilience and adaptability despite facing challenges such as the potential adverse effects of chemical-laden cosmetic products.

Since COVID-19, cosmetics market has gained huge popularity among the young generation, particularly women and girls, owing to rise in beauty consciousness among people and increase in trend of using variety of skin care, hair care, beauty care products. Cosmetic products help to build up the self-confidence and esteem of an individual. In 2024, it is anticipated that the value beauty consumers place on products will increase the importance of quality. The emerging beauty trend will emphasize the quality of ingredients, proven effectiveness of products and reassurance of simplicity. Some of the widely used cosmetic products include lipsticks, perfumes, creams, eye shadows, and nail polishes. Moreover, growing popularity of Korean skincare brands across the world is predicted to boost the cosmetics market size in the upcoming years.

Cosmetics are materials or products that are used to clean or improve the appearance of skin, hair, nails, and other body parts. Cosmetics are a blend of chemical substances that are either synthesized or taken from natural sources. They have become necessary products in life since they may improve an individual's overall look, therefore, can have a positive impact on the personality. Some of the widely used cosmetic products include face care, hair care, and lip care that are necessary to meet

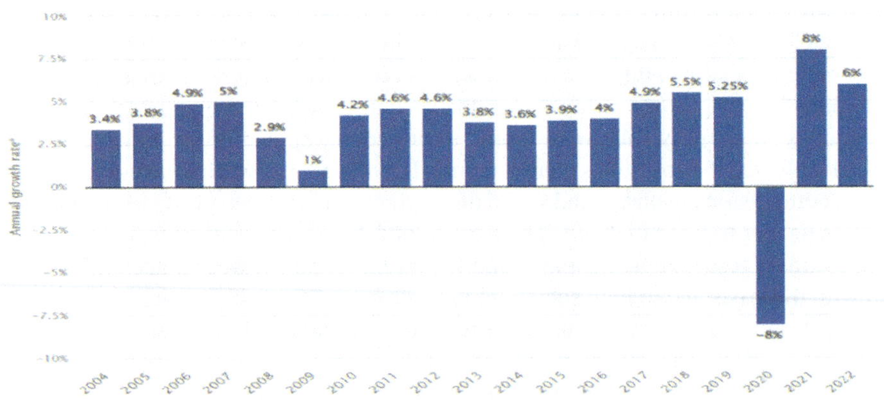

Fig. 1 Annual growth of the global cosmetics market from 2004 to 2022. *Source* Statista 2023 https://www.statista.com/statistics/297070/growth-rate-of-the-global-cosmetics-market/

the end-specific user's needs. Furthermore, growth in demand for anti-aging and anti-acne, and fairness products with attractive packaging drive the popularity of cosmetics market.

Issues like acne breakouts, clogged pores, and skin allergies are of concern and could pose constraints on market expansion. However, these limitations are being counterbalanced by the industry's rapid technological advancements, including augmented reality (AR) and artificial intelligence (AI), which enhance customer experiences and product customization. For instance, in July 2020, Amorepacific, leading South Korean cosmetics brand, installed AR mirrors at their stores. These AR mirrors can be used to analyze the skin type of the customers to recommend the appropriate products based on skin type.

The global cosmetics industry is rapidly growing owing to an increase in beauty consciousness among people and surge in demand for different cosmetic goods, skin care products, beauty care products, and hair care products. The spread of Korean cosmetic companies into Western nations, innovative cosmetic products with natural ingredients, and other factors are expected to offer significant market development potential. For example, consumer preferences have shifted swiftly from synthetic and chemical laden cosmetic products toward organic and natural products that can be safely used by the people. In addition, the popularity of "Green labeling" which indicates the usage of bioengineered substances in cosmetics is becoming highly popular. These bioengineered chemicals are derived from plants due to which they are natural and safer for use. These factors are anticipated to boost the cosmetics market share during the projection period.

As of 2021, skincare accounts for 60% of the market, but there is also a rapid increase in hair care related trends (Research Dive Analysis, 2022). The rise in awareness among consumers regarding the use of natural cosmetic products such as natural skin care products is anticipated to drive excellent opportunities in the market. This is due to the fact that 100% natural skin care products have zero side-effects, prevent premature ageing of skin, and make the skin radiant & glowing. For instance, skincare products such as lotions and facewash made from natural & pure ingredients do not have any harmful side-effects or allergies. Natural cosmetic products are made directly from natural ingredients such as aloe vera, sandalwood, rose, turmeric, & coconut milk and do not contain any complex chemicals, synthetic chemicals, or artificial fragrance. Moreover, the use of natural ingredients such as Quinoa and Jajoba oil is highly effective and prevents premature ageing. These factors are anticipated to drive the cosmetics market growth during the forecast period.

By customer orientation, the market is divided into men and women. The women segment accounted for the highest market share in 2021 whereas the men segment is estimated to show the fastest growth during the forecast period. When looking at the market share by gender for the year 2021, there is a rapid increase in the trend of men's cosmetics. The Women segment had a dominant market share in 2021. Primary factors contributing to the market growth include the growing popularity of skincare and makeup among women. Women spend more money on cosmetics and beauty items than males. Moreover, wide range of cosmetic products from various brands are available and some brands specifically cater to women cosmetics products including hair care and skin care. Furthermore, steady rise in the number of working women population is anticipated to boost the popularity of cosmetics among women. These aspects are anticipated to drive the growth of the women segment during the forecast period.

The men segment is anticipated to show the fastest growth rate during the forecast period. This growth is majorly attributed to emerging demand for men beauty products as the shift to white-collar jobs has increased the consciousness among men to look well-groomed and presentable. Earlier, the beauty segment among men was largely dominated by the shave care products. However, in recent years, the increase in adoption of facial scrubs, face wash, sunscreen, moisturizers, and cleansers has boosted the popularity of cosmetics among men. In August 2020, Shiseido and YA-MAN entered into a joint venture agreement and established EFFECTIM with the goal of open innovation and a strategy to strengthen both companies' business models.

Figure 2 presents the projected market sizes in billions of dollars for four different regions within the global cosmetics market, spanning from 2021 to 2031. The Asia–Pacific region (red line) is projected to experience significant growth over the forecast period. It starts slightly below North America (dark blue line) in 2021 but is expected to surpass it around 2024, ultimately becoming the largest market by 2031. North America is forecasted to show a steady increase, yet it consistently trails behind Asia–Pacific during this period. Europe's market (black line) also expands, albeit at a more moderate pace than Asia–Pacific and North America, reflecting a smaller yet considerable market size. Lastly, the LAMEA region (orange line) shows a continuous growth trajectory, improving its share in the global market.

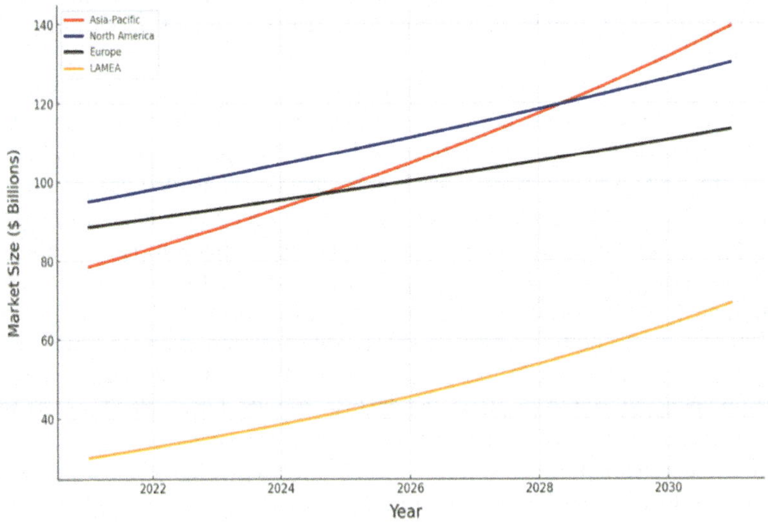

Fig. 2 Regional cosmetics market growth trajectories (2021–2031). *Source* Research Dive Analysis

It underscores the Asia–Pacific region's dominance in the cosmetics industry, with a notable contribution from the popularity of Korean beauty (K-beauty) brands known for their innovative and high-quality products. Factors fueling this regional market's growth include increased disposable income, a burgeoning beauty-conscious demographic, the entrance of new market players, and a surging demand for organic and natural cosmetic products. Simultaneously, the Latin America, Middle East, and Africa (LAMEA) region are experiencing a notable upswing in cosmetic sales. Cultural trends, such as the widespread use of perfumes and a high valuation of personal appearance, especially in countries like Saudi Arabia and the UAE, are significantly contributing to this increase. The graph projects a particularly robust future for the Asia–Pacific cosmetics sector, poised for ongoing innovation and market responsiveness, anchored by a forecasted market valuation of $78.6 billion in 2021 and an expected CAGR of 5.9%.

In summary, the global cosmetics market is on a path of dynamic growth. The industry is evolving to meet the diverse needs and preferences of consumers worldwide, leveraging both technological advancements and regional market trends, as clearly reflected in the projected market size figures.

1.3 Resilience and Reinvention: The Cosmetics Market in the Wake of COVID-19

The novel coronavirus pandemic had a significant impact on the cosmetics market owing to complete lockdown imposed across several countries that have temporarily halted the manufacturing process. To cope up with the crisis and to help society in recovering from the pandemic, the cosmetic manufacturers have started manufacturing cleaners and hand sanitizers. For instance, in March 2020, Coty Inc., the leading beauty brand introduced hydro-alcoholic hand sanitizer that was distributed for free to the people working in healthcare sector and pharmacy staffs.

Figure 3 displays the market share of two segments: Skin and Sun Care, and Hair Care. Skin and Sun Care products cover 60% of the market which indicates that a majority of consumers are purchasing products related to skincare and protection from sun exposure. The remaining 40% is dedicated to Hair Care products, suggesting a significant but smaller segment of the market focused on hair treatment and maintenance products.

From a practical standpoint, cosmetic companies need to invest more in research and development for Skin and Sun Care products, expecting a higher return due to the larger market share. They could also use this information to plan marketing campaigns, supply chain logistics, and sales forecasts. For Hair Care products, the company might explore opportunities to capture a greater share of the market, such as product innovation or targeted marketing strategies, to entice customers from the Skin and Sun Care segment.

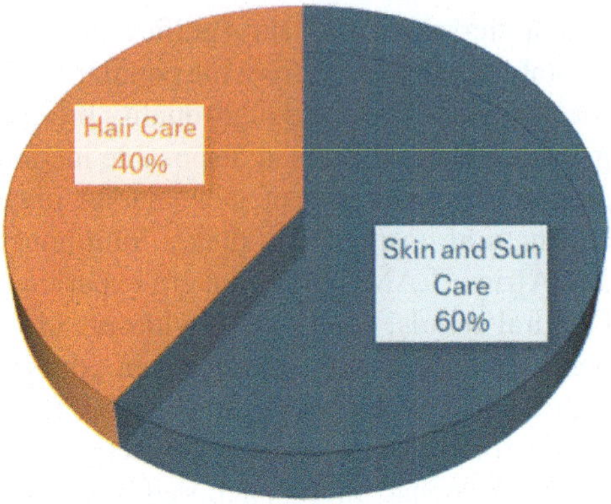

Fig. 3 Global cosmetics market share of skin and sun care versus hair care products. *Source* Research Dive Analysis

2 The Rising Sun of Beauty: Innovations in the Japanese Cosmetics Market

The Japanese cosmetics market has long been intertwined with the global cosmetic industry, its fluctuations and trends echoing the broader international landscape. As illustrated in Fig. 4, the Japanese cosmetics market experienced a significant downturn, plummeting from 1.7953 trillion yen (approximately 17.9 billion dollars) in 2019 to 1.2984 trillion yen (about 12.9 billion dollars) by the end of 2022, primarily due to the far-reaching impact of the COVID-19 pandemic. However, beneath this apparent setback lies a pivotal story of resilience and growth. The Japanese cosmetic market, despite its momentary contraction, remains a crucial player on the global stage, known for its innovative products, cutting-edge technology, and unwavering commitment to quality. Several Japanese cosmetic firms have consistently expanded their domestic boundaries, not only reinforcing the importance of the Japanese market but also asserting their influence internationally. This strategic dynamism in the face of adversity underscores the Japanese cosmetics market's enduring significance in terms of size and its global reach. As we delve deeper into this dynamic sector, we will unravel the intricate tapestry of the Japanese cosmetics market's evolution and its profound implications for the beauty industry worldwide.

Figure 4 shows how the Japanese cosmetics market (sales amount) decreased sharply due to the impact of COVID-19. However, it is expected to rapidly recover from 2023, with projections estimating a rebound to around 2.1 trillion yen based on export data.

Figure 5 represents the distribution of different segments within the digital beauty market for the fiscal year. The proportion of skincare is nearly 50%, a characteristic shared with markets in the United States, Europe, and other parts of Asia. Each segment of the market is represented by a different color and labeled with both a name and a percentage, signifying its share of the total market. The largest segment is the Skincare Market, occupying nearly half of the chart at 47.9%. This indicates that nearly half of the digital beauty market's revenue comes from skincare products,

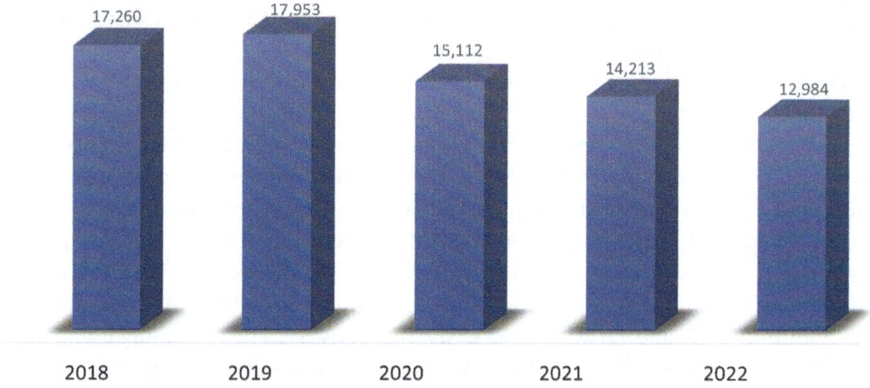

Fig. 4 Trends in the Japanese cosmetics market (Sales Amount by Business Type and By Year). *Source* Made from METI statistics

showing the segment's dominance within the industry. The next largest segment is the Haircare Market with a significant 20.3% share, followed by the Makeup Market at 17%. These sizable portions suggest that these markets are also key players in the beauty industry, with makeup and haircare products being important to consumers.

The Fragrance Market has a smaller slice of the pie at 5.5%, and an even smaller segment is the Selfcare Market at 1.2%, indicating these are more niche markets within the digital beauty industry. The category labeled other accounts for 8.2% of the market, suggesting there are additional segments not specified in the chart that collectively make up a non-negligible portion of the market. Overall, the visual breakdown of the digital beauty market indicates which product categories are most

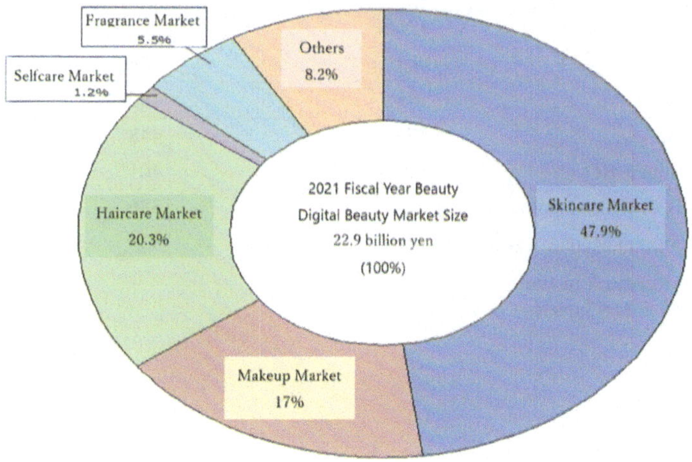

Fig. 5 2021 fiscal year digital beauty market distribution by segment. *Source* Yano Research Institute

popular among consumers and where businesses might focus their efforts for the highest potential returns.

Table 1 is a ranking of the top 10 Japanese cosmetics companies based on their sales revenue from 2021 to 2022. The leftmost column lists the companies' rankings, the middle column presents the company names, and the subsequent columns display their sales revenue in two different currencies: Japanese yen (in 100 million units) and U.S. dollars (in million). The Shiseido Company leads the list, significantly outperforming the others with a sales revenue of 10,351 hundred million yen, equivalent to approximately 8,100 million USD. This is followed by Kao with 2,393 hundred million yen and Kose with 2,249 hundred million yen, translating to 1,873 million USD and 1,760 million USD, respectively. The remaining companies, from Pola Orbis HD to Nippon Menard Cosmetic, show a descending order of sales revenues, ranging from 1,786 hundred million yen (or 1,398 million USD) to 426 hundred million yen (or 333 million USD).

Table 1 also provides a snapshot of the competitive landscape within the Japanese cosmetics industry and reflects the market dominance of established brands. Shiseido's position at the top suggests a strong brand presence and consumer trust in its products. The practical implication for businesses within this sector is the importance of brand development and innovation to secure a significant share of the market.

Table 1 Top ten Japanese cosmetics firms (2021–2022)

Ranking	Company name	Sales revenue (100 million Yen)	USD as of 2022 (in million USD)
1	Shiseido Company	10,351	8,100
2	Kao	2,393	1,873
3	Kose	2,249	1,760
4	Pola Orbis HD	1,786	1,398
5	DHC	901	705
6	Fancl	588	460
7	Mandom	573	448
8	Noevir HD	512	401
9	TOA (Nihon Kolmar)	493	386
10	Nippon Menard Cosmetic	426	333

Source Yano Research Institute
Note 1USD($) is 128 Japanese Yen (as of 2022)

2.1 Navigating the New Wave: Japanese Cosmetics Trends and Digital Transformation Challenges

Japan's population trend is strongly characterized by low birthrates and an aging population, similar to South Korea. Figure 6 offers a comprehensive view of the shifting demographics in Japan over a century, from 1960 to 2060. It highlights the population size and composition across three distinct age groups: children (0–14), adults (15–64), and the elderly (65 and above). The population size for the adult segment (depicted by green bars) maintains a dominant presence throughout the timeline, suggesting it forms the backbone of Japan's demographic structure. However, there is a noticeable trend where the adult population peaks around 2010 and then begins to plateau, which is mirrored by a gradual decline in the youth population (represented by dark blue bars). In contrast, the elderly population (grey bars) appears to expand steadily, reflecting a growing segment that surpasses the other age groups in growth rate.

The line graph overlay provides further insight into the proportional changes within the population, painting a picture of a society undergoing significant aging. The increasing orange line indicates an uptrend in the percentage of the elderly, suggesting a longevity revolution but also signaling potential socioeconomic challenges ahead. Simultaneously, the declining green line, representing the workforce-aged population, raises concerns about future labor shortages and the economic implications of a contracting pool of workers. The yellow line's downward trajectory further emphasizes the issue, pointing to a diminishing proportion of young

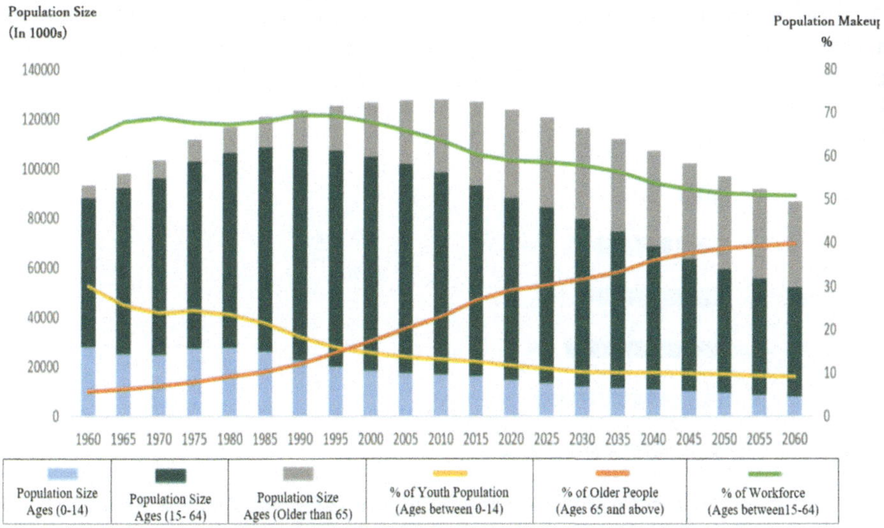

Fig. 6 Japan's demographic trend: size and % of age groups. *Source* Yano Research Institute and Ministry of Health, Labour and Welfare in Japan

people that could lead to a long-term demographic imbalance. This visual forecast of Japan's population dynamics underscores the critical need for policy adaptations to support an increasingly aged society with a shrinking workforce.

Figure 7 shows distribution channels of cosmetic products in Japan before the COVID-19 pandemic. The landscape of cosmetic product distribution was characterized by a strong preference for drug stores, which dominated the market with a 42% share. Consumers favored these convenient outlets for their wide range of accessible beauty products. Meanwhile, department stores carved out a 14% niche, appealing to those seeking a more upscale shopping experience with luxury brands and personalized service. Door-to-door sales remained surprisingly robust at 12%, underscoring the value of direct and personal engagement in the cosmetics industry. Official mail orders, including online sales, captured a 10% share, reflecting a growing trend towards digital shopping. Mass retailers and specialty stores, with 9% and 8% respectively, catered to everyday shoppers and beauty enthusiasts looking for a tailored selection. Variety shops and select cosmetics stores, with smaller footprints at 3 and 2%, offered discounted and niche products, rounding out a diverse pre-pandemic market where convenience, quality, and shopping experience were key drivers of consumer preference.

Figure 8 showcases the robust expansion of Japan's Business-to-Consumer (B2C) E-Commerce market from 2013 to 2021. By 2021, the market size surged to over 13 trillion yen, equivalent to approximately 130 billion USD, highlighting a substantial upward trajectory in the digital consumer space. Notably, the e-commerce penetration rate stood at 8.78%, a reflection of e-commerce's increasingly integral role in retail commerce. The year-on-year growth rate from 2020 to 2021 was an impressive 8.61%, more than doubling the growth accumulated over the eight preceding years. Despite this general market upswing, certain segments such as cosmetics and pharmaceuticals trailed with sales of 855.2 billion yen and a penetration rate of 7.5%.

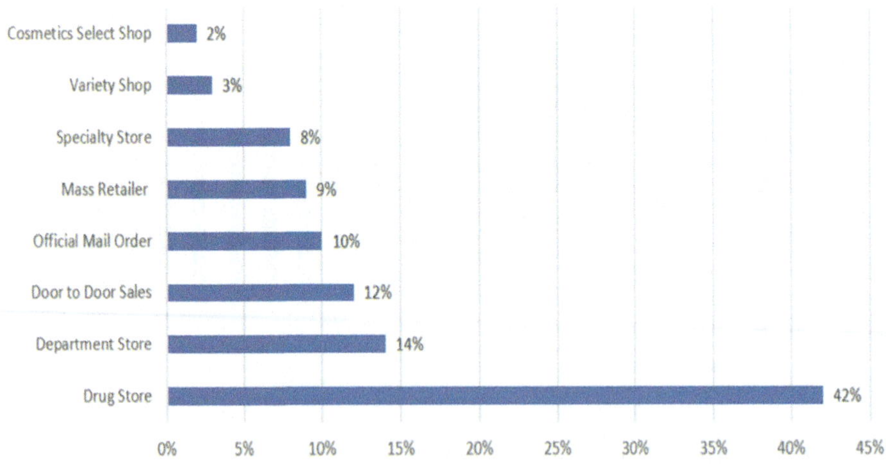

Fig. 7 Japan's distribution channels for cosmetic products in 2020. *Source* Yano Research Institute

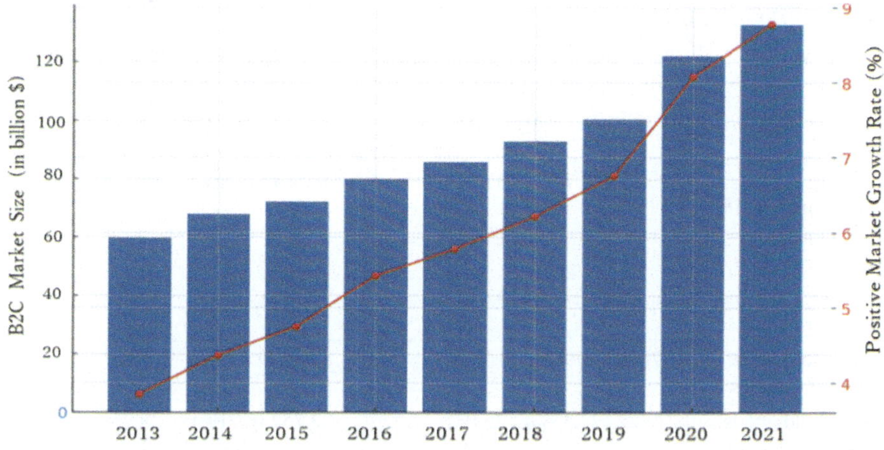

Fig. 8 Japanese B2C EC market size (in billion $). *Source* Yano Research Institute

Although these figures are modest compared to other sectors like books, household appliances, furniture, and clothing, the continuous increase indicates a growing consumer confidence in online shopping for these categories as well.

Table 2 presents a detailed breakdown of the Japanese Business-to-Consumer (B2C) E-Commerce sector's sales and online market penetration across various product categories for the years 2020 and 2021. In both years, categories such as Daily Necessities, AV Equipment, PC, Communication Equipment, and Clothing, Footwear, Accessories not only commanded a substantial share of the market but also exhibited high e-commerce penetration rates, indicating a significant consumer shift towards online purchases in these segments. The table highlights the growth in sales across all categories, with the total market sales rising from 122,333 million USD in 2020 to 132,865 million USD in 2021, alongside an increase in the overall e-commerce ratio from 8.08 to 8.78%. This reflects the broader trend of digital adoption in the Japanese retail space, with e-commerce becoming an increasingly preferred shopping channel.

Table 2 highlights the pivotal role of the cosmetics and personal care goods sector within the Japanese B2C e-commerce landscape for 2020 and 2021. Despite the broader array of product categories, the cosmetics industry stands out with significant sales figures, totaling 22,203 million USD in 2020 and rising substantially to 24,279 million USD in 2021. This growth is noteworthy, representing a 9.35% year-over-year increase and accounting for a sizable portion of the overall market. Furthermore, the e-commerce penetration rate for cosmetics and personal care goods increased from 19.44% to 21.15%, evidencing a robust consumer shift to online shopping in this category. This trend is particularly impressive, reflecting Japanese consumers' trust and growing inclination to purchase such items online, which is crucial for understanding the dynamics of the country's e-commerce evolution.

Table 2 2020–2021 Japanese B2C e-commerce sales and penetration by product category

Category	2020 sales (in millions $)	2020 EC ratio (%)	2021 sales (in millions $)	2021 EC ratio (%)
Food, beverages, alcohol	22,086 (21.13%)	3.31	25,199 (14.10%)	3.77
Daily necessities, AV equipment, PC, communication equipment	23,489 (28.79%)	37.45	24,584 (4.66%)	38.13
Clothing, footwear, accessories	16,238 (24.77%)	42.97	17,518 (7.88%)	46.20
Pharmaceuticals, medical supplies	7,787 (17.79%)	6.72	8,552 (9.82%)	7.52
Household goods, furniture, interior	21,322 (22.35%)	26.03	22,752 (6.71%)	28.25
Cosmetics, personal care goods	**22,203 (16.25%)**	**19.44**	**24,279 (9.35%)**	**21.15**
Toys, hobbies, sporting goods, pets	2,784 (16.17%)	3.23	3,016 (8.33%)	3.86
Other	6,423 (16.95%)	1.85	6,964 (8.42%)	1.96
Total	122,333 (21.71%)	8.08	132,865 (8.61%)	8.78

Source Compiled from METI statistics. *Unit* Japanese Yen

2.2 *Unveiling Varieties: Price Dynamics and Product Diversification in the Global Cosmetics Arena*

The global cosmetics market is a tapestry of varied price points and product offerings, catering to a diverse consumer base with unique preferences and needs. Price dynamics in this industry are crucial as they define the affordability and accessibility of beauty products. Economically priced items appeal to a broad demographic, offering value for money, while premium products cater to a niche market seeking luxury and exclusivity. This segmentation by price range enables brands to strategically position themselves and tailor their products to different consumer segments. Product diversification, meanwhile, refers to the extensive range of beauty products available, addressing various consumer demands from skincare and makeup to hair care. This diversification not only broadens consumer choice but also allows companies to innovate and specialize in specific categories. The variety in product types and formulations—from organic and natural to technologically advanced solutions—reflects the dynamic nature of consumer needs and the industry's agility in responding to these evolving preferences.

The global cosmetics market's landscape in 2021 was predominantly shaped by these two aspects: the dominance of the economy segment and the rising prominence of premium brands. In an industry marked by fierce competition, the ability to cater to a wide array of price points and product types is not just a strategy, but a necessity for survival and growth. This approach enables brands to navigate consumer trends effectively, whether it's the growing inclination towards affordable beauty solutions or the increasing desire for high-end, specialized products. The segmentation of the market based on product type underlines this diversity. Skincare, for instance, has become a cornerstone of the industry, addressing various consumer concerns from hydration to sun protection. The rising popularity of anti-aging products highlights a shift towards wellness and preventative care in beauty regimes. Meanwhile, the hair care segment's growth mirrors the evolving consumer understanding of hair health and the importance of targeted treatments.

The cosmetics market's embrace of these dynamics reflects a keen understanding of consumer behavior and market trends. Brands that successfully navigate this landscape do so through a blend of innovation, strategic marketing, and adaptability—ensuring they stay relevant and resonant with their target audiences. This ability to adapt and thrive amid changing consumer preferences and technological advancements is what sets successful brands apart in the fiercely competitive beauty industry. The global cosmetics market is delineated by price range into two primary segments: economy and premium. In 2021, the economy segment dominated in revenue, indicating a consumer preference for affordable beauty products. This segment's supremacy is credited to cost-effective offerings by both established and emerging companies, enabling them to capture a substantial consumer base. Conversely, the premium segment, represented by brands such as L'Oréal, Estée Lauder, and Clinique, is anticipated to experience the fastest growth, with consumers willing to invest in high-quality products like Tresemme shampoo, which boasts enhanced surfactants and conditioning agents.

Segmentation by product type reveals that skin and sun care products led the market in 2021 due to their wide utilization for various skin conditions and protection from UV rays. These products, including lotions, gels, facewash, and brightening serums, are integral to consumers' skincare routines, contributing to their skin's health and appearance. The popularity of makeup and color cosmetics, part of this segment, is expected to propel its growth further. Moreover, the anti-aging sub-segment within skin and sun care products enjoyed a significant market share, attributed to its benefits like hydration, improved radiance, and reduction in signs of aging, which resonates with consumers seeking alternatives to invasive cosmetic procedures.

In the hair care segment, anticipated to be the fastest-growing, products are designed to nourish, protect, and cleanse hair. The anti-hair fall and loss care sub-segment, in particular, holds a commanding market share with products that combat scalp issues and promote hair health, exemplified by shampoos from L'Oreal Paris and Dove. Product launches, acquisitions, and innovations are strategic approaches employed by market leaders to expand and solidify their presence, as seen in the joint venture between Shiseido and YA-MAN Ltd. This analysis points to a beauty industry that is at the forefront of retail innovation. Digital marketing strategies have been pivotal for brands to engage and expand their customer base, reflecting the industry's adaptability and responsiveness to evolving consumer demands and technological advancements.

2.3 *Innovating Allure: Trailblazing Marketing Tactics in the Beauty Industry*

The beauty industry has been at the forefront of incorporating Augmented Reality (AR) and Virtual Reality (VR) into their marketing strategies, revolutionizing traditional retail models.

Internally, beauty giants like L'Oreal are utilizing VR to refine in-store consumer approaches. Their 'L'Oreal Beauty Lab' employs VR for better product merchandising and branding decisions, resulting in quicker market improvements. The power of video is undeniable in the beauty industry, as evidenced by the significant portion of makeup tutorial views. Influencers have become pivotal, with brands like Clinique witnessing substantial increases in ad recall and product awareness through concise video content. Engaging 'content in motion' is another cost-effective strategy that has doubled viewer engagement compared to static images.

Beauty influencers are reshaping retail, with their authentic demonstrations leading to direct consumer purchases. Collaborations with the right influencers can position beauty brands quickly and effectively. It is crucial to align with influencers whose criteria match the brand's ethos, as genuine partnerships result in a more authentic endorsement of products. Streamlining the consumer path to purchase is another innovative approach, as demonstrated by Glossier, which leverages customer data from its blog Into the Gloss to enhance the consumer experience and boost sales.

Finally, the evolution of the Original Brand Manufacturer (OBM) model in the beauty industry is characterized by subscription-based models like Birchbox and Ipsy, which cater to consumer preferences and encourage brand loyalty through personalized offerings (Park et al., 2023). These subscription services have rapidly adapted to mobile and online platforms, growing faster than traditional retailers. They overcome initial trust barriers by offering flexible return policies and no-purchase commitments, fostering a loyal customer base. In summary, the beauty sector's marketing innovation is reshaping retail by leveraging cutting-edge technologies like AR and VR, harnessing the power of video and influencers, personalizing the consumer journey, and redefining business models to meet modern consumers' expectations.

3 Navigating the New Norm: Cosmetic Trends in the Digital Transformation Era

As the beauty industry transitions online, entrepreneurs are quick to capitalize on new consumer behaviors, embracing a wave of digital transformation. This shift, catalyzed by the COVID-19 pandemic, has not only reshaped sales channels but also consumer expectations, leading to a surge in e-commerce within the cosmetics sector. The industry's quick adaptation to online platforms and innovative marketing strategies underscores its responsiveness to changing market dynamics.

3.1 Shaping Beauty: Market Trends and Segmentation Dynamics in the Global Cosmetics Industry

In the dynamic world of the cosmetics industry, market trends and segmentation dynamics play a pivotal role, each profoundly influencing the other. Market trends, which encompass the evolving patterns and behaviors of consumers, dictate the types of products that gain popularity, the marketing strategies brands adopt, and the industry's overall evolution. For instance, the shift towards natural and organic cosmetics has not only increased demand for these products but also compelled companies to realign their product lines to meet this new consumer preference.

On the flip side, segmentation dynamics involve categorizing the market into distinct groups based on criteria like price range, product type, consumer demographics, or geographical location. This segmentation enables brands to effectively target and cater to specific market niches. The dichotomy of economy and premium segments is a prime example, with the former appealing to cost-conscious consumers and the latter to those seeking luxury and high-end products. The success of these segments is inherently tied to prevailing market trends, which can either bolster or diminish their appeal based on shifting consumer preferences.

The symbiotic relationship between market trends and segmentation dynamics is crucial in understanding the cosmetics industry's landscape. Market trends can catalyze the emergence of new market segments or transform existing ones. Conversely, the performance of certain market segments can significantly influence emerging trends. A case in point is the growing popularity of anti-aging products, which has not only carved out a lucrative market niche but also fostered a broader trend towards wellness-oriented skincare solutions.

The global cosmetics market's segmentation into economy and premium categories exemplifies this interplay. In 2021, the economy segment led in revenue, indicating a strong consumer predilection for affordable beauty solutions, supplied by a diverse range of products from established and emerging companies. In contrast, the premium segment, backed by esteemed brands like L'Oréal, Estée Lauder, and Clinique, is anticipated to see rapid growth, driven by consumers' willingness to invest in high-quality, luxurious products.

Diving deeper into product-type segmentation, 2021 saw skin and sun care products leading the market due to their versatile applications for various skin conditions and sun protection. These products form an integral part of daily skincare routines, contributing significantly to skin health and aesthetics. The anticipated growth in the makeup and color cosmetics domain, especially the anti-aging sub-segment, underscores the consumers' quest for products offering hydration, radiance, and anti-aging benefits. In the hair care category, products designed for hair health and anti-hair fall solutions, such as those by L'Oreal Paris and Dove, are gaining traction, reflecting the market's dynamic nature. This dynamism is further evidenced by strategic collaborations like Shiseido's partnership with YA-MAN Ltd., highlighting the industry's continuous innovation.

In conclusion, the cosmetics industry stands as a model of innovation within the retail sector. Its agility in adapting to consumer preferences and technological advancements is central to its sustained growth and resilience. Digital marketing strategies play a critical role for brands aiming to expand their consumer base, showcasing the industry's ability to stay at the forefront of the evolving retail landscape.

3.2 *Beauty Leaders Unveiled: Key Insights from 2022's Top-Tier Cosmetics Brands and Companies*

The 2021 Beauty Industry Trends and Cosmetics Marketing Report underscores a significant shift in consumer priorities, where there's an increasing emphasis on product quality and ethical considerations, rather than solely on price. This shift is especially apparent in the growing preference for natural and sustainable products. As consumer incomes rise, there's a notable trend towards valuing the effectiveness and ingredients of cosmetics over their cost. This evolving consumer consciousness is driving brands to adapt their marketing strategies, placing greater emphasis on showcasing their products' quality through customer reviews and user-generated content (UGC), and highlighting their commitment to sustainability in product formulation.

In this context, terms like 'natural', 'organic', and 'clean' have become more than mere marketing buzzwords; they represent core value propositions that resonate deeply with today's consumers. Brands that can authentically align with these values find themselves at a competitive advantage (Bach et al., 2018). The challenge for these brands is twofold: ensuring their products meet these standards, and effectively communicating these attributes to a discerning customer base. The projected growth in the global value of natural cosmetics, expected to reach $54.5 billion by 2027, underscores the economic potential of this shift (Bach et al., 2018). As the cosmetics industry continues to evolve, seamlessly integrating quality, sustainability, and ethical manufacturing into both product development and marketing strategies will be crucial for capturing and retaining the modern, environmentally and health-conscious consumer (Bonnet & Westerman, 2020).

This growing demand for natural and sustainable cosmetics has led to a significant shift in the market dynamics of the beauty industry (Sahota, 2014). Consumers are now more informed and selective about their cosmetic choices, prioritizing health, safety, and environmental impact over traditional beauty standards. This trend reflects a broader societal shift towards sustainability and ethical consumption, rather than being a mere passing fad. As a result, brands are increasingly compelled to be transparent about their product ingredients, sourcing, and manufacturing processes. This transparency is essential not just for meeting consumer expectations, but also for building trust and credibility in a market that is increasingly conscious of its environmental footprint and health implications.

Furthermore, this shift has profound implications for the marketing strategies of cosmetic brands. Traditional advertising tactics are no longer sufficient to engage consumers. Brands must now engage in meaningful dialogues with their customers, educating them about the benefits of natural ingredients, and demonstrating their commitment to sustainability through actionable initiatives. This approach helps build a loyal customer base that values the brand's ethical practices as much as the quality of its products. As the market for natural cosmetics continues to grow, companies that can effectively navigate these changes and align with the evolving values of their consumers will be best positioned for success. The global beauty industry is at a pivotal crossroads, and the way brands respond to these changing consumer preferences will be a defining factor in their future success.

3.3 The Green Wave: Assessing the Global Market Value of Natural Cosmetics in the Modern Era

The global market for natural cosmetics is experiencing a dynamic shift, driven by evolving consumer awareness and preferences. The definition of 'natural' in cosmetics is crucial yet often ambiguous due to the lack of stringent regulations. This uncertainty around what truly constitutes a 'natural' product presents both a challenge and an opportunity for emerging brands in the cosmetics industry. To capitalize on this growing segment, companies must focus on developing products that not only meet non-toxic standards in terms of ingredients and processing but also resonate with the growing consumer demand for authenticity and sustainability. The trend toward natural cosmetics is fueled by increasing consumer concerns over the potential toxicity of synthetic ingredients. Products that are safe, fragrance-free, and made with natural ingredients and essential oils are expected to see substantial growth, as consumers continue to prioritize health and safety in their beauty choices.

Furthermore, the global color make-up cosmetic market is also witnessing a shift, driven by demographic changes and evolving customer experiences. As purchasing power increases in non-western countries, these markets are exerting a more significant influence on the global beauty landscape. Diversity in ethnicity, culture, and beauty rituals is shaping the product offerings and marketing strategies of cosmetic brands.

In addition to ethnicity, age plays a crucial role in consumer behavior in the personal care market. Younger consumers, in particular, are looking for products that align with their values, including sustainability, inclusivity, authenticity and personal service care (Park & Kwon, 2022).This changing demographic landscape is prompting cosmetic brands to rethink their product lines and marketing strategies to cater to a more diverse and discerning customer base. As the global cosmetic market continues to evolve, brands that can adapt to these changes and meet the nuanced needs of a diverse consumer base will be the ones to thrive in the competitive landscape of natural cosmetics.

The landscape of makeup purchasing in the United States has seen a significant shift with the rise of Millennials and Generation Z as the dominant consumer groups. These younger generations, having entered the job market, are now key drivers of new business in the personal care sector. Their impact is particularly notable in the U.S., where their spending on personal care products, including cosmetics, significantly exceeds the national average. Millennials and Gen Z exhibit a unique shopping behavior, marked by a heightened focus on product quality, value, and brand reputation. This trend reflects their discerning purchasing habits and their willingness to invest more in personal care products, aligning with their lifestyle and values.

The preferences of Millennials in the makeup market are distinctly different from those of the previous generations, like Baby Boomers. Millennials show a strong inclination towards organic and eco-friendly products, indicating a deep-seated concern for environmental sustainability and product ingredients. This preference is more than just a passing trend; it's a fundamental shift in consumer values, with Millennials opting for products that align with their ethical and environmental ideologies. Moreover, the role of digital media and online reviews in shaping Millennials' purchasing decisions is substantial. This reliance on digital media not only highlights the importance of online presence for makeup brands but also underscores the shift towards a more informed and digitally connected consumer base. Brands that recognize and adapt to these changing preferences are more likely to resonate with this influential demographic, fostering brand loyalty and driving future business growth and configure their distribution channels (Oh & Rugman, 2007).

In the United States, the leading make-up purchase criteria have undergone a significant transformation, particularly in the context of the millennial demographic. This shift has been largely influenced by the advent of social media and the increasing reliance on digital platforms for product discovery and validation. Millennials, a generation that is deeply integrated with social and digital media, have shown a marked preference for make-up products that are not only high in quality but also boast strong social proof. This trend has set the stage for brands that can effectively leverage social proof - through customer reviews, influencer endorsements, and peer recommendations - to build trust and loyalty among this key demographic. Brands that are adept at navigating the digital landscape, therefore, find themselves in a favorable position to meet and exceed the expectations of these socially-savvy consumers.

The emphasis on social proof among millennial buyers signals a shift in how make-up brands need to approach their marketing and engagement strategies. For brands, this means moving beyond traditional advertising and embracing a more community-oriented approach that resonates with the values and habits of the millennial audience. The success of a make-up product in the U.S. market now hinges on its ability to generate positive word-of-mouth, create engaging social media content, and foster a sense of community among its users. This approach not only helps in building brand credibility but also plays a crucial role in influencing the purchasing decisions of millennials. In this digital era, where opinions are often formed and swayed by online narratives, brands that can effectively harness the power of social proof are poised to build lasting relationships with their millennial customers, turning them into loyal advocates for their products.

3.4 Titans and Trailblazers: Unearthing Major Players and Emerging Movements

The beauty industry is marked by a distinct hierarchy where, for over a century, legacy brands have reigned supreme. With a strong presence in physical retail spaces where 81% of US consumers still prefer to shop, these top 10 legacy brands have enjoyed prime product placements in drugstores and brick-and-mortar chains, finding lucrative success in traditional retail methods. However, this era of dominance is seeing a shift. The longstanding belief that youth equates to beauty is being challenged as consumer loyalty to these giants begins to falter. The rise of more youthful brands is displacing the old guard, signaling a transformative period in the beauty sector.

Despite the formidable legacies of companies like L'Oréal, Estée Lauder, and Chanel, they are finding that reverence for their past triumphs doesn't guarantee future loyalty. Today's consumers, empowered by the digital age, are gravitating towards direct-to-consumer (DTC) brands that they discover on social media. These brands, such as IPSY, Fenty, and Kylie Cosmetics, among others, are quickly coming to market and resonating with a younger audience that values innovation, inclusivity, and a personal connection with the brands they support.

The "new guard," as identified by 2PM Inc.'s DTC Power List, comprises companies like Glossier, Curology, and Drunk Elephant. These brands represent a new wave in the beauty industry, one that champions direct engagement with consumers and relies on social media platforms to build their presence (Palmié et al., 2022). As they grow, these brands are not just offering products but are fostering communities, setting new trends, and reshaping the landscape of beauty commerce for the modern consumer.

4 Digital Influence: Social Media Dynamics Shaping Today's Conversations

Digital platforms, such as social media and online communities, are capable of shaping consumer behavior, opinions, and purchasing decisions within the cosmetics industry. Digital influence encompasses the ability of individuals, brands, and content creators to impact and guide the choices made by consumers when it comes to beauty products. This influence extends beyond traditional advertising and marketing, as it often relies on authentic engagement, credibility, and relatability. In the cosmetics sector, digital influence is manifested through strategies like influencer marketing, user-generated content, and viral trends that leverage the power of online platforms to reach and resonate with a global audience. It signifies a shift in the dynamics of brand-consumer relationships, where consumers are not merely passive recipients of marketing messages but active participants in shaping beauty trends and preferences through their interactions in the digital realm.

Social media dynamics in the cosmetics industry display the ever-changing patterns, interactions, and conversations that occur on various social media platforms, including but not limited to Instagram, YouTube, TikTok, and Facebook. These dynamics involve the dissemination of beauty-related content, discussions, and trends among users, influencers, and brands (Rodner et al., 2022; Suresh et al., 2016). Key elements of social media dynamics include the rapid spread of information, the amplification of user-generated content, and the real-time feedback loop between consumers and beauty brands. In the cosmetics sector, social media dynamics play a pivotal role in setting and amplifying beauty trends, showcasing product innovations, and driving consumer engagement. It's a space where consumers share their beauty routines, reviews, and aspirations, while brands harness these dynamics to build brand awareness, foster brand loyalty, and adapt to evolving consumer preferences. Social media dynamics are a driving force behind the digital transformation of the cosmetics industry, reshaping the way beauty products are marketed, discovered, and experienced.

This social media driven ecosystem teems with potential interactions, indicated by dynamic lines and symbols of connectivity, yet the image also suggests a nascent state—a world where the complete synergy between social media leverage and the cosmetic industry's market reach has not yet been fully realized. There's a sense of motion and activity, but the pathways between products, platforms, and end-users seem to be in the process of being forged, representing a landscape ripe with opportunity for deeper integration and innovation.

The strategies behind creating engaging content, such as interactive posts or visually appealing graphics, play a significant role in attracting and retaining consumers' attention. The impact of influencer collaborations is profound, as influencers can offer a sense of authenticity and relatability, making products more appealing to their followers. Furthermore, social media platforms have become crucial for direct-to-consumer sales, offering an immediate and personal way for consumers to purchase products. These platforms also facilitate two-way communication, allowing brands to receive real-time feedback from consumers, which is invaluable for fostering brand loyalty and adapting quickly to consumer preferences.

4.1 *Social Media Advertising: Catalyst for Beauty Brand Success*

Social media platforms like Instagram, Facebook, and Twitter have become essential tools for beauty brands seeking to advertise their products effectively (Cheung et al., 2021). Glossier credits its remarkable success to a robust social media presence, and Rihanna's exclusive brand launch on these platforms underscores their pivotal role in modern marketing strategies. The key to social media marketing is to highlight the visual appeal of the product, experimenting with creative displays that go beyond basic application shots. Vincent Wu from Bambu Earth emphasizes the importance of innovatively showcasing product textures, lighting, and props to capture audience attention and drive ad success.

Developing an effective social media buying strategy requires a blend of creativity and analytical thinking. Brands should first analyze customer behavior post-purchase, such as return rates and purchasing patterns, to inform a spending strategy that aligns with cash flow and broader business goals. This data-driven approach enables brands to optimize their social media advertising efforts, ensuring they not only capture attention but also convert it into sustainable growth.

Influencers have become an invaluable asset for cosmetic brands, offering the unique ability to demonstrate product results in real-time. This contemporary approach to beauty marketing mirrors the traditional practice of in-person makeup samples at malls but with a digital twist. Bloggers and influencers now conduct live tutorials on social media, showcasing the effectiveness of products and sharing personal endorsements. This method of marketing is particularly potent because it transcends the limitations of static images and text, allowing the authenticity of the influencer's experience with the product to be fully appreciated by the audience.

The impact of influencer content is significant, with a majority of beauty-related media consumption coming directly from these digital trendsetters rather than the brands themselves. This trend highlights the importance of building trust with consumers through social proof, suggesting that the endorsement of influencers can substantially influence purchasing decisions. Brands that successfully leverage influencer partnerships can enhance their credibility and drive consumer engagement in an increasingly crowded and competitive market.

4.2 *Empowering Beauty: The Ascendancy of Solo Creators on YouTube's Cosmetic Stage*

The realm of beauty content on YouTube has witnessed a dramatic shift, with individual creators garnering a staggering 97% of total views, dwarfing the mere 3% held by established beauty brands. This shift, noted by DigitalSurgeons, opens a gateway for emerging startups to exploit influencer marketing, reaching a deeply engaged and vast audience. A prime exemplar of such influence is Jeffree Star, whose product launches and in-depth tutorials not only create immense anticipation and traffic but also showcase the power of personal branding in driving consumer purchases.

Likewise, TikTok has ascended as a formidable platform for beauty influencers, enabling brands to vividly demonstrate their products' impact. Moreover, the potential of unboxing videos to spark excitement and engagement is often overlooked, yet when utilized effectively, as seen with Fabfitfun's campaigns, they can significantly bolster brand engagement. Enhancing these experiences with personalized touches, such as special gifts or handwritten notes, can deepen the influencer-brand relationship and result in content that truly resonates with authenticity.

In the e-commerce landscape, Google Shopping stands out as a pivotal tool, where success is intricately linked to the precision of data feed management. Bridging the gap between organic and paid marketing efforts is paramount for not only driving growth but also securing customer loyalty through owned media channels. Crafting personalized email campaigns and informative blog content nurtures an organic following that feels valued and engaged.

The culmination of these marketing strategies is reflected in the on-site conversion rate, a key indicator of a brand's ability to convert interest into sales. Tactics to bolster this rate span from capturing emails to highlighting reviews and from displaying trust badges to offering subscriptions and upsells. These, combined with a focus on site speed and mobile optimization, are essential for providing a seamless and persuasive shopping experience that translates into customer retention and growth.

4.3 *Enduring Connections: Mastering Strategies for Customer Lifetime Value and Retention*

In the quest for long-term business growth, a pivotal yet frequently underestimated metric is customer lifetime value (LTV), also known as the "cash multiplier" (CM). Instead of focusing on the entire lifespan of a business, a more practical approach is to assess the worth of a customer within a specified payback period, such as 30, 60, or 90 days. Establishing this timeframe allows for the creation of strategies that align with cash flow and foster sustained business development. Engaging customers through memorable unboxing experiences or compelling content marketing with personalized care services can nurture a dedicated community of brand advocates (Merrilees, 2016; Rodner et al., 2022).

Email marketing is the linchpin of customer retention and plays an integral role in enhancing LTV and maximizing revenue potential. By leveraging strategies that drive site traffic, businesses can encourage email list subscriptions, which paves the way for future purchases. It's essential to balance educational and engaging content with promotional messages, cultivating a relationship with subscribers, whether they are potential or returning customers. Implementing loyalty or subscription programs can further solidify a sense of community around the brand, eventually leading to upselling.

Understanding variable costs (VC) is crucial, as they increase in proportion to order volume. These costs, which differ from fixed expenses like rent and operational overhead, include the cost of goods sold (COGS), platform and payment processor fees, supply chain, fulfillment, and customer acquisition costs (CAC), encompassing total expenditure inclusive of agency fees. The analysis of these costs hinges on unit economics, which involves dissecting financial inputs and outputs on a per-unit basis. To effectively measure and manage variable costs, employing a four-quarter accounting matrix can provide insights into the financial health of these components and highlight potential areas for optimization and growth.

5 Conclusion

This chapter provides an insightful analysis of the digital transformation shaping the cosmetics industry, highlighting the dynamic changes that digital technology brings to consumer interactions, product development, and market strategies. It sets the foundation for an in-depth look at the industry's evolution, as traditional retail practices give way to innovative digital solutions. The chapter emphasizes the industry's readiness to embrace digital advancements, which are redefining everything from marketing to supply chain logistics, foreshadowing a future where the cosmetics sector is increasingly tech-driven and customer-centric (Kane et al., 2015; Rogers, 2016).

The latest trends reveal the cosmetics market's immense appeal, especially among young consumers who prioritize beauty and personal care. This section underscores the global market's potential growth and acknowledges the challenges posed by the adverse effects of chemically laden products (Kumar, 2005; Łopaciuk & Łoboda, 2013; Park et al., 2023). The embrace of cutting-edge technologies like AR, AI, and 3D printing is presented as a pivotal driver for future market growth, while the chapter also acknowledges the current market dominance of the Asia–Pacific region and the rapid growth in LAMEA markets. The narrative closes with an overview of the Japanese cosmetics market, detailing the challenges and opportunities presented by an aging population and shifting consumer behaviors, and concludes with the market's resilience and growth potential post-COVID-19, further fueled by the rise in e-commerce and influencer marketing.

References

Bach, M. P., Spremić, M., & Vugec, D. S. (2018). Integrating digital transformation strategies into firms: Values, routes and best practice examples. In *Management and technological challenges in the digital age* (pp. 107–128). CRC Press.

Bonnet, D., & Westerman, G. (2020). The new elements of digital transformation. *MIT Sloan Management Review, 62*(2). https://sloanreview.mit.edu/article/the-new-elements-of-digital-transformation/

Cheung, M. L., Pires, G. D., Rosenberger, P. J., III., & De Oliveira, M. J. (2021). Driving COBRAs: The power of social media marketing. *Marketing Intelligence & Planning, 39*(3), 361–376.

Kane, G. C., Palmer, D., Phillips, A. N., & Kiron, D. (2015). Is your business ready for a digital future? *MIT Sloan Management Review, 56*(4), 37–44.

Kumar, S. (2005). Exploratory analysis of global cosmetic industry: Major players, technology and market trends. *Technovation, 25*(11), 1263–1272.

Łopaciuk, A., & Łoboda, M. (2013, June). Global beauty industry trends in the 21st century. In *Management, knowledge and learning international conference* (pp. 19–21).

Merrilees, B. (2016). Interactive brand experience pathways to customer-brand engagement and value co-creation. *Journal of Product & Brand Management, 25*(5), 402–408.

Oh, C. H., & Rugman, A. M. (2007). Regional multinationals and the Korean cosmetics industry. *Asia Pacific Journal of Management, 24*, 27–42.

Palmié, M., Miehé, L., Oghazi, P., Parida, V., & Wincent, J. (2022). The evolution of the digital service ecosystem and digital business model innovation in retail: The emergence of meta-ecosystems and the value of physical interactions. *Technological Forecasting and Social Change, 177*, 121496.

Park, E., & Kwon, K. H. (2022). A popularization of curation service for dermatological condition in Republic of Korea. *Journal of Cosmetic Dermatology, 21*(12), 6594–6604.

Park, Y. W., Hong, P., & Shin, G. C. (2023). Rising and thriving in the post COVID-19 era: A case study of COSMAX, a leader of the Korean cosmetic industry. *Asia Pacific Business Review, 29*(4), 1105–1124.

Park, Y. W., & Shintaku, J. (2022). Sustainable human–machine collaborations in digital transformation technologies adoption: A comparative case study of Japan and Germany. *Sustainability, 14*(17), 10583.

Rodner, V., Goode, A., & Burns, Z. (2022). "Is it all just lip service?": On Instagram and the normalisation of the cosmetic servicescape. *Journal of Services Marketing, 36*(1), 44–58.

Rogers, D. L. (2016). *The digital transformation playbook: Rethink your business for the digital age*. Columbia University Press.

Sahota, A. (Ed.). (2014). *Sustainability: How the cosmetics industry is greening up*. Wiley.

Suresh, V., Chitra, M., & Maran, K. (2016). A study on factors determining social media on cosmetic product. *Journal of Pharmaceutical Sciences and Research, 8*(1), 1.

Westerman, G., Bonnet, D., & McAfee, A. (2014). *Leading digital: Turning technology into business transformation*. Harvard Business Press.

Yi, H. T., Cha, Y. B., & Amenuvor, F. E. (2021). Effects of sales-related capabilities of personal selling organizations on individual sales capability, sales behaviors and sales performance in cosmetics personal selling channels. *Sustainability, 13*(7), 3937.

Chapter 4
Navigating the New Frontier: Digital Marketing Strategy in the Cosmetics Industry

Abstract This chapter explores the transformation of Japan's cosmetics sector amidst the rise of e-commerce, especially in the face of the COVID-19 pandemic. With Japan holding the third-largest cosmetics market globally, the traditionally lauded aspects of functionality, quality, and safety have been challenged by reduced domestic and foreign demand due to pandemic-related restrictions. This has compelled companies to pivot towards e-commerce for customer acquisition and retention. The discussion underscores the strategic shift from merely acquiring new customers to fostering "Genuine Loyalty," a concept that embodies both attitudinal and behavioral dimensions of consumer loyalty. By dissecting the nuances of loyalty. By examining the nuances of loyalty—cognitive, affective, and conative—the chapter outlines how Japanese cosmetics businesses can adapt to and flourish in the e-commerce era, despite the initial hesitance of consumers who prefer tactile product experiences. Further, the analysis examines the roles of customer loyalty and word-of-mouth (WOM) marketing in driving e-commerce success. It emphasizes the unique characteristics of Japanese consumers, who often desire to test cosmetics first-hand due to product-specific factors like texture and skin compatibility. Despite this, the increased reliance on e-commerce during the pandemic has necessitated strategies to maintain and boost customer loyalty. The narrative explains how leveraging digital platforms for customer engagement and satisfaction, harnessing the power of positive WOM, and utilizing innovative tools like AI for personalized experiences are critical. It also discusses the dual nature of loyalty: attitudinal, reflecting the customer's emotional connection, and behavioral, indicating their purchasing patterns. Through case studies of leading companies, the text provides insights into creating digital platforms that not only facilitate transactions but also cultivate a loyal customer base essential for long-term success in the competitive digital landscape of the cosmetics industry.

Y. W. Park and P. Hong, *Cosmetics Marketing Strategy in the Era of the Digital Ecosystem*, https://doi.org/10.1007/978-981-97-3674-4_4

1 Introduction

In an era where digitalization is not just a trend but a paradigm shift, the cosmetics industry stands at the forefront of a new frontier. This chapter delves into the essence of this transformation, highlighting the imperative of navigating through the digital landscape with agility and foresight. The digital age has revolutionized the way beauty products are marketed and sold, presenting both unparalleled opportunities and unique challenges.

At the heart of this evolution is the digital marketing strategy, a critical tool for cosmetic brands to engage with a diverse and digitally savvy consumer base. Digital marketing in this context is more than just a channel for advertising; it's a multifaceted approach that encompasses social media engagement, influencer partnerships, personalized content, and data-driven insights. This strategy enables brands to connect with customers on a more intimate level, crafting experiences that resonate and foster loyalty.

The interrelationship between navigating this new frontier and employing an effective digital marketing strategy is intricate. As traditional advertising methods become less effective in the face of changing consumer behaviors, brands must adapt by embracing digital platforms. This transition, however, is not without its challenges. Regulatory constraints, the necessity for digital agility, and the emergence of targeted consumer segments require a nuanced understanding and strategic approach. This chapter will explore these challenges in depth, offering insights into how cosmetic brands can leverage digital tools and channels effectively. The focus will be on the need for a dual-strategy approach to marketing that balances immediate gains with sustainable long-term brand building. Such an approach is indispensable for thriving in today's dynamic digital ecosystem, allowing brands to not only meet the immediate demands of consumers but also to build a resilient and enduring presence in the market.

1.1 Striking the Balance: A Dual Strategy Approach

The cosmetics industry is currently navigating a complex marketing landscape, one that demands a dual-strategy approach capable of balancing immediate needs with long-term goals. Stricter regulations on advertising have constricted traditional marketing channels, complicating the communication of product benefits through conventional slogans and imagery. Meanwhile, the digital transformation has expanded customer touchpoints, presenting both opportunities and challenges. While digital avenues such as e-commerce and social media offer direct access to consumers, they also require a cohesive strategy to achieve synergy and avoid the pitfalls of organizational fragmentation which can slow down a company's ability to respond to market changes effectively.

Simultaneously, there's an emerging 'small mass' trend that is reshaping consumer engagement. First identified by Kao in 2015, this approach targets a stable and specific consumer segment that doesn't conform to the mass market but nonetheless holds significant sales potential. As consumers increasingly seek products that resonate with their individual values rather than generic, mass-market appeals, large corporations are struggling to adapt. This shift in consumer behavior is opening doors for smaller, agile companies to carve out substantial niches by offering premium, personalized products. As a result, the ability to pivot and cater to these nuanced market segments is becoming a critical competitive edge in the cosmetics industry.

Table 1 presents a juxtaposition of marketing strategies viewed through the lenses of time: one short-term, the other long-term, each with distinct focal points and objectives. On one side, the short-term perspective zeroes in on immediate sales, targeting current customers with the goal of driving quick revenue growth. This approach is about capitalizing on what can be achieved now, leveraging existing relationships and market presence to secure a swift increase in sales figures. It's a sprint, pushing for a rapid expansion in market share and immediate financial gains. In contrast, the long-term perspective is akin to a marathon, where the focus shifts from immediate transactions to nurturing enduring relationships that bolster the brand. Here, the audience widens to encompass not just the existing customers but also potential ones who may be won over by the brand's allure in the future. The strategy pivots towards sustainable growth, investing in the brand's essence and its value proposition to ensure it remains compelling over time. It's about building a legacy and fostering a market position that can weather changes in consumer trends and market dynamics.

The essence of a dual-strategy approach in marketing lies in harmonizing these two perspectives. It's an intricate dance between seizing the day and planting seeds for the future. In practice, this means that a company might engage in aggressive promotion and sales tactics to boost short-term revenue while simultaneously crafting content and experiences that contribute to long-term brand loyalty and equity. For the cosmetics industry, this duality could manifest in the form of time-limited discounts to encourage immediate purchases and detailed, influencer-led campaigns designed to deeply embed the brand into the consumer's lifestyle narratives. Striking this balance is critical; leaning too heavily on either side can have detrimental effects. A myopic focus on the short-term can lead to a fragile brand that's overly dependent on

Table 1 Short-term and long-term perspective of marketing

	Short-term perspective	Long-term perspective
Challenge	Selling (sales)	Relationships that foster a brand that creates a system that sells itself (marketing)
Customer	Current customers	Current Customers + Potential Customers
Purpose	Speedy growth	Sustainable management and creation of corporate value

discounts and promotions, while an exclusive emphasis on the long-term can leave a company unresponsive to immediate market opportunities and financial necessities. The dual strategy ensures that a company remains agile and responsive to immediate market demands without losing sight of its ultimate ambition to build a brand that endures and prospers through changing times.

1.2 Understanding Customer Psychographics in Cosmetics

In cosmetics marketing, a deep dive into customer psychographics is crucial for uncovering their hidden needs and shaping effective strategies. This section focuses on how the cosmetics industry can utilize psychographic analysis to understand the intricate layers of consumer behavior and preferences. By examining the psychology behind customer choices, businesses can segment their audience more effectively and develop precise targeting tactics. This method goes beyond just tracking purchasing habits; it involves a detailed exploration of the motivations and desires that influence consumer behavior. Implementing this approach not only boosts customer satisfaction but also strengthens the brand's competitive standing in the market. Through this exploration, we aim to reveal the underlying factors that drive consumer decisions in the cosmetics industry.

Discovering the Hidden Needs of Customers. Understanding the psychological state of customers in cosmetics marketing involves dissecting their needs, wants, and demands. 'Needs' refer to a state of deficiency, such as dry skin concerns. 'Wants' are desires to satisfy these needs, like the yearning for moisturizing products. Finally, 'Demand' is the aspiration to purchase specific items, like choosing a particular brand's moisturizer. In the current information-rich era, customers often struggle to recognize or articulate their needs. Therefore, effective advertising and customer service that can unearth these latent needs are key to successful marketing. For instance, beauty consultants at Japanese department stores like Shiseido have boosted sales by addressing underlying customer concerns. Furthermore, the integration of AI in counseling, through smartphone applications and other technological innovations, marks a significant advancement in identifying and meeting customer needs.

Segmenting Customers with STP Analysis. Segmenting the market, targeting specific segments, and positioning the brand effectively are the core elements of STP (Segmentation, Targeting, Positioning) analysis. Segmentation involves dividing the market into groups with similar characteristics, identified through geographic or demographic variables like location, age, or income. Targeting then selects the most promising market segments. Positioning is about differentiating one's brand from competitors. A crucial aspect here is the analysis of psychographic variables, which include psychological characteristics. These are not as easily quantifiable as geographic or demographic factors; hence they often require in-depth methods like group interviews or ethnographic research to truly grasp the human condition. Web surveys, while efficient, may only capture issues that customers are already aware of.

Insights from Ethnographic Research. Kao's approach to market research exemplifies the depth of understanding achievable through ethnographic methods. When revamping their Essential shampoo line, they conducted multi-stage surveys, including interviews with 200 people, a blogging activity for 17 individuals, and a detailed ethnography of 6 women. This comprehensive study revealed nuanced insights, such as young women's concerns not just about hair tips but also the strands below their ears. Such deep understanding enabled Kao to develop a successful marketing strategy focused on "cute hair tips," resonating well with their target audience. Additionally, the rise of social media platforms like YouTube, Instagram, and TikTok, where users share beauty routines, offers a wealth of information akin to ethnographic research. Analyzing these videos with AI technology for image and video analysis can further enhance understanding of consumer lifestyles and preferences, showcasing the growing importance of digital tools in market research.

Segmenting Customers with STP Analysis allows for the market to be divided into distinct groups, chosen by geographic or demographic variables. Targeting then involves selecting the most viable segments, while positioning distinguishes a brand from its competition. The pivotal part of this strategy is analyzing psychographic variables—psychological traits of consumers that are less quantifiable and often uncovered through in-depth interviews or ethnographic research. Insights from Ethnographic Research are illustrated by Kao's approach to revamping their shampoo line. Their exhaustive research process, including interviews and observations of daily routines, uncovered specific consumer concerns, leading to a marketing strategy that resonated deeply with their target demographic. The prevalent use of social media, where individuals share beauty routines, can similarly offer insights comparable to ethnographic studies. Analysis of this content with AI technology can yield a profound understanding of consumer lifestyles and preferences.

Stages of Consumer Adoption. Building upon these insights, the adoption of new products in the cosmetics industry can be explained by consumer adoption stages. This model outlines the adoption journey from 'Innovators,' a tiny fraction of early enthusiasts, to 'Early Adopters,' community influencers who add credibility to the product. The 'Early Majority' and 'Late Majority' are more cautious but represent a larger portion of the market, while 'Laggards' are the last to adopt, resistant to change until it becomes the norm. Each group's willingness to embrace innovation is crucial for planning the introduction and scaling of new products or ideas across consumer segments.

Figure 1 delineates how a new product or idea is embraced by the market over time through distinct segments of adopters. At the outset, 'Innovators,' a small group representing 2.5% of the potential population, are the first to try the innovation. They are followed by 'Early Adopters' (13.5%), who are key opinion leaders in their communities and help the product gain market credibility. The 'Early Majority' (34%) comes next. These individuals are deliberate and pragmatic in their adoption choices, requiring more proof before commitment. Bridging the significant 'chasm'

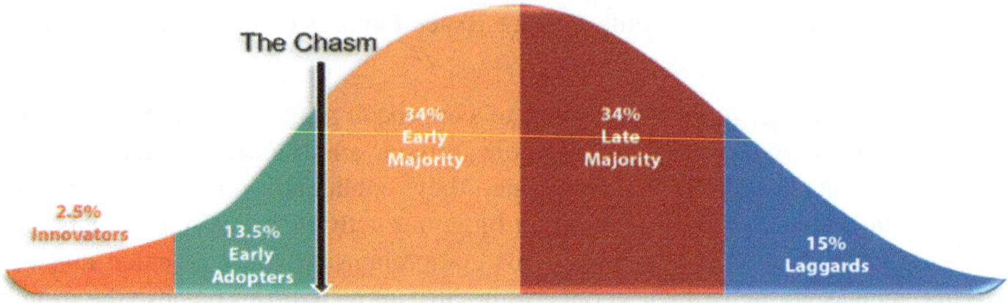

Fig. 1 Stages of consumer adoption in the diffusion of innovation

between early adopters and the early majority is crucial for an innovation's sustained market presence. The 'Late Majority' also comprises 34% of the market; these individuals are skeptical and will only adopt after the majority has tested the innovation. Finally, 'Laggards' (16%) are tradition-bound, resistant to change, and adopt innovation only when it has become a part of the traditional landscape. Each stage reflects varying degrees of willingness to adopt innovations, and understanding these segments is vital for strategizing the rollout of new products or concepts to different consumer groups.

2 Digital Marketing Tools

In the ever-evolving landscape of digital marketing, various tools have emerged as game-changers, particularly in the cosmetics industry. These tools, ranging from social media platforms to advanced analytics, have revolutionized how beauty brands engage with their audience, understand consumer behavior, and drive sales. The advent of platforms like Instagram, coupled with the strategic use of influencer marketing, has profoundly influenced consumer preferences and purchasing decisions. This section delves into the significant impact of these digital marketing tools, starting with a focus on Instagram's transformative role in the cosmetics industry. We will explore how this platform, in conjunction with influencer marketing, has not only altered the way products are presented but also how they are perceived by different demographic groups, thereby shaping the marketing strategies of cosmetic brands.

2.1 Instagram's Major Impact on the Cosmetics Industry

Influencer Marketing: Influencer marketing has been particularly effective in web promotions for cosmetics. Engaging influencers with large followings, such as YouTubers and Instagrammers, to showcase products influences consumer purchasing decisions. This strategy is known to be more effective for cosmetics than other products. According to marketing research, influencer marketing has a greater impact on point makeup products than on skincare and hair care products.

Changes Brought About by Instagram: This trend has been explosively increasing since 2017, and in Japan, the term "Insta photo editing" (Insta-bae) became a buzzword of the year. Particularly, sales of point makeup products have significantly increased. On Instagram, products with elements of surprise and transformation are visually appealing and tend to have high engagement, leading to previously unpopular products like color-changing lipsticks and colorful eyeshadow palettes becoming bestsellers.

Instagram initially required consciousness about visual media, like "Insta photo editing," but with the introduction of Stories, it has become a more life-integrated media, where people can share updates or exchange direct messages.

Generational Differences in Instagram Use: While the 30–40 age group uses Instagram as one of many social media tools, younger generations use it as a fundamental part of their daily lives. Many young people prefer Instagram's direct messages over other communication apps like LINE (equivalent to KakaoTalk in Korea), and they often search for desired products on Instagram rather than using Google, exhibiting different behavioral characteristics from older generations.

2.2 Cultivating Customer Loyalty and Amplifying Word-of-Mouth Advocacy

Customer loyalty and word-of-mouth (WOM) marketing are integral elements in modern marketing strategies, shaping consumer behavior and brand perception. Companies prioritize fostering customer loyalty, recognizing its impact as a formidable marketing asset. In today's digitally interconnected landscape, consumer choices are influenced by diverse factors, ranging from social media engagements to online reviews, ultimately converging on familiarity and trustworthiness in brands.

The extensive exploration of customer loyalty encompasses a spectrum of theories and insights, exemplified by contributions from Mikawa et al. (2007), Kaneko (2021), and Day (1999). Day highlights four advantages of customer loyalty, emphasizing its impact on service efficiency, pricing resilience, willingness to pay, and positive brand advocacy, elucidating the invaluable role of loyal customers in reducing acquisition costs and augmenting brand value.

To comprehend consumer behavior comprehensively, businesses must delve beyond sales data, encompassing customer surveys and the intricacies of online WOM. WOM operates as individuals disseminate information, as detailed by Eda (2021), driven by various motivations articulated by Rosen (2000), Lee et al. (2015), and Eda (2021), reflecting the evolving nature of motivations in digital WOM dynamics.

Recent studies delve deeply into the intricate relationship between customer loyalty and WOM. Ferguson et al. (2006) underscore the influence of positive WOM on customer retention, elucidating its role in retaining and attracting customers. Wang and Binti Omar (2023) establish links between employee satisfaction and positive WOM, advocating leveraging engaged employees for brand advocacy. Godes and Mayzlin (2009) and Haenlein and Libai (2017) reveal the impact of WOM on sales and propose metrics to measure WOM program value. Liu et al. (2021) dissect the interplay between customer experience, perceived value, and loyalty within specific platforms, emphasizing the pivotal role of physical environment and human interaction.

Psychological motives and behavioral patterns in WOM, explored by researchers like Packard and Wooten (2013), Peluso et al. (2017), Lisjak et al. (2021), and Berger and Schwartz (2011), illuminate consumer behavior in compensating for knowledge gaps, engaging in compensatory WOM, and responding to various marketing perks. Theoretical perspectives by De Angelis et al. (2012) and Dubois et al. (2016) shed light on motives driving positive and negative WOM and the impact of interpersonal closeness on WOM valence.

Managing customer-to-customer communication, as investigated by Godes and Mayzlin (2009) and Haenlein and Libai (2017), underscores the significance of less loyal customers in WOM propagation and the necessity of integrating WOM programs into broader customer management functions.

Together, these studies underscore the potency of positive WOM, primarily fueled by satisfied employees and customers, as a catalyst for nurturing customer loyalty and retention. Businesses seeking to fortify customer loyalty should prioritize enhancing service quality, fostering employee satisfaction and engagement, and devising WOM strategies leveraging these factors to cultivate a dedicated and loyal customer base.

The contrast between traditional WOM and modern, digital platforms prompted investigations into the differing nature of shared content and motivations. Research indicates a significant correlation between customer loyalty and WOM behaviors, with loyal customers often sharing positive experiences, recommendations, and information tailored to their networks, making WOM an influential factor in consumer purchasing decisions and a means for brands to turn satisfied customers into advocates for new customer acquisition (Kaneko, 2021). Oliver (2014) bifurcates customer loyalty into attitudinal and behavioral categories, with the former encompassing cognitive, affective, and conative loyalties.

Table 2 is a summary that shows the categorization of customer loyalty into various types, as delineated by Kaneko (2021), and serves as a vital framework for businesses to understand and engage with their customer base effectively. This nuanced understanding is particularly important in the cosmetics industry, where brand perception and customer experience are paramount. Understanding these different types of loyalty is indispensable for cosmetic brands. It allows them to craft targeted marketing strategies that resonate with customers at different loyalty stages. For instance, cognitive loyalty can be addressed with informative content and demonstrations of product effectiveness, while affective loyalty can be deepened through storytelling and brand experiences that evoke emotions.

Table 2 Three types of loyalty (Kaneko, 2021)

Classification of customer loyalty		Definition
Attitudinal loyalty	Cognitive loyalty	A state of customer loyalty in which the consumer logically judges that the target is in his or her best interest
	Affective loyalty	A state of customer loyalty in which the consumer has an extremely positive feeling toward the subject
	Conative loyalty	A state of customer loyalty in which consumers are strongly motivated to preferentially visit, purchase, and use the target
Behavioral loyalty	Behavioral loyalty	Customer loyalty status indicating the recency, frequency, and amounts of purchases consumers have made for the target in the last specified period

Recognizing the distinction between the types of loyalty enables cosmetic brands to personalize the customer journey. Customers exhibiting cognitive loyalty may be more receptive to data-driven communications that showcase the brand's unique selling propositions. In contrast, those with affective loyalty may appreciate more personalized interactions and exclusive offers that acknowledge their emotional connection to the brand. Lastly, customers with high affective and conative loyalty are invaluable as brand advocates, especially in an industry where word-of-mouth is a powerful tool. By leveraging these customers' willingness to share their positive experiences, cosmetic brands can amplify their reach and credibility, attracting new customers through trusted recommendations. In essence, the multi-tiered approach to customer loyalty allows cosmetic brands to engage with their customers more meaningfully, ensuring that their marketing efforts are not only seen and heard but also felt and responded to, fostering a loyal customer base that grows in both number and devotion.

Word-of-mouth communication spreads in a chain-like process, where the initial recipient becomes a new sender, further transmitting the information (Eda, 2021). The motives behind information sharing, as outlined by Rosen (2002), can be grouped into five factors. First, it aligns with our survival instinct, historically crucial for sharing vital information for survival. Second, it promotes social relationships and solidarity. Third, it reduces risk and uncertainty by distributing information. Fourth, it can yield economic benefits due to network effects. Fifth, it helps alleviate stress and anxiety (Rosen, 2002). Furthermore, Arndt (1978) identifies several motives for word-of-mouth, such as altruism, displaying situational interest, self-protection in friendships, and the need to resolve dissatisfaction. Recent studies on motivations specific to Instagram (Eda, 2021; Lee et al., 2015) reveal a range of motives that diverge from those of traditional word-of-mouth.

The investigation into the different motivations behind traditional word-of-mouth and those on interactive platforms like Instagram was prompted by the distinct nature of content shared on these platforms. Kenmochi (2017) highlights the relationship between customer loyalty and word-of-mouth behavior. Word-of-mouth, which includes sharing positive experiences, making recommendations, and disseminating tailored information, is a potent influence on consumer purchasing decisions. It leverages the voice of existing customers to evangelize the brand and draw in new ones (Kaneko, 2021).

2.3 Strategic Perks of Launching Your Own E-Commerce Platform in Cosmetics

Strategic perks refer to the advantages or benefits that a company gains by implementing a particular strategy that aligns with its long-term goals and competitive position. These perks typically provide leverage in the marketplace, enhance operational efficiency, or improve the brand's value proposition. They can be in the form of increased control over business processes, improved profit margins, enhanced customer insights and data, stronger brand identity, and the ability to respond quickly to market changes.

Cosmetics companies can gain such long-term benefits by establishing and managing their own online sales channels. The foremost strategic advantage is the control of customer data. In the digital age, data is the most valuable asset a company can possess. Selling products through third-party wholesalers or vast internet e-commerce malls often means surrendering the complete ownership of customer data, which is a significant loss. By launching an independent e-commerce platform, a cosmetics brand can implement a strategy to secure at least 16% of its target customer data, allowing for a deeper understanding of customer preferences and behavior, which is instrumental in crafting personalized marketing campaigns and product development.

The second perk is the control of marketing. While listing products on large e-commerce sites like Amazon or Rakuten Market may seem convenient, these platforms are saturated with competition—housing approximately 170,000 and 50,000 stores, respectively—making brand differentiation a formidable challenge. Communication with customers on these platforms is often impersonal, with customers typically more aware of the platform than the individual brands they purchase from. Further, constraints on packaging design make it difficult for brands to use this as a means of educating customers about their products. An independent e-commerce site becomes not just a sales channel but a marketing tool that enables brands to build a distinctive identity and directly communicate with their customers.

Lastly, control of profit margin is a significant consideration. When dealing with drugstores and specialty stores, particularly in Japan, companies are often compelled to sell their products at 60–70% of the retail price, with the potential for even lower pricing demands. Furthermore, fixed fees for product placement in stores can erode profit margins. By launching a proprietary e-commerce platform, a cosmetics company can command full price for its products, eliminating the middleman and improving profitability.

In summary, operating an own e-commerce site in the cosmetics industry provides strategic control over crucial aspects of business, from customer relationships and brand marketing to financial management. Each of these advantages is key to building a resilient brand in a market that is as competitive as it is lucrative.

3 Sephora's Trailblazing Journey: A Case Illustration

Sephora, a renowned name in the global cosmetics industry, began its journey in France in 1969, heralding a new era in beauty retail. This prestigious brand, known for revolutionizing the way beauty products are marketed and sold, has since evolved into a frontrunner in the cosmetics world. The company's trajectory took a significant turn in 1997 when it became part of the luxury conglomerate LVMH (Louis Vuitton Moët Hennessy), marking a pivotal moment that expanded its international reach. This expansion continued unabated, with Sephora establishing a strong global presence in 1998. Although it ventured into Japan in 1999, the brand later withdrew from this market, reflecting its strategic adaptability.

3.1 Innovative Direct-to-Consumer (D2C) and E-Commerce Strategies (ECS)

As we delve into the realm of the cosmetics industry, a sector constantly evolving with technological advances and shifting consumer behaviors, the move towards Direct-to-Consumer (D2C) and E-Commerce Strategies (ECS) has become not just a trend, but a pivotal component of business success. These strategies represent a transformative shift from traditional retail models, offering brands the autonomy to engage directly with their customers and the flexibility to navigate the digital marketplace on their own terms.

What sets Sephora apart is its unique store features. Each outlet is a treasure trove of beauty products, offering an extensive selection from over 3000 brands. This diversity caters to a wide range of beauty needs and preferences. More than just stores, Sephora locations are beauty hubs where staff members are experts in their field, offering personalized, unbiased advice to customers. This hybrid retail approach combines the variety of a department store with the accessibility of a drugstore, often positioned for convenient access.

The launch of Sephora.com in 1999 marked a significant leap in its journey, introducing the Beauty Insider Community. This initiative fostered a more interactive and engaging relationship with customers, featuring elements like Real Talk, Ratings & Reviews, and the Beauty Board. It signaled Sephora's commitment to creating a community around beauty, transcending the traditional retail experience.

2007 was another milestone year for Sephora as it expanded its e-commerce presence. This move was about more than just online sales; it was the creation of an integrated beauty platform. The introduction of the Beauty Insider loyalty program allowed customers to accrue points across both physical and digital realms, bridging the gap between in-store and online shopping experiences. This integration of community, membership, and e-commerce repositioned Sephora not just as a retailer but as a comprehensive beauty destination.

Sephora's evolution from a French cosmetic store to a global beauty platform underscores its dedication to innovation, customer engagement, and providing a seamless shopping experience. By continually adapting to shifts in the retail landscape and consumer preferences, Sephora has cemented its status as a trailblazer in the beauty industry.

Table 3 showcases the tiered membership benefits of the 2021 Beauty Club offered by Sephora, providing a clear comparison between the three levels of membership: Basic, Premier VIP, and First Class VIP.

At the foundational level, the Basic membership, which is free to join, offers a modest set of benefits. Members at this level do not receive beauty club cash but are eligible for a 10% discount during Seasonal Saving Events. Additionally, Basic members can enjoy free standard shipping on orders that meet a minimum of $50 and a Dollar Savings Offer of $15 off, presumably on eligible purchases. Points for Discount Events are not available at this level, nor are First Class VIP Rewards.

Moving up to the Premier VIP tier, which requires a $350 membership fee, members enjoy enhanced benefits. They receive an increased discount of 15% off during Seasonal Saving Events and a lower free shipping threshold of $45. The Dollar Savings Offer is also more generous, providing $20 off. Similar to the Basic tier, there is no mention of beauty club cash or Points for Discount Events, and First-Class VIP Rewards are not part of this package either.

Table 3 2021 beauty club member benefits

Benefit parameters	Basic (free to join)	Premier VIP ($350 membership fee)	First class VIP ($1,000 membership fee)
Beauty club cash	○	○	○
Seasonal saving event	10% off	15% off	20% off
Free standard shipping	$50 min	$45 min	No min
Dollar savings offer	$15 off	$20 off	$25 off
Points for discount events	○	○	○
FIRST class VIP reward			○

Source Adapted from Sephora Beauty Insider

The First-Class VIP level represents the highest tier of membership with a $1,000 membership fee. Members at this level receive the most substantial benefits, including a 20% discount during Seasonal Saving Events and the luxury of having no minimum purchase requirement for free standard shipping. The Dollar Savings Offer is the highest at this tier, granting $25 off. While beauty club cash and Points for Discount Events are not explicitly provided at this level either, the mention of First-Class VIP Rewards suggests exclusive perks that are reserved for the highest-paying members.

Each tier is carefully crafted to incentivize higher spending with greater rewards, a strategy designed to foster brand loyalty and encourage recurrent spending among Sephora's customer base. The structure reflects a commitment to rewarding customer loyalty with progressively valuable benefits as they move up the membership ranks. The absence of certain perks like beauty club cash across all tiers may indicate a strategic choice by Sephora to emphasize direct discounts and savings. It's worth noting that the table is adapted from Sephora's Beauty Insider program, indicating that these benefits are part of a larger loyalty strategy aimed at enhancing customer retention and engagement.

3.2 Beyond Beauty Club Perks: Sephora's Personalized Customer Experience

Having examined the tiered advantages that Sephora's Beauty Club offers, it becomes clear that these benefits are just the beginning of a much more expansive strategy. The Beauty Club sets the foundation for a deeper, more engaging customer relationship—one that is further enriched by Sephora's cutting-edge digital initiatives and personalized services. This seamless blend of loyalty perks and innovative shopping tools exemplifies Sephora's commitment to creating an unparalleled beauty experience for every customer.

Enter the Sephora To Go app, launched in 2013, which represents a leap forward in the company's digital evolution. It's not merely a mobile extension of the Beauty Club Member Benefits; it's an integral part of Sephora's ecosystem that brings the in-store experience into the digital age. The app's functionality, from purchase points to AR technology, enhances the existing Beauty Club perks by adding layers of convenience and personalization. It's a prime example of how Sephora uses technology not just to sell products, but to create a comprehensive beauty journey tailored to the individual needs of its users.

Further expanding on the notion of personalized shopping, Sephora's 'One Team Service' epitomizes the brand's innovative spirit. By leveraging insights from the Beauty Insider program, Sephora personalizes every interaction—whether in-store or online—to reflect the unique preferences of each customer. This strategic use of data enriches the benefits of being a club member and positions Sephora at the forefront of customer-centric retail in the cosmetics industry.

As we delve into Sephora's strategic initiatives, from the Sephora To Go app to the personalized 'One Team Service,' we see a brand that has mastered the art of customer engagement, setting a new benchmark for the retail experience. These strategies not only complement the Beauty Club's structure but elevate it, ensuring that every touchpoint with the brand is as informative and enjoyable as it is exclusive and rewarding.

This transition underscores the connection between the loyalty program benefits and Sephora's broader strategic initiatives, providing a smooth segue into discussing the company's innovative approaches that have revolutionized the cosmetic shopping experience.

3.3 E-Commerce Strategies (ECS)

Sephora's E-Commerce Strategies (ECS) have been finely tuned to recognize and cater to the various types of customer loyalty, understanding that each segment interacts with the brand differently. By dissecting customer data, Sephora identifies cognitive loyalty within shoppers who seek value and quality, offering them in-depth product information and comparison tools. Affective loyalty is nurtured through personalized recommendations and a rewards system that resonates with customers' emotional connections to the brand. For those demonstrating conative loyalty, Sephora enhances the convenience of repurchase with features like subscription services and reordering ease. The company's strategic segmentation ensures that customers feel understood and valued at each stage of their loyalty journey, reinforcing their commitment to the brand and encouraging the transition from one loyalty type to the next.

Sephora's social media strategies are a testament to its innovative approach to ECS. The brand leverages platforms like Instagram and YouTube to create vibrant communities around beauty. They employ user-generated content and influencer partnerships to foster a sense of trust and authenticity. Campaigns like #SephoraSquad utilize social listening tools to identify and collaborate with micro-influencers, tapping into diverse customer segments and driving engagement. By creating hashtag challenges and interactive content, Sephora turns its social media channels into a space for customers to share their experiences and become brand advocates, effectively utilizing WOM in the digital age.

Lastly, the development and implementation of Sephora's digital marketing platform illustrate the brand's forward-thinking approach. Sephora's Beauty Insider Community is a digital marketing marvel, combining forums, rewards programs, and interactive content to build a loyal customer base. The 'Virtual Artist' app feature using AR technology exemplifies how Sephora integrates the latest tech to provide value, allowing customers to try on products virtually from anywhere. The brand's commitment to a seamless omnichannel experience is evident through initiatives like the Sephora To Go app, which synchronizes in-store and online shopping preferences and history, ensuring that every customer interaction is personalized and data-driven. These digital touchpoints illustrate Sephora's prowess in creating an ecosystem where digital marketing is not an afterthought but a central component of the customer experience.

Sephora, a visionary leader in the global cosmetics industry, is renowned for its trailblazing e-commerce strategy that has transformed the retail landscape. The brand's journey in digital commerce is characterized by its innovative use of technology and data to create a customer-centric shopping experience that is both seamless and personalized. Sephora has been at the forefront of integrating digital tools such as augmented reality for virtual try-ons, a robust mobile app that complements in-store experiences, and a sophisticated loyalty program that connects with consumers beyond the transactional level.

This approach is considered trailblazing because Sephora was among the first in its sector to truly understand and leverage the full potential of digital channels to enhance customer engagement and loyalty. Their strategy effectively combines the tactile allure of in-store shopping with the convenience and personalization of online retail. By doing so, Sephora has not only set a high standard for digital innovation within the beauty industry but has also raised the bar for retailers across all sectors, demonstrating the power of embracing digital transformation to meet and exceed consumer expectations in the digital age.

4 Conclusion

In the realm of modern commerce, the adoption and integration of digital marketing strategies are not just innovative steps but foundational ones for any successful online marketing framework. These strategies, when harnessed effectively, serve as the linchpins in unifying various marketing channels and activities, ensuring a cohesive approach that supports and amplifies the overarching business goals. The ultimate aim is to create a harmonious digital ecosystem where methods such as digital word-of-mouth enhance the customer experience, leading to robust acquisition and retention. For organizations of all types and sizes, the ability to intertwine digital initiatives with traditional marketing tactics is not just beneficial; it is essential for sustained growth and the achievement of communication objectives.

Furthermore, when operating on a global scale, the strategic employment of six key digital marketing communication tactics becomes increasingly critical. Search Engine Marketing and Social Media Marketing are at the forefront, driving visibility and engagement in an ever-competitive digital landscape. Display Advertising and Digital PR extend a brand's reach and build its narrative, while Digital Partnerships open avenues for collaborative success. Lastly, Digital Messaging personalizes the conversation with the audience, making each interaction count. Together, these tactics form the bedrock of effective digital outreach, each contributing uniquely to solidifying a firm's digital presence and maximizing its impact in a connected world.

Sephora exemplifies this strategic prowess, having revolutionized the beauty industry with its adept use of digital marketing strategies. From employing augmented reality to enhance online shopping to curating a robust loyalty program that intersects seamlessly with both online and in-store experiences, Sephora's approach is a benchmark in digital marketing excellence. Thus, in conclusion, while the digital marketing landscape is vast and dynamic, Sephora's trailblazing journey in e-commerce stands as a prime illustration of how a coherent, innovative digital strategy can lead to unparalleled customer engagement and commercial success. Their ability to consistently adapt and implement these digital tactics cements their status as a leader, not just within the beauty sector but as a beacon of digital innovation across the retail industry.

References

Arndt, J. (1978). How broad should the marketing concept be? Should it be developed into a full-fledged behavioral science?. *Journal of Marketing, 42*(1), 101–103.

Berger, J., & Schwartz, E. M. (2011). What drives immediate and ongoing word of mouth? *Journal of Marketing Research, 48*(5), 869–880.

Day, G. S. (1999). *The market driven organization*. Free Press.

De Angelis, M., Bonezzi, A., Peluso, A. M., Rucker, D. D., & Costabile, M. (2012). On braggarts and gossips: A self-enhancement account of word-of-mouth generation and transmission. *Journal of Marketing Research, 49*(4), 551–563.

Dubois, D., Bonezzi, A., & De Angelis, M. (2016). Sharing with friends versus strangers: How interpersonal closeness influences word-of-mouth valence. *Journal of Marketing Research, 53*(5), 712–727.

Eda, A. (2021). *Cosmetics industry word-of-mouth marketing strategy*. Saitama University Graduation Thesis.

Ferguson, R. J., Paulin, M., & Leiriao, E. (2006). Loyalty and positive word-of-mouth: Patients and hospital personnel as advocates of a customer-centric health care organization. *Health Marketing Quarterly, 23*(3), 59–77.

Godes, D., & Mayzlin, D. (2009). Firm-created word-of-mouth communication: Evidence from a field test. *Marketing Science, 28*(4), 721–739.

Haenlein, M., & Libai, B. (2017). Seeding, referral, and recommendation: Creating profitable word-of-mouth programs. *California Management Review, 59*(2), 68–91.

Kaneko, E. (2021). *Strategies for an e-commerce platform business in cosmetics industry*. Saitama University Graduation Thesis.

Kenmochi, M. (2017). Antecedents and consequential behavior of customer loyalty: A case study of a convenience store. *Mizuho Information & Research Institute Report, 14*, 1–19. https://www.mizuho-ir.co.jp/publication/report/2017/pdf/mhir14_royalty.pdf

Lee, E. J., Lee, J. A., Moon, J. H., & Sung, Y. J. (2015). Pictures speak louder than words: Motivations for using Instagram. *Cyberpsychology, Behavior, and Social Networking, 18*(9), 552–556.

Lisjak, M., Bonezzi, A., & Rucker, D. D. (2021). How marketing perks influence word of mouth. *Journal of Marketing, 85*(5), 128–144.

Liu, F., Lai, K.-H., & Duan, W. (2021). Listening to online reviews: A mixed-methods investigation of customer experience in the sharing economy. *Decision Support Systems, 149*(October), 1–16. https://doi.org/10.1016/j.dss.2021.113609

Mikawa, K., Takahashi, T., & Goto, M. (2007). Study of a structure analysis method for customer loyalty based on text data. *Japan Industrial Management Association, 57*(3), 182–192.

Oliver, R. L. (2014). *Satisfaction: A behavioral perspective on the consumer* (2nd ed.). Irwin/McGraw-Hill.

Packard, G., & Wooten, D. B. (2013). Compensatory knowledge signaling in consumer word-of-mouth. *Journal of Consumer Psychology, 23*(4), 434–450.

Peluso, A. M., Bonezzi, A., De Angelis, M., & Rucker, D. D. (2017). Compensatory word-of-mouth: Advice as a device to restore control. *International Journal of Research in Marketing, 34*(2), 499–515.

Rosen, E. (2000). *The anatomy of buzz: How to create word-of-mouth marketing*. Currency, Doubleday Business.

Rosen, S. (2002). Markets and diversity. *American Economic Review, 92*(1), 1–15.

Wang, X., & Binti Omar, N. A. (2023). Nexus between brand love, loyalty, affective commitment and positive word of mouth: In the context of social identity theory. *Sustainability, 15*, 3813. https://doi.org/10.3390/su15043813

Chapter 5
Boosting Customer Loyalty and WOM Marketing in Japan's Cosmetics Sector

Abstract This chapter investigates how Japan's leading cosmetics companies are redefining customer loyalty strategies amidst the rise of digital platforms and evolving customer behavior. Unlike the broader focus of previous analysis, the discussion specifically addresses the critical role that personalized experiences and community building efforts play in cultivating sustainable customer loyalty. The chapter delves into strategies for nurturing such loyalty, highlighting the indispensable role of customer relationships in sustaining a brand's success. The discussion further extends to customer loyalty's intricate relationship with Word-of-Mouth (WOM) marketing, where personal recommendations and shared consumer experiences play a pivotal role in influencing purchasing decisions. In a market where e-commerce had initially struggled due to the consumers' preference for physically trialing products, the pandemic has inadvertently boosted online sales, making the understanding and harnessing of digital WOM more critical than ever. Analyzing loyalty through the lens of companies like Shiseido, FANCL, and Orbis, provides a framework for optimizing digital platforms to foster a loyal customer base. This analysis, rooted in Dick and Basu's loyalty matrix, reveals varying degrees of loyalty, each with strategic implications for brand stability and growth. The chapter concludes by reinforcing the value of a digital platform not just as a sales channel, but as a community space for engagement, information exchange, and reinforcing customer bonds, setting the foundation for future research and strategy development in the post-pandemic cosmetics industry.

We acknowledge the contribution of Eri Kaneko in preparing this chapter in text mining and data analysis support.

Y. W. Park and P. Hong, *Cosmetics Marketing Strategy in the Era of the Digital Ecosystem*, https://doi.org/10.1007/978-981-97-3674-4_5

1 Introduction

The cosmetics industry in Japan, recognized for its quality and safety, has undergone a significant shift, particularly with the rise of e-commerce. In 2019, Japan's cosmetics market was the third largest globally, valued at 1.7953 trillion yen ($17.9 billion). However, the COVID-19 pandemic led to a downturn, with the market value dropping to 1.2984 trillion yen ($12.9 billion) by 2022. Despite this decline, a recovery is anticipated after 2023. The pandemic's impact was marked by decreased demand due to restrictions and self-quarantine measures, affecting both inbound tourism and domestic consumption (Kaneko, 2021).

In response to these challenges, cosmetics companies are increasingly turning to e-commerce for customer acquisition and retention. With rising advertising costs, it is becoming imperative to nurture existing customer relationships for sustained profitability (Kaneko, 2021). The concept of 'Genuine loyalty' as proposed by Dick and Basu (1994), where customers develop strong positive sentiments towards a brand leading to repeated purchases, is particularly relevant (Kufakunesu & Kapesa, 2018). This loyalty encompasses both attitudinal and behavioral aspects, emphasizing customers' attitudes and purchasing behaviors over specific timeframes. This chapter aims to explore tailored strategies for the cosmetics e-commerce sector in Japan, leveraging these concepts to adapt and succeed amidst the evolving market landscape.

2 Cultivating Devoted Advocates: Customer Loyalty and Word-Of-Mouth Dynamics in Marketing

The body of research on Word-of-Mouth (WOM) and its relationship with customer loyalty encompasses various dimensions. Studies conducted by Ferguson et al. (2006), Wang and Binti Omar (2023), and Dubois et al. (2016) highlight the intricate interplay between customer loyalty and WOM. Ferguson et al. (2006) emphasize how positive WOM advocacy, stemming from satisfied customers, contributes to retaining existing customers and attracting new ones. In a similar vein, Wang and Binti Omar (2023) delve into the relationship between employee loyalty and brand love, underscoring how satisfied and loyal employees indirectly affect customer loyalty through positive WOM. Dubois et al. (2016) investigate the influence of interpersonal closeness on the valence of WOM, suggesting that high closeness might lead to more negative WOM, possibly due to the desire to protect others.

Furthermore, studies such as Berger (2014), De Angelis et al. (2012), and Chen (2017) provide deeper insights into the psychological motivations driving WOM. Berger (2014) outlines five self-serving functions driving WOM, emphasizing how these motivations significantly influence conversation content. De Angelis et al. (2012) reconcile contradictory findings about positive and negative WOM, attributing them to self-enhancement motives in WOM generation and transmission. Meanwhile,

Chen (2017) explores the motivations behind sharing content with strangers versus friends, highlighting the role of self-enhancement and emotional connections in these interactions.

Several studies also focus on the strategic implications of WOM in marketing and management. Lisjak et al. (2021) introduce the concept of "contractuality" in marketing perks, suggesting that low-contractuality perks are more effective in fostering WOM. Berger and Schwartz (2011) shed light on product characteristics, environmental cues, and promotional giveaways in WOM campaigns, offering practical insights into WOM strategies.

Moreover, theoretical perspectives and research by Godes and Mayzlin (2009), Haenlein and Libai (2017), Hennig-Thurau et al. (2004), Libai et al. (2013), Packard and Wooten (2013), and Peluso et al. (2017) contribute significantly to understanding WOM dynamics. They delve into customer-to-customer communication, measurement of WOM program value, eWOM behavior, and compensatory behavior in WOM communications. These studies offer theoretical frameworks and practical implications, guiding businesses on leveraging WOM effectively.

In synthesis, the collective body of research accentuates the crucial role of positive WOM in fostering customer loyalty. They emphasize the importance of employee satisfaction, service quality, strategic WOM initiatives, and psychological drivers in shaping WOM behaviors, ultimately influencing customer loyalty and business success.

The relationship between Word-of-Mouth (WOM) and customer loyalty is vital. A loyalty matrix provides a framework for businesses to understand the varied impacts of different types of WOM on customer loyalty and helps strategize approaches to maximize positive WOM while mitigating the effects of negative WOM on loyalty and retention (Liu et al., 2021; Madzik & Shahin, 2020). Madzik and Shahin (2020) classified customer categorization using a three-dimensional loyalty matrix. Liu et al. (2021) integrate WOM within a more comprehensive framework highlighting the pivotal influence of overall customer experience on loyalty in the sharing economy. Positive WOM significantly boosts loyalty by fostering trust and brand perception. Conversely, negative WOM can erode loyalty by damaging brand reputation. Neutral WOM has limited impact unless combined with other factors. Employee-generated WOM, influenced by engaged employees, moderately impacts loyalty. Strategically, businesses should prioritize generating positive WOM through exceptional experiences, address negative WOM promptly, and focus on employee satisfaction to leverage its impact on customer loyalty.

The Japanese cosmetics industry, renowned worldwide for its quality and safety, is experiencing a decline in demand due to the pandemic's impact. In response, companies are increasingly focusing on e-commerce to acquire and retain customers, recognizing the importance of high-loyalty customers in an environment of escalating advertising costs (Kaneko, 2021). The concept of "Genuine loyalty" is particularly relevant in this context, where customers with strong attitudinal and behavioral loyalty are seen as holding significant lifetime value (Day, 1999). Attitudinal loyalty includes cognitive, affective, and conative aspects, while behavioral loyalty is characterized by measures such as purchase recency, frequency, and monetary value (Kaneko, 2021; Kenmochi, 2017).

This research applies Dick and Basu's (1994) loyalty theory to the cosmetics industry, examining strategies for companies to acquire high-loyalty customers and thrive amid the competitive digital landscape. The chapter also explores how the cosmetics industry's unique characteristics, such as customers' preference for trial-based purchases and exploring product texture, scent, and skin compatibility, impact loyalty and sales strategies on digital platforms. Despite the shift to e-commerce during the pandemic, these customer preferences persist, making the study of loyalty enhancement on digital cosmetic platforms particularly intriguing. The chapter delves into customer loyalty within digital word-of-mouth platforms, defining these platforms as online spaces that facilitate e-commerce and connect customers with companies (Kaneko, 2021; MarkeZine, 2016; Mimuro et al., 2007). Customer loyalty, encompassing both attitudinal and behavioral aspects, brings benefits like ease of service provision, increased brand understanding, reduced price sensitivity, and enhanced word-of-mouth promotion (Day, 1999; Oliver, 2014). The relationship between attitudinal and behavioral loyalty is further explored through the lens of Dick and Basu's (1994) framework, which posits that relative attitude and repetitive purchase behavior form four distinct loyalty quadrants.

Table 5.1 presents a conceptual framework for analyzing customer loyalty by plotting attitudinal loyalty against behavioral loyalty, forming four distinct quadrants. At the high end of both dimensions is 'Genuine loyalty,' where customers not only repeatedly purchase but also have a strong, positive relationship with the brand. 'Spurious loyalty' occurs when there is frequent purchasing behavior but without a strong positive attitude toward the brand, often driven by convenience rather than preference. 'Latent loyalty' captures those customers who have a favorable view of the brand but do not consistently purchase, indicating a potential for conversion into more active customers. Lastly, the 'No loyalty' quadrant reflects a lack of both purchase behavior and a positive attitude, signifying disengagement from the brand. This matrix is instrumental for businesses in strategizing customer relationship management by identifying where customers lie within these loyalty spectrums and tailoring their marketing efforts accordingly.

Genuine loyalty in the cosmetics industry signifies a deep, enduring connection between customers and brands, characterized by both strong positive sentiments and consistent repeat purchases. This level of loyalty indicates a profound and meaningful relationship where customers are not only satisfied but also actively choose the brand repeatedly. Genuine loyalty is a vital asset for brands, as it represents a reliable and

Table 5.1 Mapping customer loyalty: understanding attitudinal and behavioral dimensions

Behavioral loyalty	High	Spurious loyalty	Genuine loyalty
	Low	No loyalty	Latent loyalty
		Low	High
		Attitudinal loyalty	

stable customer base (Kufakunesu & Kapesa, 2018). In contrast, latent loyalty and spurious loyalty present unique challenges. Latent loyalty is where customers hold positive feelings towards a brand but do not consistently translate these feelings into purchases. This disconnect between sentiment and action suggests potential barriers in the purchasing process or external factors influencing consumer behavior. Spurious loyalty, on the other hand, involves repeated purchases without a strong emotional connection to the brand. This type of loyalty is often driven by practical considerations, such as convenience or lack of alternatives, rather than genuine brand affinity (Kufakunesu & Kapesa, 2018). Understanding these different loyalty types is crucial for brands to develop strategies that not only attract but also retain customers by fostering a genuine connection with them.

3 Case Study Methods

Case study methods stand out as a deeply investigative tool, particularly adept at unraveling the intricacies of phenomena like customer loyalty in the dynamic realm of cosmetics e-commerce, especially in the wake of the COVID-19 pandemic. This method's strength lies in its ability to conduct a detailed examination of complex issues where the environment plays a critical role in influencing outcomes. By engaging with case studies, researchers can delve into the granular details of consumer behavior, business strategy adaptations, and the shifting digital marketplace. The inherent value of case studies becomes even more pronounced when considering their contextual relevance. They provide a canvas to paint the full picture of how consumer interactions with digital platforms have evolved due to the pandemic and how the cosmetics industry has navigated these changes. This approach not only captures the essence of the consumer's journey but also sheds light on the strategic pivots that businesses have had to undertake to maintain and grow customer loyalty in a market that has been fundamentally changed by external forces.

Case study methods are particularly valuable in the cosmetics industry, where the consumer-brand relationship is often nuanced and deeply personal. Through their process-oriented nature, these studies delve into the customer's journey with a cosmetic brand over time, tracing the development of loyalty from the initial product experience to the formation of a long-lasting bond. This is especially crucial in understanding the unique challenges and opportunities that have arisen in the post-pandemic era, where customer expectations and shopping behaviors have seen significant shifts. The temporal exploration offered by case studies is critical in assessing the effectiveness and long-term viability of innovative e-commerce strategies introduced by cosmetics companies. Observing these strategies in action, as they evolve and adapt to the changing market, provides a clear picture of what drives consumer loyalty in a digital context. Moreover, these studies provide a rich source of empirical insights that can inform both current practices and future initiatives, linking theoretical constructs to practical, actionable outcomes.

In the rapidly evolving beauty sector, case studies offer the flexibility needed to keep pace with emerging trends and shifting consumer preferences. This adaptability is a powerful asset, ensuring that the insights gained are not just snapshots of a moment in time but are also capable of guiding companies through the ongoing transformations of the cosmetic landscape. As case studies continue to document how cosmetic brands navigate these complexities, they become an essential tool for companies looking to solidify customer loyalty and thrive within the vibrant and competitive post-pandemic e-commerce arena.

3.1 Case Selection Criteria

This case study aims to investigate the strategies cosmetic digital platforms employ to attract and maintain loyal customers in the aftermath of the COVID-19 pandemic. The selection of the firms for this study was guided by a set of criteria that reflect strong digital sales performance and a high propensity for customer loyalty, inspired by the principles outlined by Mikawa et al. (2007). These criteria prioritize customer autonomy in product evaluation and the measurable satisfaction ratings of those products. Furthermore, the timing of customer reviews was incorporated as an essential variable, which is critical for the RFM (Recency, Frequency, Monetary value) analysis that precedes the application of Dick and Basu's loyalty framework. Within the scope of these rigorous selection conditions, Shiseido, FANCL, and Orbis emerged as the companies whose digital platforms met all requirements, thereby becoming the focal point of our research.

Table 5.2 showcases the e-commerce sales of Japan's top cosmetic companies in fiscal years 2019 and 2020, with Shiseido at the forefront, displaying a significant 45% growth. FANCL follows with an impressive 14.2% decrease, while Kao maintains its position with stable sales. Orbis and DHC also report decrease of 10.5% and 18%, respectively. The closing dates for each company provide a timeframe for the reported financial data, reflecting the impact of e-commerce on the beauty industry. This data, provided by the Japan Net Keizai Paper Editorial Department in 2021, illustrates the critical role of online platforms in the cosmetic sector's revenue generation.

Table 5.2 Ranking cosmetic giants in E-commerce sales (FY 2019 & 2020 snapshot)

Company	Sales (million yen)	Percentage change (from FY2019 to FY2020)	Closing
Shiseido	230,222	45	12/2020
FANCL	65,140	▲14.2	03/2021
Kao	52,000	–	12/2020
Orbis	45,415	▲10.5	12/2020
DHC	41,053	▲18	07/2020

Source Japan Net Keizai Paper Editorial Department (2021)

3.2 Data Collection

In this study, user reviews were collected from the e-commerce platforms of three prominent cosmetics companies: Shiseido, FANCL, and Orbis. This approach was chosen to prioritize direct consumer-brand interactions, rather than relying on general reputation sites. A total of 300 reviews were analyzed, focusing on ten lotion products from each company. These products were selected based on the volume of reviews they received. A slight adjustment was made in the case of Orbis to maintain consistency in the number of reviews across all companies.

The analytical framework for this study was grounded in the theories of Dick and Basu (1994) and Mikawa et al. (2007). The main objective was to identify reviews that demonstrated high customer loyalty, characterized by expressions of utmost satisfaction. The data, which was collected up to December 31, 2023, included comprehensive details such as the contributor's information, product rating, review count, and price. This allowed for a nuanced analysis of consumer engagement and satisfaction. Additionally, the reviews underwent sentence decomposition using "MeCab" software for morphological analysis, which helped in removing regional terms and refining the data for more accurate interpretation.

3.3 Data Analysis

In this analysis, the items from the customer loyalty structure diagram were carefully aligned with the definition of customer loyalty as outlined in Kenmochi's (2017) research. This alignment allowed for a precise measurement of diverse types of loyalty as expressed in user reviews. To quantify this, a binary system (0 for absence and 1 for presence) was utilized to evaluate the occurrence of words related to the structure diagram's most detailed items within the reviews. This method enabled the calculation of a numerical loyalty score for each review, based on the presence of specific loyalty-indicative terms.

The scoring system for customer loyalty was structured into distinct categories. Cognitive loyalty could reach a maximum score of 16 points, emotional loyalty was capped at 8 points, and conative loyalty at 6 points. These scores were combined to form a total of 30 points, representing attitudinal loyalty. Additionally, behavioural loyalty was assessed using RFM (Recency, Frequency, Monetary) analysis, with each of these parameters having a maximum score of 5 points, culminating in a total of 15 points. These calculated values were then plotted on the customer loyalty matrix, a framework proposed by Dick and Basu in 1994, to provide a comprehensive visual representation of the varying degrees of customer loyalty.

Table 5.3 presents a framework for evaluating customer engagement using an RFM (Recency, Frequency, Monetary) model, which scores customers based on three criteria: Recency, Frequency, and Monetary (RFM). Recency is scored on a scale from 1 to 5, with 5 being a review posted within the past month and 1 being a

Table 5.3 Customer engagement scoring via RFM analysis for E-Commerce in Japan

Point	Recency of review	Frequency of review	Monetary
5	In past 1 month	10 times and above	~8,000 Yen
4	In past 3 months	8~9 times	~6,000 Yen
3	In past 6 months	4~7 times	~4,000 Yen
2	In past 1 year	2~3 times	~2,000 Yen
1	Older than past 1 year	1 time	~1,000 Yen

Source Environmental Systems Research Institute (ESRI)

review older than a year. Frequency also ranges from 1 to 5, with scores given based on the number of times a customer has reviewed, where a score of 5 represents 10 or more reviews. The Monetary aspect correlates with the approximate expenditure in yen, with higher spenders receiving a higher score. ESRI (Environmental Systems Research Institute) is an international supplier of geographic information system (GIS) software, web GIS, and geodatabase management applications. The company is known for producing tools that are used for spatial analysis, data management, and mapping. ESRI software is used in various fields, including urban planning, environmental science, resource management, and logistics to manage and analyze spatial data effectively. By integrating RFM data with geographic information, companies can gain deeper insights into customer behavior patterns and tailor their marketing strategies more effectively to different regions and demographics.

4 Unravelling the Secrets of E-Commerce Customer Dynamics

In our journey through the e-commerce landscape, we've uncovered fascinating patterns and trends in customer behavior, specifically within the cosmetics industry. This exploration has shed light on the complex nature of online consumer engagement, offering valuable benchmarks for strategic decision-making in the digital marketplace. The richness of our data provides a robust foundation for understanding the nuances of customer loyalty and purchasing behaviors, especially in the post-pandemic era. Our findings serve as a compass for navigating the evolving currents of e-commerce customer interactions.

4.1 Decoding the Digital Cosmetics Marketplace

Our meticulous selection of digital platforms for this study was guided by specific criteria to ensure the most accurate insights. We sought platforms that allowed customers to freely rate their purchases and provided a clear method for gauging product satisfaction through user scores. The transparency of review timestamps was also a key factor. Initially, five major cosmetic brands—Shiseido, FANCL, Kao, Orbis, and DHC—were under consideration. However, the platforms of Kao and DHC did not meet our stringent criteria and were excluded from our analysis. This careful selection process highlights the critical role of transparent and independent customer feedback in evaluating the effectiveness of e-commerce strategies. Our study emphasizes the importance of these factors in gaining a true understanding of digital consumer behavior in the cosmetics sector.

Our exploration of the e-commerce sector has revealed measurable patterns and trends in customer behavior. The findings elucidate the intricacies of online consumer engagement, providing critical benchmarks to guide strategic decision-making within the digital sphere of the cosmetics industry. The extensive data we have gathered forms a solid foundation, enabling a deeper understanding of customer loyalty and purchasing patterns in the aftermath of the pandemic.

4.2 *Variations in Digital Cosmetics Platforms*

The criteria for selecting an appropriate digital platform for our analysis were stringent: the platform needed to allow customers to independently rate their purchases and provide a mechanism for quantifying product satisfaction through user scores. Additionally, the posting dates and times of reviews had to be transparent. Originally, five prominent cosmetic companies—Shiseido, FANCL, Kao, Orbis, and DHC—were considered. However, the platforms of Kao and DHC did not fulfill these criteria and were subsequently omitted from the analysis. This selection process underscores the importance of transparent customer feedback mechanisms in assessing e-commerce effectiveness.

Table 5.4 delineates the features of e-commerce websites from five prominent cosmetic brands, indicating the presence of customer engagement elements such as satisfaction ratings and comments, which are universally adopted across Shiseido, FANCL, Orbis, Kao (RMK), and DHC. The table reveals a disparity in the depth of customer data collected; Shiseido, FANCL, and Orbis gather detailed personal and lifestyle information to potentially enhance user experience and inform product customization, while Kao RMK and DHC show a more reserved data approach, possibly to streamline user experience or due to strategic priorities. Although most brands omit in-depth data like occupation or living environment, suggesting potential areas for advancing customer personalization, the strategic collection of these details varies, likely due to privacy policies or the perceived relevance of such information for each brand's market approach.

In the digital age, e-commerce platforms are the new battleground for customer loyalty and engagement. Here is how five major Japanese cosmetics companies—Shiseido, FANCL, Orbis, Kao, and DHC—have tailored their digital strategies to adapt to the evolving consumer landscape and the unique challenges they face:

Table 5.4 Comparison of E-commerce website

	Shiseido	FANCL	Orbis	Kao (RMK)	DHC
Customer name	○	○	○	○	○
Date	○	○	○	○	-
Satisfaction Level	○	○	○	○	-
Comment	○	○	○	○	○
Age	○	○	○	–	○
Purchased store	○	–	–	–	–
Skin condition	○	○	○	–	–
Skin problems	○	○	–	–	–
Living environment	○	○	–	–	–
Frequency of makeup	○	–	–	–	–
Occupation	○	–	–	–	–
Purpose of use	–	–	○	–	–
Usage history	–	○	○	–	○
Place of living	–	–	–	–	○

- **Shiseido** has leveraged its Watashi + platform to create a paradigm of customer-centric services since its inception in 2012 (Leelapanyalert et al., 2015). Embracing the concept of "customer-centric services," the platform seeks to forge deeper connections between the brand and its clientele (MarkeZine, 2016). The integration of the Salesforce Marketing Cloud in 2015 marked a strategic pivot towards crafting personalized customer experiences, utilizing email and LINE for direct marketing. This shift in strategy moves beyond merely driving sales, focusing on delivering a consistently superior brand experience (MarkeZine, 2016). The corporate philosophy, "Be beautiful in every moment and throughout your life," reflects their dedication to enhancing lifetime customer value (LTV). Watashi + collects extensive user information, ensuring the brand remains attuned to the evolving preferences of its customers. It also offers robust review filtering options, catering to specific needs such as age and living environment, effectively leveraging positive customer feedback to attract new users (Day, 1999).
- FANCL has evolved from a mail-order pioneer to a modern e-commerce contender, revamping its online presence in 2018 to boost user engagement with personalized content (Mizuochi, 2019). The company's review system as of 2021, which displays only the 100 most recent reviews, limited the depth of customer feedback available for analysis and lacked the advanced sorting capabilities of competitors like Shiseido, potentially increasing the effort required for customers to find relevant reviews. However, the company took the opportunity of the intensifying competition for customers, driven by the penetration of product purchases via e-commerce sites into daily life, to reflect on its own UX policies, and as of January 2024, the company's review system has removed the restriction on

the number of reviews available for viewing, and has added sorting and filtering capabilities similar to competitors (BeBit, 2023).

- **Orbis** provides a simplified, yet efficient review system compared to its counterparts, focusing on user-friendly filtering tools that allow customers to tailor their search according to their preferences. The platform's "Everyone's Reviews" section fosters a community environment by rewarding high-quality feedback, thus recognizing the power of positive reviews in driving sales, a correlation supported by Day (1999).
- **Kao**, despite its extensive skincare brand portfolio, has not fully capitalized on the e-commerce trend, with only a select few brands offering online review capabilities (Nakamura, 2019). This fragmented digital strategy, coupled with a dearth of customer feedback, resulted in Kao's exclusion from this analysis due to inadequate data.
- **DHC** faces similar challenges with its e-commerce site, lacking a system to gauge customer satisfaction levels and clear review timelines, essential features for evaluating consumer engagement. The absence of review sorting and filtering mechanisms makes it difficult for customers to sift through the abundance of feedback for pertinent insights.

Each company's approach to digital engagement and customer feedback reflects the diverse strategies within the cosmetics industry, underscoring the importance of a comprehensive and customer-centric online presence in today's market.

5 Unveiling the Landscape of Brand Loyalty in the Cosmetics Industry

This section introduces the findings from a comprehensive Customer loyalty Matrix Analysis, applying the renowned framework of Dick and Basu (1994) across various leading cosmetic firms. We'll explore the synergy between customers' emotional connections to these brands and their actual purchasing behaviors, providing a multidimensional perspective on brand loyalty. As we proceed to examine the specific outcomes for each company, it's essential to contextualize these results within the broader industry narrative.

The insights gleaned from the loyalty matrices of Shiseido and other cosmetic giants offer a revealing snapshot of the industry's current state of customer allegiance. These matrices act as strategic windows, through which we can observe the effectiveness of loyalty-building initiatives and identify potential for growth. They serve as a testament to how these brands resonate with their customers on both an attitudinal and behavioral level, offering valuable lessons for enhancing customer engagement and driving sustained business growth in the competitive landscape of cosmetics e-commerce.

5.1 Shiseido

As Japan's largest and most esteemed cosmetics firm, Shiseido not only represents the pinnacle of the Japanese cosmetic industry but also serves as its global ambassador. Esteemed for its premium quality and high pricing strategy, Shiseido has long been synonymous with luxury and exclusivity in skincare and beauty. In this context, analyzing customer loyalty is particularly meaningful. It reveals how a brand that operates at the higher end of the market spectrum maintains its customer base. A Customer loyalty Matrix analysis offers valuable insights into the relationship Shiseido fosters with its customers—how it balances the premium quality of its products with its pricing strategies to maintain and grow a loyal customer base that appreciates the brand's value and continues to engage with it actively.

Figure 5.1 presents a Customer loyalty Matrix for Shiseido, mapping out the relationship between attitudinal loyalty and behavioral loyalty among its customers. It visualizes customer data points on a two-dimensional plane, where the horizontal axis represents attitudinal loyalty, gauged by customers' sentiments towards the brand, and the vertical axis denotes behavioral loyalty, indicated by the frequency and recency of purchases. Each point on the graph corresponds to a customer's loyalty score, with the cluster of points suggesting a trend in Shiseido's customer base. In the past, the cluster of data points predominantly aligns in the higher range for both attitudinal and behavioral loyalty, indicating Shiseido's success in nurturing a customer base deeply appreciative of the brand, actively making purchases. These strategic insights into customer loyalty serve as pivotal guides for Shiseido, aiding in refining marketing strategies and bolstering efforts to retain customers. However, as of 2023, a decline in attitudinal loyalty data points is mirrored by a reduction in behavioral loyalty scores.

Table 5.5 provides a quantitative breakdown of Shiseido's customer loyalty, categorized into four distinct segments based on their attitudinal and behavioral loyalty. The matrix reveals that 34% of customers exhibit spurious loyalty, characterized

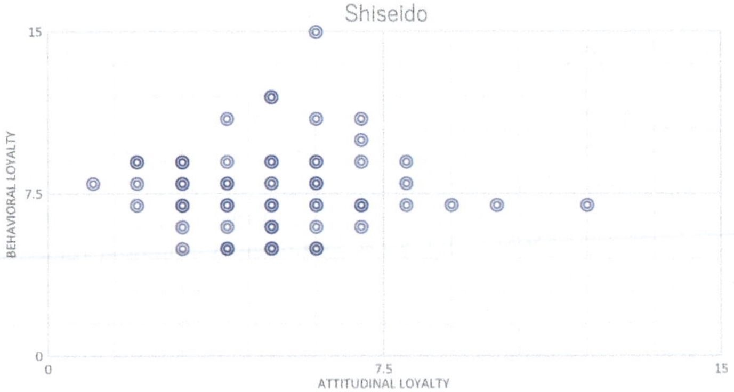

Fig. 5.1 Shiseido's customer engagement spectrum: analyzing loyalty dimensions

Table 5.5 A quantitative breakdown of Shiseido's customer loyalty

Behavioral loyalty	High	Spurious loyalty (34%)	Genuine loyalty (2%)
	Low	No loyalty (60%)	Latent loyalty (4%)
		Low	High
		Attitudinal loyalty	

by high purchase frequency but low emotional attachment, while the genuinely loyal segment—those with both high attitudinal and behavioral loyalty—accounts for only 2%. A significant 60% of customers are in the no loyalty quadrant, showing low scores in both dimensions, and the remaining 4% display latent loyalty, indicating strong potential for brand allegiance despite lower purchasing activity. Alarmingly, the genuinely loyal segment dwindles to a mere 2%, a stark decline. Moreover, a substantial 60% of customers reside in the 'no loyalty' quadrant, indicating low scores in both dimensions, while the remaining 4% display latent loyalty. This shift in the loyalty matrix indicates a decline in Shiseido's marketing strategy, signaling challenges in sustaining customer loyalty and brand connection.

This loyalty matrix serves as a strategic tool for Shiseido, offering insights into customer segments that could be nurtured towards genuine loyalty, thus enhancing overall customer retention and brand affinity.

As of 2023, there has been a gradual decline in customer loyalty. To recuperate this decline, Shiseido needs to focus on bolstering both attitudinal and behavioral loyalty. Watanabe (2020) underlines the significance of uplifting customer spirits as a strategy to secure enduring loyalty towards Shiseido's brand and products. The integration of Salesforce Marketing Cloud has empowered Shiseido to personalize individual customer journeys, nurturing one-on-one marketing relationships and comprehending evolving customer preferences through continuous engagement (MarkeZine, 2016). Nevertheless, to genuinely solidify customer loyalty, Shiseido must ensure a comprehensive and data-backed customer experience, alongside an effective PDCA (Plan-Do-Check-Act) cycle to dynamically refine and enhance the customer journey strategy.

5.2 *FANCL*

FANCL Corporation stands out in Japan's cosmetic industry as a pioneer of preservative-free skincare products, which has carved a unique niche for the brand. Established in 1980, FANCL's philosophy revolves around the concept of delivering fresh skincare and supplements to its customers, ensuring efficacy and safety by eliminating preservatives that can cause skin irritation. This approach has not only earned it a loyal customer base but also differentiates it within a market that is highly competitive and innovation-driven.

The company also leads in direct marketing and personalized skincare solutions, leveraging advanced technology and scientific research to cater to individual customer needs. FANCL's retail strategy includes a strong presence both online and through a network of physical stores, including its flagship FANCL Ginza Square. In the broader wellness and beauty sector in Japan, FANCL maintains a strong position by offering holistic health and beauty solutions, demonstrating a commitment to both product purity and environmental sustainability, which resonates well with the globally increasing demand for clean beauty products.

Figure 5.2 presents a scatter plot visualizing the relationship between attitudinal and behavioral loyalty for FANCL customers. Attitudinal loyalty is plotted along the x-axis, with a possible score ranging up to 15 points, while behavioral loyalty is charted along the y-axis, with scores up to 15 points. Each dot represents aggregated customer feedback, with its placement indicating the degree of loyalty: horizontal placement for attitudinal loyalty and vertical placement for behavioral loyalty. As of 2023, the analysis reveals a shift where most customers exhibit spurious loyalty, marked by frequent purchases but lacking emotional attachment, while the genuinely loyal segment is growing with both high attitudinal and behavioral loyalty. These numbers indicate a successful marketing strategy for FANCL.

Table 5.6 illustrates the distribution of FANCL's customer base across four distinct loyalty categories, presented as a percentage of the total customer sample. The matrix is divided into quadrants that cross-reference attitudinal loyalty with behavioral loyalty. Starting with 'Spurious loyalty' (68%), these customers exhibit high behavioral loyalty but low attitudinal loyalty, indicating that their repeat purchases may not reflect a deep commitment to the brand.

In contrast, 'Genuine loyalty' (19%) represents a smaller yet significant segment where high levels of both attitudinal and behavioral loyalty intersect, suggesting these customers are both committed to and active purchasers of the brand. The 'No loyalty'

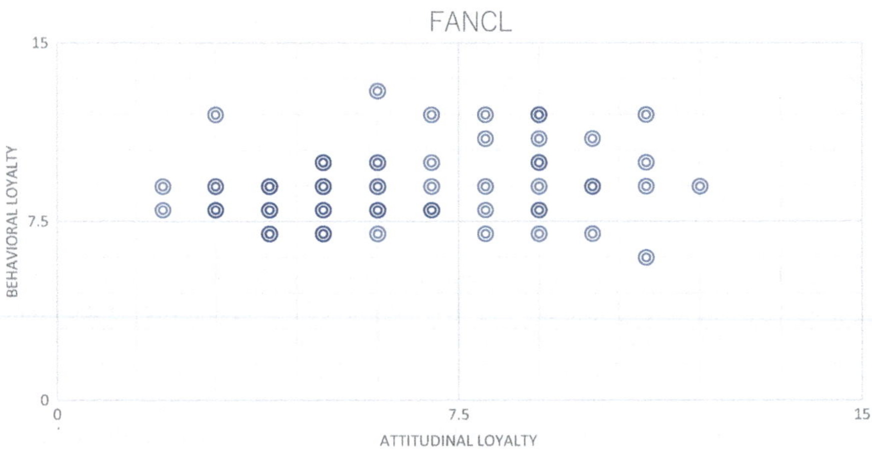

Fig. 5.2 FANCL customer engagement analysis: attitudinal vs. behavioral loyalty scatter plot

Table 5.6 Proportional analysis of FANCL customer loyalty dimensions

Behavioral loyalty	High	Spurious loyalty (68%)	Genuine loyalty (19%)
	Low	No loyalty (9%)	Latent loyalty (4%)
		Low	High
		Attitudinal loyalty	

quadrant encompasses 9% of customers showing low scores in both dimensions, pointing to a lack of connection with the brand. Lastly, 'Latent loyalty' (4%) captures those with high attitudinal loyalty but low behavioral loyalty, highlighting a group that may favor the brand but not necessarily translate this preference into frequent purchases. This matrix is a strategic tool for FANCL to identify areas of strength and potential growth within their customer engagement strategies.

5.3 *Orbis*

Orbis, a distinguished player in Japan's skincare and health product market, is renowned for its oil-free skincare philosophy, which is a cornerstone of its product development. Established in 1987, Orbis has cultivated a unique identity by offering a comprehensive line of oil-free skincare products that cater to customers seeking simplicity and purity in their beauty routines. This distinctive feature sets the brand apart in a crowded marketplace, where consumers are increasingly aware of and concerned about the ingredients in their skincare. Furthermore, Orbis emphasizes the inner health-beauty connection, offering a range of health foods and supplements alongside its skincare lines. By integrating skincare with nutritional science, Orbis has secured a holistic approach to beauty and wellness. The company has also capitalized on the direct sales model, creating a robust online presence that complements its physical stores across Japan. Its commitment to a health-conscious, oil-free beauty regimen has enabled Orbis to establish a strong industry position, particularly among consumers who prioritize ingredient-conscious products and holistic well-being.

Figure 5.3 maps out the dimensions of customer loyalty for Orbis, a key player in the Japanese skincare market. In order to apply Dick and Basu's (1994) customer loyalty matrix, we have attitudinal loyalty on the x-axis, which can score up to 30 points, representing customers' psychological commitment to the brand. The y-axis shows behavioral loyalty with a maximum score of 15 points, indicating the tangible actions of repeat purchases and brand patronage. Each dot in the plot symbolizes a composite score from individual customer reviews. The distribution of dots suggests that Orbis's behavioral loyalty in 2023 has notably increased, signifying the brand's focus on strengthening customer relationships.

The plot reveals that while many customers appreciate the brand, their buying patterns vary in loyalty levels, spanning from low to high. This detailed mapping

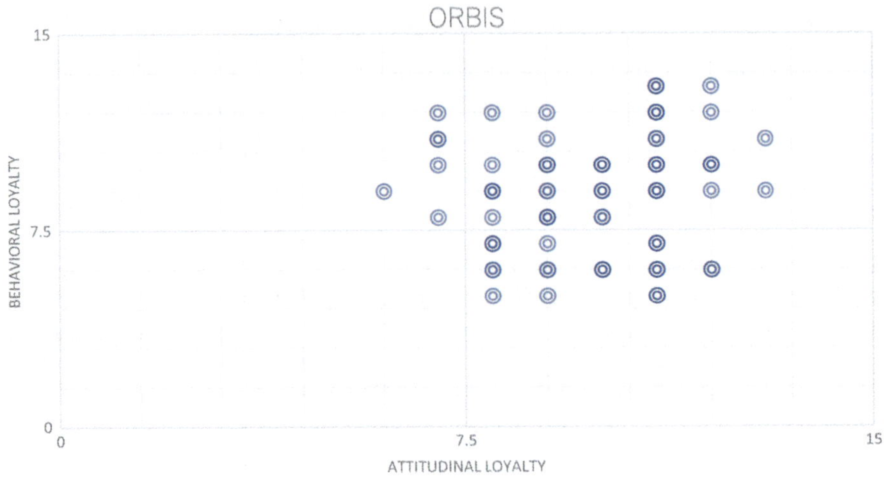

Fig. 5.3 The Orbis loyalty landscape: visualizing consumer engagement depth

is critical for Orbis to customize its marketing and customer relationship strategies, aiming to cultivate higher attitudinal alignment and stronger purchasing behaviors. The goal is to move more customers towards the upper right quadrant of the matrix, where both attitudinal and behavioral loyalty are high.

Table 5.7 offers a comprehensive look at Orbis's customer loyalty, categorizing it into four segments based on attitudinal and behavioral loyalty. The horizontal axis of the matrix measures attitudinal loyalty, reflecting customers' emotional connection to the Orbis brand, while the vertical axis assesses behavioral loyalty, indicative of customers' actual purchasing patterns.

Within this matrix, 6% of customers fall under 'Spurious loyalty', showcasing high purchase frequency but low emotional attachment to the brand. In contrast, the 'Genuine loyalty' segment makes up 70% of the base, representing those who are both emotionally invested and consistently purchase Orbis products. The smallest segment, 'No loyalty', encompasses 0% of customers, showcasing a strong brand affinity among Orbis's customer base. Meanwhile, 'Latent loyalty', at 24%, includes customers who exhibit a strong affinity for the brand, yet this has not translated into regular purchasing behavior. This loyalty matrix is a valuable analytic tool for Orbis, providing clear insights for enhancing customer engagement and identifying areas ripe for targeted marketing initiatives to foster increased loyalty.

Table 5.7 Orbis loyalty quadrants: decoding customer allegiance

Behavioral loyalty	High	Spurious loyalty (6%)	Genuine loyalty (70%)
	Low	No loyalty (0%)	Latent loyalty (24%)
		Low	High
		Attitudinal loyalty	

Orbis's digital platform, resembling a social media environment, allows for easy customer-to-customer communication. This setting enhances the likelihood that positive endorsements from genuinely loyal customers could influence the potential loyalists, making them more inclined to make purchases, as suggested by Day in 1999. The goal for Orbis would be to strategize on ways to elevate customers from moderate attitudinal loyalty to higher behavioral loyalty, thus enhancing the overall customer devotion to the brand.

5.4 *Synthesis of Customer Loyalty Across Leading Beauty Brands*

In this section, we undertake a comparative analysis to delineate the varying degrees of customer loyalty among three prominent beauty brands: Shiseido, FANCL, and Orbis. By juxtaposing these brands, we glean insights into the loyalty distribution among their customer bases, illuminating the effectiveness of each brand's engagement strategies. This comparative study not only reflects the unique market positioning of each company but also underscores the challenges and opportunities they encounter in cultivating robust customer relationships.

Table 5.8 offers an insightful perspective on the distribution of customer loyalty across Shiseido, FANCL, and Orbis. Orbis leads with an impressive 70% in 'Genuine loyalty,' indicating a robust alignment between customers' brand sentiments and their purchasing behavior. Conversely, FANCL demonstrates a significant 68% in 'Spurious loyalty,' suggesting that repeated purchases may not necessarily arise from strong brand attachment. Shiseido faces a notable challenge, with 60% of its customer base categorized under 'No loyalty', signaling the need for enhanced engagement strategies. Notably, Orbis also possesses the highest percentage in 'Latent loyalty' at 24%, highlighting customers with a strong emotional inclination towards the brand not yet fully reflected in their buying patterns. This table underscores distinct customer relationship dynamics, guiding targeted marketing and loyalty initiatives. This table underscores distinct customer relationship dynamics, guiding targeted marketing and loyalty initiatives.

Table 5.9 presents a comparative overview of customer loyalty among Shiseido, FANCL, and Orbis. FANCL's customer base predominantly exhibits 'Spurious loyalty,' indicating frequent purchases without strong emotional connections to the brand. In contrast, Shiseido has a larger proportion of customers categorized under

Table 5.8 Brand loyalty spectrum: a comparative analysis

	Genuine loyalty (%)	Latent loyalty (%)	Spurious loyalty (%)	No loyalty (%)
Shiseido	2	4	34	60
FANCL	19	4	68	9
Orbis	70	24	6	0

Table 5.9 Comparative customer loyalty dynamics amongst beauty industry leaders

	1st	2nd	3rd	4th
Shiseido	No loyalty	Spurious loyalty	Latent loyalty	Genuine loyalty
FANCL	Spurious loyalty	Genuine loyalty	No loyalty	Latent loyalty
Orbis	Genuine loyalty	Latent loyalty	Spurious loyalty	No loyalty

'No loyalty,' suggesting an opportunity to enhance customer relationships and retention strategies. 'Genuine loyalty' remains significant for Orbis, reflecting a core group of dedicated consumers, a segment less prevalent for Shiseido. Orbis also stands out with a significant percentage of customers in 'Latent loyalty,' showcasing admiration for the brand without consistent purchase behavior.

The focus on 'Genuine loyalty' as a driver of long-term revenue stability (Watanabe, 2020) underscores its importance for loyalty programs. Orbis, with a relatively high percentage of 'Genuine' and 'Latent' loyal customers, seems well-positioned for sustained stability. FANCL emerges as the next potential candidate for fostering long-term customer allegiance.

The pivotal role of a company's digital platform is underscored, especially platforms that extend beyond simple e-commerce. Features such as user review sorting, filtering, and community interaction are instrumental in cultivating genuine customer loyalty. Hence, platforms that foster active customer communication and information exchange are integral to nurturing a robust base of truly loyal customers.

6 Conclusion

In the realm of Japan's cosmetics sector, this chapter navigates the evolving e-commerce landscape, a shift intensified by the challenges brought about by the COVID-19 pandemic. As the world's third-largest cosmetics market, Japan has witnessed a dramatic pivot from traditional sales channels to digital platforms. This transformation is driven by an imperative to maintain consumer engagement amid travel restrictions and a decline in physical store traffic. However, the focus extends beyond mere customer acquisition; it emphasizes customer retention as a means to bolster sales and profitability in the increasingly competitive digital space. A key strategy highlighted is the development of "Genuine loyalty," which denotes customers with a deep and positive brand connection, underpinned by frequent purchases and a synthesis of attitudinal and behavioral loyalty. The chapter presents insights into fostering such loyalty, underscoring the critical importance of customer relationships in sustaining brand viability.

The nexus between customer loyalty and Word-of-Mouth (WOM) marketing is also thoroughly explored, noting how personal endorsements and consumer narratives significantly sway purchasing behaviors. The pandemic has unexpectedly propelled online sales in a market traditionally dominated by in-store experiences, thus magnifying the significance of digital WOM. The case studies of Shiseido, FANCL, and Orbis illuminate how digital platforms can be optimized to nurture a devoted customer base. This analytical approach, informed by the Dick and Basu loyalty matrix, distinguishes different degrees of loyalty, each bearing distinct strategic implications for a brand's enduring success and expansion. The chapter concludes by affirming the multifaceted role of digital platforms, not just as conduits for sales but as community hubs for robust engagement, knowledge sharing, and strengthening customer ties. This foundational work serves as a guidepost for future research and strategic planning in the cosmetics industry's digital transformation post-pandemic. The insights offered herein are invaluable, providing a reference point for other cosmetic firms aiming to forge or enhance their digital platforms in the wake of COVID-19.

References

BeBit. (2023). FANCL implements "UX Growth Ops Lite" to improve user experience on official E-commerce site (Dec 19th). Retrieved from https://www.agara.co.jp/article/332830

Berger, J. (2014). Word of mouth and interpersonal communication: A review and directions for future research. *Journal of Consumer Psychology, 24*(4), 586–607.

Berger, J., & Schwartz, E. M. (2011). What drives immediate and ongoing word of mouth? *Journal of Marketing Research, 48*(5), 869–880.

Chen, Z. (2017). Social acceptance and word of mouth: How the motive to belong leads to divergent WOM with strangers and friends. *Journal of Consumer Research, 44*(3), 613–632.

Day, G. S. (1999). *The Market Driven Organization.* Free Press.

De Angelis, M., Bonezzi, A., Peluso, A. M., Rucker, D. D., & Costabile, M. (2012). On braggarts and gossips: A self-enhancement account of word-of-mouth generation and transmission. *Journal of Marketing Research, 49*(4), 551–563.

Dick, A. S., Basu, K. (1994). Customer loyalty: Toward and integrated conceptual framework. *Journal of The Academy of Marketing Science* 99–113.

Dubois, D., Bonezzi, A., & De Angelis, M. (2016). Sharing with friends versus strangers: How interpersonal closeness influences word-of-mouth valence. *Journal of Marketing Research, 53*(5), 712–727.

Ferguson, R. J., Paulin, M., & Leiriao, E. (2006). Loyalty and positive word-of-mouth: Patients and hospital personnel as advocates of a customer-centric health care organization. *Health Marketing Quarterly, 23*(3), 59–77.

Godes, D., & Mayzlin, D. (2009). Firm-ation: Evidence from a field test. *Marketing Science, 28*(4), 721–739.

Haenlein, M., & Libai, B. (2017). Seeding, referral, and recommendation: Creating profitable word-of-mouth programs. *California Management Review, 59*(2), 68–91.

Hennig-Thurau, T., Gwinner, K. P., Walsh, G., & Gremler, D. D. (2004). Electronic word-of-mouth via consumer-opinion platforms: What motivates consumers to articulate themselves on the internet? *Journal of Interactive Marketing, 18*(1), 38–52.

Kaneko, E. (2021). Strategies for an E-commerce platform business in cosmetics industry. Saitama University Graduation Thesis.

Kenmochi, M. (2017). Antecedents and consequential behavior of customer loyalty: A case study of a convenience store. Mizuho Information & Research Institute Report, 14, 1–19. Retrieved from https://www.mizuho-ir.co.jp/publication/report/2017/pdf/mhir14_royalty.pdf

Kufakunesu, F., & Kapesa, T. (2018). Customer loyalty, a reality or an allegory: Exposing Dick and Basu (1994) loyalty segmentation model in Bindura fast-food industry. (2018). *International Journal of Scientific Research and Management (IJSRM), 6*(4), 282–293. https://doi.org/10.18535/ijsrm/v6i4.em07

Leelapanyalert, K., Tanpradit, N., Khiewvan, C., Sakhonchaicharoen, P. (2015). Shiseido group: The turning points, challenges and future opportunities. *Academy of Asian Business Review, 1*(2), 69–97. https://doi.org/10.26816/aabr.1.2.201512.69

Libai, B., Muller, E., & Peres, R. (2013). Decomposing the value of word of mouth seeding programs: Acceleration versus expansion. *Journal of Marketing Research, 50*(2), 161–176.

Lisjak, M., Bonezzi, A., & Rucker, D. D. (2021). How marketing perks influence word of mouth. *Journal of Marketing, 85*(5), 128–144. https://doi.org/10.1177/0022242921991798

Liu, F., Lai, K.-H., & Duan, W. (2021). Listening to online reviews: A mixed-methods investigation of customer experience in the sharing economy. *Decision Support Systems, 149*, 1–16. https://doi.org/10.1016/j.dss.2021.113609

Madzik, P., & Shahin, A. (2020). Customer categorization using a three-dimensional loyalty matrix analogious to FMEA. *International Journal of Quality & Reliability Management, 38*(8), 1833–1857.

MarkeZine. (2016). Shiseido Watashi+'s Accompanying Marketing that capture the present based on customer preferences and support beauty for a long time. MarkeZine Editorial Department (Dec 1st). Retrieved from MarkeZine: https://markezine.jp/article/detail/25595

Mikawa, K., Takahashi, T., & Goto, M. (2007). Study of a structure analysis method for customer loyalty based on text data. *Japan Industrial Management Association, 57*(3), 182–192.

Mimuro, K., Suzumura, K., & Kanda, H. (2007). Customer voice management: "Seeing" what customers really think through text mining. Japan, Ohm, Tokyo

Mizuochi, E. (2019). Learning from FANCL, how to use chatbots without ending up as a disappointing case. Retrieved from IT Media Marketing (April 18th): https://marketing.itmedia.co.jp/mm/articles/1904/18/news005.html

Nakamura, Y. (2019). Kao's lagging e-commerce strategy: Targeting distressed consumers with its first ever online product line. Retrieved from Nikkei X Trend (August 6th): https://xtrend.nikkei.com/atcl/contents/18/00192/00002/

Oliver, R. L. (2014). Satisfaction: A behavioral perspective on the consumer (2nd edn.). Irwin/McGraw-Hill.

Packard, G., & Wooten, D. B. (2013). Compensatory knowledge signaling in consumer word-of-mouth. *Journal of Consumer Psychology, 23*(4), 434–450.

Peluso, A. M., Bonezzi, A., De Angelis, M., & Rucker, D. D. (2017). Compensatory word-of-mouth: Advice as a device to restore control. *International Journal of Research in Marketing, 34*(2), 499–515.

Wang, X., & Binti Omar, N. A. (2023). Nexus between brand love, loyalty, affective commitment and positive word of mouth: In the context of social identity theory. *Sustainability, 15*, 3813. https://doi.org/10.3390/su15043813

Watanabe, H. (2020). Structuralization and quantification of loyalty. *The 11th Oukan union conference*.

Chapter 6
Mastering Digital WOM: Innovative Strategies in Japan's Cosmetic Market

Abstract This chapter presents an in-depth exploration of digital Word-of-Mouth (WOM) marketing within Japan's cosmetic sector, focusing on the dynamics between consumer interaction and language use on digital platforms. It dissects the content and intent behind WOM on two popular platforms: @cosme—a comprehensive beauty website with a vast database of products and brands—and Instagram, which is favored by a younger demographic for its visual-centric sharing. The analysis underscores the distinction between the unilateral consumption of reviews on @cosme and the interactive dialogue facilitated by Instagram. It delves into the structural differences in posting reviews on both platforms, with @cosme allowing for detailed categorization and Instagram offering a more straightforward, visual-focused approach. The research then shifts to the trends and impacts of WOM in Japan, highlighting its significant influence on purchasing decisions. WOM remains a crucial determinant in product selection, with a notable gender difference in its impact—women are more influenced by WOM than men. The motives behind sharing WOM are also explored, revealing that the type of language used (cognitive or emotional) is closely tied to the poster's intent, whether it's to inform or engage in a pleasurable conversation. The study culminates with a comparative analysis of WOM content across @cosme and Instagram, revealing that @cosme posts are more inclined towards functional usage, while Instagram content emphasizes aesthetic appeal and purchase experiences. The findings suggest that the motive behind posting WOM significantly shapes the language and content of the reviews, offering critical insights for companies aiming to harness WOM effectively for marketing purposes.

We acknowledge the contribution of Akari Eda who provided with data gathering and analysis support in preparing this chapter content.

Y. W. Park and P. Hong, *Cosmetics Marketing Strategy in the Era of the Digital Ecosystem*, https://doi.org/10.1007/978-981-97-3674-4_6

1 Introduction

The nature and intention behind word-of-mouth communication can vary significantly based on the platform used for interaction. This chapter focuses on analyzing the language, motives, and purposes of word-of-mouth content posted on two platforms: @cosme, a cosmetics word-of-mouth site, and Instagram, a globally popular platform, especially among young individuals. The goal is to examine the distinctions between a cosmetics-specific word-of-mouth site, where information is primarily read unilaterally, and Instagram, which enables interactive communication through word-of-mouth.

The subjects of this chapter are @cosme, Japan's largest comprehensive cosmetics and beauty website, boasting a database with extensive brand and product information. It serves over 1 billion users globally, with more than 3300 active users in Japan. The second platform is Instagram, a social media service that allows users to post photos and videos. These platforms were chosen for their proficiency in collecting word-of-mouth data, particularly from younger demographics, and their abundant cosmetic sample data.

1.1 Unlocking @Cosme's Influence: A Deep Dive into Japan's Premier Beauty Platform

@cosme is a service used monthly by nearly 30% of women in their 20s and 30s in Japan. It operates physical stores nationwide and offers a wide range of beauty-related information and services. This chapter delves into the cosmetics-specific word-of-mouth section of @cosme. Here, users follow a structured process to contribute reviews: starting with a product search, categorizing based on various criteria, and providing detailed feedback including images or videos. Additionally, users can tag products based on their efficacy, function, or color, making them easily accessible and recommendable to others.

@cosme not only stands as a repository of vast beauty information but also as a social barometer for the latest trends and consumer preferences in the beauty sector. Its user-generated content provides invaluable insights into product popularity, user satisfaction, and emerging beauty trends, making it a crucial tool for both consumers and industry players. Marketers and product developers closely monitor @cosme's user reviews and ratings to gauge market responses and identify potential areas for product innovation or improvement. The platform's influence extends beyond mere product reviews, shaping the beauty industry's dynamics by creating a space where consumers' voices directly impact brand reputation and product success.

1.2 *Instagram's Pivotal Role: Shaping Trends and Engagement in Japan's Young Demographic*

Instagram, launched in 2010 by Kevin Systrom and Mike Krieger, has over 1 billion global users and sees more than 80 million posts daily. Particularly popular among young Japanese females, it boasts over 20 million daily users in this demographic. Instagram serves both individuals and businesses, with the latter using it as a key marketing tool. The platform facilitates sharing photos and videos, engaging with content via likes and comments, and using hashtags for increased discoverability. This chapter will focus on standard posting practices, excluding the story function, which is ephemeral.

Instagram's role in the beauty industry is multifaceted, serving not only as a platform for personal expression but also as a vital marketing and branding tool. It has become a space where beauty trends are born and propagated, often influenced by popular influencers and celebrities. Brands leverage Instagram for product launches and campaigns, utilizing its visual-centric nature to showcase their offerings attractively. The interactive features of Instagram, like polls and Q&A in stories, further allow for direct engagement with consumers, fostering a two-way conversation. This level of interaction and immediate feedback makes Instagram an indispensable tool for understanding and engaging with the younger demographic, especially in the dynamic and visually driven world of beauty and fashion.

2 Word-Of-Mouth Marketing Trend in Japan

The evolution of word-of-mouth marketing in Japan reflects a broader shift in communication and information dissemination. With the advent of digital technology and the internet, the traditional boundaries of word-of-mouth have expanded significantly. This transformation has led to the rise of digital platforms as the new epicenters of word-of-mouth marketing. Japanese consumers, known for their discerning and community-oriented consumption patterns, have embraced these digital platforms, making them an integral part of their decision-making process. This shift has not only changed the way word-of-mouth is shared but also the scope and impact of such communications, with digital word-of-mouth having the potential to reach a far wider audience than traditional methods ever could.

2.1 *Understanding Word of Mouth*

Certainly, these studies provide a comprehensive understanding of Word-of-Mouth (WOM) dynamics and its evolution. Initially face-to-face, WOM has transformed, now encompassing digital platforms like Instagram and Twitter (Ando, 2010). Its influence on consumer behavior is notable, with NTT Com Research (2011) underscoring that 80% of consumers are impacted by WOM when making purchasing decisions. Interestingly, gender disparities are evident, with 75% of men and 90% of women considering WOM in their buying choices (NTT Com Research, 2011).

Specific sectors showcase unique WOM dynamics. Cosmetics, for instance, are profoundly impacted by WOM, especially among the 18–29 age group, leveraging platforms like Instagram for decision-making (BMRITE survey). In customer-centric environments, studies like Liu et al. (2021) emphasize the intricate relationship between customer experience, perceived value, and loyalty, particularly highlighting the role of physical environments and human interaction.

Employee engagement, as explored by Wang and Binti Omar (2023), stands as a significant factor affecting PWOM, elucidating the interplay between employee brand love, loyalty, and positive WOM in the tourism sector. Even in healthcare settings, positive WOM advocacy significantly correlates with patient satisfaction and hospital personnel contentment (Ferguson et al., 2006).

Psychological underpinnings of WOM are revealed by Berger (2014), who identifies five self-serving functions driving WOM and their influence on consumer behavior. Chen (2017) theorizes that social acceptance drives content sharing, impacting WOM differently in interactions with strangers versus friends.

Studies explore the metrics of WOM program value (Haenlein & Libai, 2017), electronic WOM motives (Hennig-Thurau et al., 2004), and how WOM seeding programs generate value (Libai et al., 2013). Additionally, research delves into knowledge signaling (Packard & Wooten, 2013) and compensatory word of mouth (Peluso et al., 2017), revealing how consumers navigate knowledge gaps and exert control through WOM.

Together, these studies offer a comprehensive portrayal of WOM's evolution, sector-specific dynamics, psychological drivers, and the intricate interplay between context, motives, and WOM dynamics across various domains.

2.2 Gender Disparities in Word of Mouth

Gender differences significantly affect the impact of word-of-mouth. The same survey indicated that about 75% of men and 90% of women take word-of-mouth into account when making purchasing decisions. Additionally, 60% of men and 75% of women have confirmed making purchasing decisions based on word-of-mouth. Notably, women show a higher susceptibility to and belief in word-of-mouth compared to men.

2.3 *The World of Cosmetic Word-Of-Mouth*

Cosmetics occupy a unique place in women's word-of-mouth behavior. As an integral part of daily life and subject to trends, individuals, especially those who are trend-sensitive, actively seek information about cosmetics. A BMRITE survey revealed that individuals aged 18–29, particularly those engaged with cosmetics, often rely on platforms like Instagram for information sharing. Word-of-mouth, store recommendations, and magazines are the top sources of information for cosmetics, underscoring the importance of platforms like cosmetic word-of-mouth sites and Instagram in shaping consumer choices.

3 Word-Of-Mouth Motivation and Language Types

Moore (2012) classifies word-of-mouth (WOM) into explanatory and experiential language types, reflecting cognitive and emotional tones, drawing from the LIWC (Linguistic Inquiry and Word Count) category model (Pennebaker et al., 2015). However, there are limitations with LIWC's adaptation and time constraints, utilizing J-LIWC2015 for cognitive word classification and an in-depth analysis of appreciative words.

Ando (2010) connects language types in WOM to motivational factors, suggesting individuals lean toward explanatory language when aiming for recognition and adopt experiential language for rapport-building. This hypothesis is supported through surveys exploring the purpose behind transmission and conversation, validating distinct motives: imparting knowledge and relationship-building.

Several studies delve into the influence and implications of WOM in various sectors. For instance, Ferguson et al. (2006) emphasize the impact of positive WOM on customer retention in healthcare. Wang and Binti Omar (2023) focus on employee loyalty and its mediation between employee brand love and WOM in the tourism sector. Their findings underline the importance of engaged employees in driving positive brand advocacy.

Berger (2014) outlines five self-serving functions driving WOM, while De Angelis et al. (2012) reconcile contradictory findings about positive and negative WOM, attributing them to self-enhancement motives. Chen (2017) explores motivations behind sharing content with strangers versus friends, highlighting self-enhancement and emotional connection as influential factors.

Psychological motives and behavioral patterns in WOM are explored by various studies, such as Packard and Wooten (2013), who examine how consumers compensate for knowledge gaps through WOM communications, and Peluso et al. (2017), who introduce "compensatory word of mouth" as a means to restore control when faced with threats.

Studies like Lisjak et al. (2021) discuss leveraging low-contractuality perks for WOM, while Berger and Schwartz (2011) analyze drivers of immediate and ongoing

WOM, emphasizing the impact of product characteristics and environmental cues. Dubois et al. (2016) explore the influence of interpersonal closeness on WOM valence, highlighting psychological motives.

Furthermore, Godes and Mayzlin (2009) investigate customer-to-customer communication in driving sales, emphasizing the significance of less loyal customers in spreading WOM. Haenlein and Libai (2017) propose methods to measure WOM program value and its impact on customer equity, integrating WOM programs into broader customer management functions.

Collectively, these studies contribute to understanding WOM's psychological underpinnings and practical implications in marketing and management strategies, highlighting the significance of positive WOM fueled by satisfied employees and customers in driving customer loyalty and retention.

4 Research Methods

This section outlines the methodology employed in this chapter. The primary objective is to explore the structural dimensions of consumer motivations on Instagram and to establish connections between specific motivations, attitudes, and behaviors. The study involved 212 Instagram users in a comprehensive survey, assessing motivations, main activities, usage intentions, and attitudes. The findings reveal five primary social and psychological motives among Instagram users: social interaction, archiving, self-expression, escapism, and curiosity. Building upon previous research, two hypotheses were formulated. @cosme, a cosmetic word-of-mouth site, lacks direct communication means between information senders and recipients. In contrast, Instagram provides an interactive platform for sender-recipient engagement through comments. Hypothesis 1 suggests that @cosme primarily uses explanatory language, employing cognitive words to ensure clear information understanding and recognition by the recipient. Hypothesis 2 proposes that Instagram favors conversational, experiential language, rich in emotions and sensory words, to facilitate enjoyable conversations and foster relationship-building.

This research aimed at understanding the language styles used on two different digital platforms, @cosme and Instagram, and how these styles impact user engagement and communication. The following two hypotheses are important as they provide insights into the communication strategies that are most effective on different types of digital platforms. Understanding these differences can help content creators, marketers, and platform developers to tailor their communication strategies to align with user preferences and behaviors, ultimately enhancing user engagement and satisfaction.

Hypothesis Statements:

H1: @cosme utilizes explanatory language, employing cognitive words for clarity and understanding by the recipient.

H1 posits that @cosme, a cosmetics word-of-mouth website, primarily uses explanatory language that includes cognitive words. The hypothesis suggests that this language style is chosen to ensure that the information is clear and easily understood by the recipient. This is important to test because it addresses how clarity and cognitive processing influence user interaction on a platform primarily focused on information dissemination. By validating H1, researchers can gain insights into how effective communication is achieved on informational platforms and how it influences user behavior, such as decision-making or perception of products.

H2: Instagram employs experiential language, using emotional and sensory words, to enhance conversations and build relationships.

H2, on the other hand, proposes that Instagram, a social media platform known for its visual content and interactive nature, utilizes experiential language rich in emotional and sensory words. This language style is believed to enhance conversations and foster relationship-building among users. Testing H2 is crucial because it helps to understand the role of emotional and sensory engagement in social media interactions. It examines how this language style contributes to building a sense of community, user engagement, and the strength of relationships formed on the platform. This is particularly relevant for Instagram, where the nature of interaction goes beyond mere information exchange to include social connection and personal expression.

4.1 Study Subjects

This study conducts an analysis of word-of-mouth data from the @cosme and Instagram platforms, focusing on three cosmetic products: Paul Cezanne's "Lasting Gloss Lip," "Fair Glow Highlight," and Cosmetic Décolleté's "Face Powder." The products were chosen based on their rankings on @cosme. The selection criteria aimed to ensure a balanced representation by including both lower-priced and higher-priced items, thereby minimizing any potential bias in the analysis.

4.2 Analysis Items

The analysis covers word-of-mouth posts made from January 1, 2019, to June 30, 2019. This comprehensive analysis focuses on several key elements essential for understanding the nature and impact of the content submitted. First, it involves identifying the presence of words that convey positive and negative appraisals, as well as those that relate to cognitive and sensory experiences within the submitted content. This step is crucial for assessing the overall tone and emotional impact of the posts.

Following the identification process, the analysis proceeds to calculate the frequency of these identified words. This quantification allows for a more objective measurement of the sentiments expressed across the posts, offering insights into how often specific types of expressions are used by contributors.

Another important aspect of the analysis is determining the commonalities and differences in the content submitted on both platforms. By comparing the submissions across different platforms, it becomes possible to understand the unique or shared characteristics of the posts, highlighting platform-specific trends or universal themes among the users.

Lastly, evaluating the most frequently used words in the submissions is a critical part of the analysis. This evaluation aims to discern prevalent trends and sentiments among the submissions, offering a snapshot of the dominant themes and emotional undercurrents present in the word-of-mouth posts. By focusing on these key elements, the analysis seeks to provide a thorough understanding of the nature of the content shared between January 1, 2019, and June 30, 2019, shedding light on the sentiments, perceptions, and experiences conveyed by users during this period.

4.3 Methodology

The methodology section outlines the approach taken to analyze the data collected from @cosme and Instagram for the specified period. The process is divided into two primary methods: a manual analysis using Excel and an AI-based analysis using the "UserLocal" tool.

In the manual analysis using Excel, data are randomly collected from both @cosme and Instagram. This step ensures a diverse and representative sample of the content shared on these platforms. Following the collection, a morphological analysis is applied to decompose the gathered data into individual words. This breakdown into component words is crucial for a detailed examination of the language and terminology used in the posts. Subsequently, a comparative evaluation is conducted to determine word matches for the survey items across both samples and platforms. This comparison aims to identify common terms and phrases, highlighting similarities and differences in the content shared on @cosme and Instagram.

The AI-based analysis involves the use of the "UserLocal" tool. In this method, the collected data is inputted into "UserLocal," which then employs its analysis function to systematically analyze and interpret the results. This advanced tool allows for a more sophisticated examination of the data, leveraging artificial intelligence to uncover patterns, trends, and insights that may not be immediately apparent through manual analysis alone. By combining both manual and AI-based methodologies, the study aims to achieve a comprehensive understanding of the content dynamics on @cosme and Instagram, providing a thorough investigation of the language and themes present in the data from the specified period.

4.4 Research Materials and Analysis Method

The method focus is on the systematic comparison of words found in submissions against established frameworks and tables of positive/negative appraisal words, cognitive classifications, and reference materials for sensory words. This detailed comparison is foundational to understanding the nuanced expressions of sentiment, cognitive processes, and sensory experiences conveyed in the submissions related to selected cosmetic products.

The methodology for identifying positive and negative words is based on the emotion polarity table created by Takamura Daiya, Inui Takashi, and Okumura Manabu in 2006. This table serves as a critical tool for categorizing words according to their emotional valence, enabling a structured analysis of how positive and negative sentiments are expressed in word-of-mouth communication.

Cognitive words are categorized according to a set of predefined factors, including insight, cause, deviation point, ambiguity, certainty, and differentiation. This classification scheme allows for a detailed examination of the cognitive aspects of the submissions, shedding light on the thought processes, reasoning, and levels of certainty or ambiguity expressed by the contributors.

When it comes to sensory words, the analysis involves consulting specific reference materials to resolve cases of ambiguity. These references aid in accurately identifying and categorizing words that describe sensory experiences, ensuring that the analysis captures the full spectrum of sensory impressions communicated in the submissions.

Collectively, these methods aim to provide a comprehensive and multi-faceted analysis of word-of-mouth communication for the selected cosmetic products. By evaluating both the content and linguistic style across different digital platforms, this approach seeks to uncover insights into how consumers express their opinions, experiences, and perceptions regarding cosmetic products, offering valuable perspectives on consumer behavior and product reception in the digital age.

5 Results

Before delving into the specifics of the analysis using Excel, it's important to note the methodological approach that underpins this analysis. The research aimed to dissect and quantify the types of language used in word-of-mouth communication on the two digital platforms, @cosme and Instagram. By categorizing words into positive and negative sentiments, cognitive aspects, and sensory expressions, the study sought to uncover the underlying tone and style of communication prevalent in user reviews and comments. This methodical breakdown serves as a lens through which the distinct communication styles of the two platforms are compared and contrasted, revealing insights into how users engage with and perceive cosmetic products in digital spaces.

5.1 Analysis Using Excel

The analysis results for each sample are presented below. We analyze the proportions of positive sentiment words, negative sentiment words, cognitive words, and sensory words (onomatopoeia/imitation) appearing on @cosme and Instagram platforms. Let's begin with the analysis of Paul Cezanne's "Lasting Gloss Lip". The analysis reveals that on Instagram, positive appraisal words are roughly twice as prevalent, while @cosme sees about a fivefold increase in negative appraisal words. @Cosme tends to use more cognitive words, whereas Instagram shows a higher frequency of onomatopoeia and sensory expressions. In summary, Instagram demonstrates a higher likelihood of featuring positive sentiment and onomatopoeic expressions, whereas @cosme leans towards negative sentiment and cognitive language.

Moving on to Paul Cezanne's "Far Glow Highlights", Instagram exhibits a higher frequency of positive appraisal words, nearly five times more than @cosme. Similar to the previous sample, Instagram demonstrates a prevalence of both onomatopoeia and sensory expressions. Positive sentiment words, cognitive words, onomatopoeia, and sensory expressions tend to be prominent on Instagram, while @cosme primarily features negative sentiment words.

Lastly, in the analysis of Cosmetics Decollete's "Face Powder", Instagram reveals a surplus of positive appraisal words compared to @cosme, which features a higher occurrence of negative appraisal words. Similar to the prior samples, Instagram shows a prevalence of onomatopoeia and sensory expressions. Positive sentiment words, cognitive words, onomatopoeia, and sensory expressions stand out on Instagram, while @cosme predominantly features negative sentiment words.

When considering the analysis of the three samples collectively, Instagram demonstrates a higher likelihood of featuring positive appraisal words and onomatopoeia/imitation, whereas @cosme tends to showcase negative appraisals. However, concerning cognitive words, while Instagram indicates higher prevalence in two samples, the results for another sample indicate no such trend. Thus, it's inconclusive to assert Instagram's overall prevalence in using cognitive words.

5.2 Analysis Using the Text Mining Tool

This section delves into the analysis results utilizing Text Mining, referred to as an Air Network. An air network can be defined as a network formed by connecting words appearing in documents, thereby establishing links between closely related concepts. Words in proximity within a document typically share similar contexts, indicating a semantic relationship. The color scheme in the analysis denotes green for adjectives and pink for verbs. Nouns were excluded from the comparison due to considerable fluctuations across samples.

Upon examining Paul Cezanne's 'Lasting Gloss Lip', the @cosme air network reveals a concentration of larger nodes in the upper right corner (Fig. 6.1). Clustered

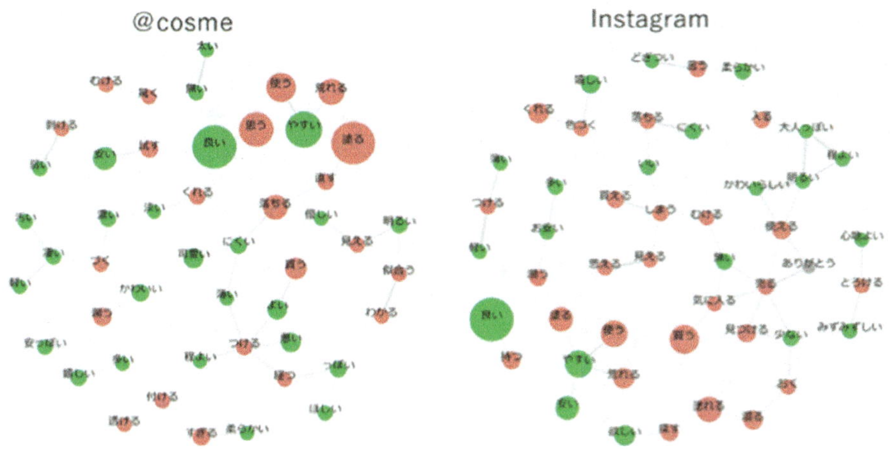

Fig. 6.1 Lipstick

words such as ‘apply,’ ‘rough,’ ‘use,’ ‘think,’ ‘good,’ and ‘cheap’ suggest a focus on usability and practical aspects. In contrast, Instagram’s air network displays a thicker line connecting words in the upper right, emphasizing terms like ‘adult,’ ‘appropriate,’ ‘bright,’ and ‘lovely,’ which highlight appearances. Moreover, more purchasing-related words like ‘buy,’ ‘find,’ and ‘panda’ are prominent compared to @cosme, indicating a different focus in user discussions.

Continuing with the analysis results for Paul Cezanne’s ‘Far Glow Highlight’ (Fig. 6.2), the @cosme air network reveals two areas of significant clustering. The first cluster, located in the top right corner, comprises three prominent words: ‘to put on,’ ‘to apply,’ and ‘to finish.’ When grouped, these words collectively express the user’s experience, conveying sentiments akin to ‘too attached’ or ‘used and discarded.’ Another cluster towards the lower part centers around the word ‘to think,’ featuring phrases like ‘it is good,’ ‘it is cheap,’ and ‘we use.’ These phrases collectively convey a user-friendly experience, with sentiments such as ‘easy to use’ or ‘I think it’s easy to use and good.’

In contrast, examining Instagram’s air network shows significant prominence with the word ‘live.’ Additionally, several terms related to appearance, such as ‘looks good,’ ‘cheap-like,’ and ‘grown-up,’ are prevalent. Furthermore, there is a cluster of words in the upper part indicating a desire to purchase, including terms like ‘high,’ ‘I want to have,’ ‘cheap,’ and ‘I can afford.’

The final discussion focuses on the analysis results of Cosmetic Décolleté’s ‘Foundation’ (Fig. 6.3). Upon reviewing the @cosme air network, similar to the previous samples, there is a notable frequency of words related to user experience, such as ‘use’ and ‘breakdown.’ Additionally, there is an increased appearance of terms like ‘it is dull,’ ‘like,’ and ‘completed.’ In contrast, on Instagram, there is a heightened frequency of the word ‘give.’ Interestingly, when considering the connected

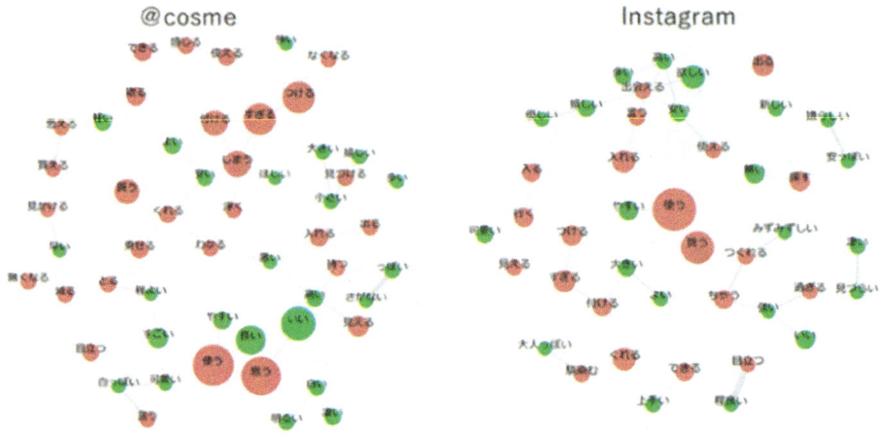

Fig. 6.2 Highlight

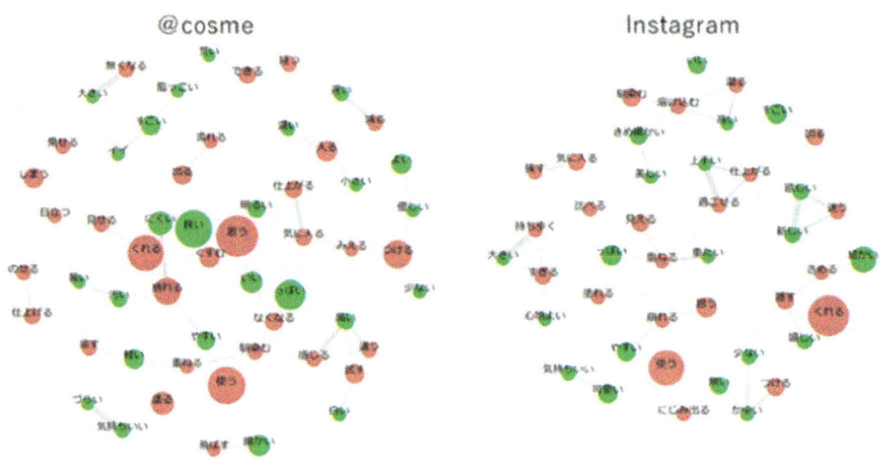

Fig. 6.3 Foundation

words 'determining' and 'hide' together, they form phrases that express the notion of 'hiding' and 'giving determination'.

5.3 Results of Hypothesis Testing

Regarding Hypothesis 1, although there were observed differences in the results, the appearance rate of cognitive words was predominantly higher on Instagram. This suggests that Instagram users tend to communicate in a more detailed and analytical manner than initially anticipated, challenging the assumption that @cosme would be the primary platform for cognitive, information-driven discourse. Therefore, Hypothesis 1, which posited that @cosme would predominantly utilize explanatory language using cognitive words, lacks support due to Instagram's unexpectedly high usage of such language.

Concerning Hypothesis 2, Instagram exhibited a prevalence of sensory words across all three samples. However, while positive appraisal words were notably higher on Instagram, negative appraisal words were more frequent on @cosme. In essence, although Instagram employed an experiential language using emotional and sensory words, it predominantly used positive emotional words and fewer negative ones. Therefore, Hypothesis 2, albeit conditionally, was not fully supported.

Regarding the analysis via text mining and air networks, @cosme displayed a higher presence of words expressing product usage experiences, whereas Instagram showed a higher occurrence of words related to product appearance and purchase decisions. This contrast suggests that users on @cosme are more focused on practical aspects and real-life utility of products, while Instagram users emphasize aesthetics and the shopping experience. Additionally, this difference may reflect the distinct user communities and objectives of the two platforms, with @cosme catering to in-depth reviews and Instagram to visually driven, lifestyle-oriented content.

In the hypothesis test implementation, Instagram demonstrated a higher appearance rate of cognitive words in two out of three samples. This suggests that, compared to @cosme, Instagram tends to use descriptive language employing cognitive terms more frequently presence of users aiming to increase their followers, known as 'Insta Glamors,' who wield significant influence and can earn income by promoting products, likely influences the appearance of cognitive words.

Furthermore, analyzing the tendency for negative emotional words, @cosme had fewer positive appraisal words but more negative ones compared to Instagram. This disparity might be due to Instagram's tendency to share information among acquaintances, while @cosme caters to a broader audience of anonymous users. The anonymity on @cosme possibly facilitates the easier expression of negative emotions, unlike Instagram, where the fear of rejection is minimal.

Lastly, the air network analysis highlighted that @cosme focuses on usability descriptions, while Instagram features more appearance and purchase-related descriptions. @cosme's platform structure encourages tagging effects and functions, facilitating word-of-mouth based on these tags. Conversely, the abundance of appearance-related content on Instagram might stem from fashion-conscious users who frequently post about appearance. Additionally, the simplicity of posting on SNS may contribute to the platform's emphasis on purchase-related content, attracting highly actionable users who make prompt purchases upon product release.

6 Conclusion

The methodology described herein involves a thorough collection of word-of-mouth data, followed by the utilization of the morpheme analysis software, MeCab, to dissect this data into individual words. This analytical step is crucial for understanding the granular level at which consumers communicate their opinions and experiences. Following the dissection, the data undergoes a categorization process, where words are classified into cognitive, positive, and negative emotion words based on vocabulary dictionaries and emotion polarity correspondence tables. This classification allows for a systematic calculation and comparison of how frequently each category of word appears within the dataset. Such a methodical approach is instrumental in identifying prevailing word-of-mouth models, revealing patterns in how consumers express their views on cosmetics products.

This research offers practical insights for cosmetics-related companies, highlighting the importance of leveraging customer opinions for marketing purposes and to enhance customer satisfaction. By understanding the word-of-mouth model, companies can more effectively target potential customers and extract valuable information, such as product usage experiences and perceptions related to appearance. This understanding fosters improved engagement with consumers throughout their consumption journey, enhancing the overall value provided to them. Furthermore, applying the insights gained from the word-of-mouth model can significantly benefit companies in the cosmetics industry by elevating the customer experience and, subsequently, buyer satisfaction.

Additionally, the research emphasizes the pivotal role of digital platforms in influencing consumer perceptions and behaviors within the cosmetics sector. Through an analysis of word-of-mouth models on platforms such as @cosme and Instagram, companies can discern how different styles of communication and types of content resonate with their audience. This understanding is crucial for developing more effective marketing strategies and creating content that meets consumer preferences and expectations. In the competitive landscape of the cosmetics market, strategic application of word-of-mouth analysis can be a key differentiator, aiding in the cultivation of brand loyalty and enhancing consumer engagement. This chapter, therefore, not only contributes to academic knowledge but also offers valuable, actionable insights for practitioners in the cosmetics industry.

References

Ando, H. (2010). Effect of the goal of word-of-mouth transmission on the audience evaluation of storytellers. *Chiba Opponent Nonchong, 48*(1), 87–100.

Berger, J. (2014). Word of mouth and interpersonal communication: A review and directions for future research. *Journal of Consumer Psychology, 24*(4), 586–607.

Berger, J., & Schwartz, E. M. (2011). What drives immediate and ongoing word of mouth? *Journal of Marketing Research, 48*(5), 869–880.

Chen, Z. (2017). Social acceptance and word of mouth: How the motive to belong leads to divergent WOM with strangers and friends. *Journal of Consumer Research, 44*(3), 613–632.

De Angelis, M., Bonezzi, A., Peluso, A. M., Rucker, D. D., & Costabile, M. (2012). On braggarts and gossips: A self-enhancement account of word-of-mouth generation and transmission. *Journal of Marketing Research, 49*(4), 551–563.

Dubois, D., Bonezzi, A., & De Angelis, M. (2016). Sharing with friends versus strangers: How interpersonal closeness influences word-of-mouth valence. *Journal of Marketing Research, 53*(5), 712–727.

Ferguson, R. J., Paulin, M., & Leiriao, E. (2006). Loyalty and positive word-of-mouth: Patients and hospital personnel as advocates of a customer-centric health care organization. *Health Marketing Quarterly, 23*(3), 59–77.

Godes, D., & Mayzlin, D. (2009). Firm-created word-of-mouth communication: Evidence from a field test. *Marketing Science, 28*(4), 721–739.

Haenlein, M., & Libai, B. (2017). Seeding, referral, and recommendation: Creating profitable word-of-mouth programs. *California Management Review, 59*(2), 68–91.

Hennig-Thurau, T., Gwinner, K. P., Walsh, G., & Gremler, D. D. (2004). Electronic word-of-mouth via consumer-opinion platforms: What motivates consumers to articulate themselves on the internet? *Journal of Interactive Marketing, 18*(1), 38–52.

Libai, B., Muller, E., & Peres, R. (2013). Decomposing the value of word of mouth seeding programs: Acceleration versus expansion. *Journal of Marketing Research, 50*(2), 161–176.

Lisjak, M., Bonezzi, A., & Rucker, D. D. (2021). How marketing perks influence word of mouth. *Journal of Marketing, 85*(5), 128–144. https://doi.org/10.1177/0022242921991798

Liu, F., Lai, K.-H., & Duan, W. (2021). Listening to online reviews: A mixed-methods investigation of customer experience in the sharing economy. *Decision Support Systems, 149*, 1–16. https://doi.org/10.1016/j.dss.2021.113609

Moore, S. G. (2012). Some things are better left unsaid: How word of mouth influences the storyteller. *Journal of Consumer Research, 38*(6), 1140–1154.

NTT Com Research. (2011). Influence of word of mouth on purchasing behaviour. Retrieved on 27 Dec 2019 https://research.nttcoms.com/database/data/001436/

Packard, G., & Wooten, D. B. (2013). Compensatory knowledge signaling in consumer word-of-mouth. *Journal of Consumer Psychology, 23*(4), 434–450.

Peluso, A. M., Bonezzi, A., De Angelis, M., & Rucker, D. D. (2017). Compensatory word-of-mouth: Advice as a device to restore control. *International Journal of Research in Marketing, 34*(2), 499–515.

Pennebaker, J. W., Boyd, R. L., Jordan, K., Blackburn, K. (2015). The development and psychometric properties of LIWC2015. University of Texas at Austin. https://repositories.lib.utexas.edu/bitstream/handle/2152/31333/LIWC2015_LanguageManual.pdf?sequence=3). Viewed on 26 Dec 2019.

Takamura, D., Inui, T., & Okumura, M. (2006). Extraction of emotional polarity of words by spin model. *Journal of the Journal of Information Processing Society, 47*(2), 627–637.

Wang, X., & Binti Omar, N.A. (2023). Nexus between brand love, loyalty, affective commitment and positive word of mouth: In the context of social identity theory. *Sustainability, 15*, 3813. https://doi.org/10.3390/su15043813

Chapter 7
Behind the Beauty: Unveiling COSMAX's Game-Changing ODM Strategy

Abstract This chapter examines COSMAX's transformative strategy as an Original Design Manufacturer (ODM) in the cosmetic industry, highlighting its success amidst the post-pandemic shifts in consumer behavior and technological advancements. As the middle class in East Asia expands, there is an increased demand for personalized self-care and beauty products, coupled with a reliance on digital solutions and sustainable practices. COSMAX has harnessed these trends, leveraging big data, IoT, and AI to enhance its value chain and meet the sophisticated demands of its global customer base. The analysis underscores the agility and innovative spirit of COSMAX, which, despite the challenges posed by the pandemic, has continued to thrive by adapting to the evolving digital landscape and consumer priorities in the cosmetic sector. COSMAX's journey from a modest start-up to a global ODM leader is a testament to its strategic emphasis on research, innovation, and customer-centric approaches. It has effectively merged skincare and makeup, pushing the boundaries of product development through its R&D efforts. By embracing the Fourth Industrial Revolution, COSMAX has optimized its operations for speed and flexibility, significantly reducing product development time and enhancing manufacturing processes. This case study exemplifies how a forward-thinking business model, grounded in technological innovation and global market awareness, can drive a company to industry leadership and offer valuable lessons for businesses navigating the complexities of the post-pandemic market.

Part of this paper incorporates the content from Park, Y. W., Hong, P., & Shin, G. C. (2023). Rising and thriving in the post COVID-19 era: a case study of COSMAX, a leader of the Korean cosmetic industry. Asia Pacific Business Review, 29(4), 1105–1124.

Y. W. Park and P. Hong, *Cosmetics Marketing Strategy in the Era of the Digital Ecosystem*, https://doi.org/10.1007/978-981-97-3674-4_7

1 Bridging the Gap: From Pandemic Challenges to Market Opportunities

The post-pandemic scenario presents a unique blend of challenges and opportunities, especially for the cosmetic industry in East Asia. The pandemic, while posing significant hurdles, has also acted as a catalyst for change, pushing industries to innovate and adapt. This innovation is not merely a response to immediate challenges but a strategic realignment towards emerging market dynamics. The cosmetic industry, in particular, finds itself at the forefront of this transformation. With the growing middle class in East Asia increasingly focused on wellness, beauty, and self-care, there is a burgeoning demand for products and services that cater to these evolving needs. This demand, coupled with the rapid digitalization of consumer habits, sets the stage for a significant overhaul in how cosmetic products are developed, marketed, and distributed.

1.1 Post-pandemic Business Opportunities in East Asia

Despite the COVID-19 pandemic, growing business opportunities in East Asia are expected to continue to expand, driven by the growing middle class in this vibrant region. The post-pandemic era is marked by an increasing focus on individualized self-care, green technology, digital markets, and a surge in venture firms. Weaknesses exposed by the pandemic could catalyze greater human innovation, aligning with the quality-of-life aspirations of the growing middle class (Alexandri & Janoschka, 2020; Beane & Brynjolfsson, 2020; Kochhar, 2020). Long-term trends also indicate reasons for optimism in creative industries after the pandemic (Dharmani et al., 2021; Goldberg & Reed, 2020; Park et al., 2023).

In this new era, the increasingly affluent middle class is likely to prioritize values centered around beauty, cleanness, nutrition, and healthcare development (Byun and Gardner, 2021; Kaiser et al., 2021; Leach et al., 2021; Shin, 2017). Although growth rates slowed during the pandemic, the long-term prospects for Asian economies remain robust (Dieppe, 2021; Maliszewska et al., 2020). Various industries, particularly cosmetics, are addressing the needs of these expanding segments. Cosmetics firms are leveraging big data, establishing brand partnerships across industries, and integrating IoT and AI into their product and process development (Čirjevskis, 2020; Faria-Silva et al., 2020; Nguyen et al., 2020). This utilization of big data, collected through IoT devices, improves value chain operations and creates a digital thread through the global value chain (GVC) (Baines & Lightfoot, 2013; Demil & Lecocq, 2010; Frederick et al., 2018).

1.2 The Evolving Cosmetic Industry Challenges in a Digital Age

GVC research is rapidly growing, with Kano et al. (2020) highlighting GVCs and digitization as essential future research topics. While previous studies have examined the impact of new technologies on GVC configurations, future studies could explore how digital technologies transform GVC governance structures (Foster & Graham, 2017; Foster et al., 2018; Laplume et al., 2016). Additionally, research might focus on various aspects such as power dynamics in digital value chains, business model innovation through platformization, and the integration of digital and brick-and-mortar scenarios within the same network (Foster & Graham, 2017; Foster et al., 2018; Jarvenpaa & Leidner, 1999; Kano, 2018; Kano et al., 2020; Li et al., 2019a, 2019b). However, there is still much to learn about the post-COVID-19 era rise of Asian cosmetics firms catering to the growing Asian middle class, especially in terms of business model evolution.

As of 2020, the top ten global cosmetics firms include four from the USA, three from Europe, two from Japan, and one from Korea. The US and European firms continue to maintain their competitive edge in the industry. The global cosmetics market share indicates Asia as the largest region, followed by Western Europe and North America. With the rapid growth of the middle class in Asia, increased sales are expected more in this region than on other continents (Morea et al., 2021; Spieth et al., 2019). This dynamic market environment poses a challenge for the cosmetic industry in developing and adopting unique business models.

This chapter aims to explore how cosmetics firms are transitioning into technology-enabled beauty companies to meet changing customer demands. It presents the context of cosmetic industry growth in the post-pandemic world and suggests a research framework for the Original Design Manufacturer (ODM) business model. A case study of COSMAX provides insights into the changing dynamics of the industry, the key success factors of this hidden champion, and the theoretical and managerial implications.

2 Reimagining Business Models in the Cosmetic Industry

The cosmetic industry is undergoing a transformative phase, characterized by a shift in business models driven by digitalization and the complexities of modern market demands. This transition is not just about incorporating new technologies but redefining the very essence of how cosmetic companies operate, create value, and connect with consumers. The traditional business models, while effective in the past, are now being challenged by the rapid advancements in technology and changing consumer preferences. This necessitates a more dynamic and flexible approach to business modeling, one that can adapt to the fast-paced changes in the industry and leverage digital technologies to their fullest potential.

2.1 *The Business Model in the Cosmetic Industry*

The business model concept in the cosmetic industry refers to the strategic alignment of different areas of a firm's activity to deliver value to customers. This concept can be approached in two ways: a static view, seeing it as a blueprint for coherence between core business model components, and a transformational approach, which uses the concept as a tool to address change and innovation within the organization or the model itself. The evolution of business models reflects the new strategic emphasis and direction of innovation for firms in dynamic market contexts, increasingly influenced by digital technologies such as IoT and AI (Chang et al., 2021; Demil & Lecocq, 2010; Jacobides & Reeves, 2020; Park, 2017, 2020). The IoT, for instance, interconnects all things to make them more intelligent and capable of interacting with humans and each other.

The rise of big data from IoT devices is transforming GVCs, particularly after-sales data-driven knowledge services. Global value chains involve various services at each stage, including R&D, product design, procurement, production, and marketing, generally carried out by inter-firm networks on a global scale (Frederick et al., 2017; Gereffi & Fernandez-Stark, 2016; Low & Pasadilla, 2016). Thus, IoT creates new challenges and opportunities for evolving business models, with standardization playing a crucial role in ensuring global interoperability and reliability.

2.2 *Digital Transformation in the Cosmetic Industry*

Contemporary products are adding complexity to systems, while consumers demand increasing uncertainty, diversity, and sophistication in business processes (Fujimoto & Park, 2012; Park, 2017; Park & Hong, 2012; Reeves et al., 2020). Managing this complexity is a significant challenge for manufacturers across various industries. In the cosmetics industry, a realistic customer experience requires the application of IoT and AI to existing complex design and manufacturing processes. The traditional closed system business model is inadequate for such requirements; instead, a more open, holistic, and adaptive approach is needed in the digital ecosystem environment (Li, 2020; Liu et al., 2021; Park, 2017). Traditionally, cosmetic firms have managed all value creation processes through vertical integration, from product development to logistics. This approach is similar to the OEM and ODM business models of the 1990s, like Apple's relationship with Foxconn. However, manufacturers are increasingly turning to specialized service providers for various functions in their chains, such as raw material procurement, production planning, and logistics (Coronado Mondragon & Coronado Mondragon, 2018; Frederick et al., 2017; Hong & Park, 2014; Low & Pasadilla, 2016; Hong & Park, 2020; Seyoum, 2021).

Unlike assembled manufacturing products, cosmetics products use highly integrated processes, making it challenging to delegate design know-how and manufacturing processes (Lim & Fujimoto, 2019; Park, 2017; Park et al., 2019). The COVID-19 pandemic has accelerated online sales in the cosmetic industry and wellness-related micro-trends, leading consumers to search for products that promote health, safety, and overall wellness. In response, cosmetics manufacturers have diversified their product offerings and shifted towards digital markets, creating online platforms and communities for product discovery, advice, and sharing during these uncertain times (Chouhan et al., 2021; Kwon, 2020).

3 COSMAX: Trailblazing in the Global ODM Market

COSMAX stands as a paradigm of success in the Korean beauty industry, transitioning from a modest startup in 1992 to becoming the global leader in Original Design Manufacturing (ODM) for cosmetics. With a robust annual growth rate of 35%, COSMAX has made remarkable strides, particularly in the Chinese market, where it has established itself as the top ODM company. Its global production and distribution system is a testament to its expansive reach, with subsidiaries and factories across five countries and an impressive annual capacity of 1.85 billion units. The company's financial success is reflected in its group sales, which amounted to $2173 million in 2020, with cosmetics sales contributing $1383 million.

COSMAX's journey to international prominence includes significant milestones, such as its expansion into the United States with the acquisition of L'Oréal's Ohio Solon plant. The company has adeptly adapted to the diverse needs of American consumers, blending Korean innovation with local preferences. Its product development includes collaborations with renowned brands like Estee Lauder and Stila. COSMAX's commitment to enhancing its customer focus is further evidenced by its acquisition of NuWorld, the third-largest color cosmetics ODM company in the US, in 2017. This strategic move not only diversified COSMAX's production capabilities but also expanded its customer base, further solidifying its position in the competitive US market.

3.1 Fostering Innovation: COSMAX's Beauty Scientists and the ODM Business Model

COSMAX is a Korean "hidden champion" company. It was established in 1992 with four employees. In 2004, it became the first Korean ODM company in China. Since then, it has achieved an average annual growth rate of 35%. It is positioned as the indisputable number of ODM companies in China. It became the global No. 1 ODM firm from 2015. COSMAX has a global production and distribution

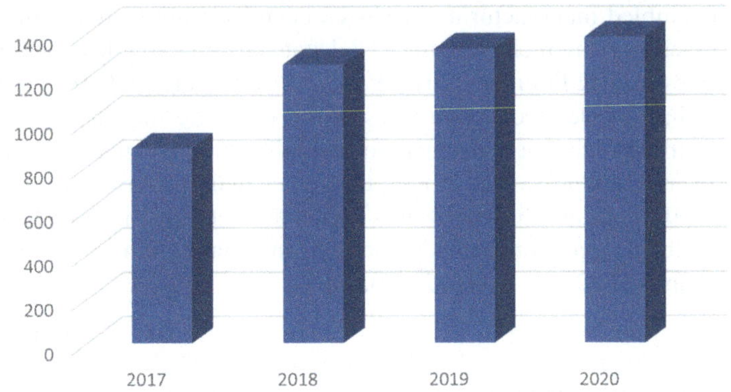

Fig. 1 2017–2020 cosmetics sales of COSMAX (Million USD) (*Source* COSMAX. *Note* 1$ USD = 1,000 Korean Won)

system by which it produces, supplies, and delivers to customers from its overseas subsidiaries. COSMAX's subsidiaries and factories are located in six cities in five countries (Korea, China, the United States, Indonesia, and Thailand). Based on the annual production capacity, the total annual capacity is 1.85 billion units, including 410 million units in Korea, 210 million units in the United States, 990 million units in China, 140 million units in Indonesia, and 90 million units in Thailand as of 2021. It achieved $2173 million in group sales ($1383 million in cosmetics sales) in 2020 (see Fig. 1).

After successfully making inroads into China, it opened COSMAX USA in 2013. The US plant acquired facilities from Loréal, the largest cosmetics company in the world, after acquiring the Ohio Solon plant, and transformed it to produce diverse product lines that satisfy US customers. With the establishment of a local Research and Innovation (R&I) Center in New Jersey, it focused on meeting the changing requirements of American consumers with Korean innovativeness through collaboration with the R&I Center in Korea. It is currently developing or producing about 50 brands of products, including Estee Lauder and Stila. Its cosmetics sales achieved $884 million in 2017 and $1383 million in 2020.

COSMAX is making efforts to strengthen its customer focus to become the best ODM company in the United States. As part of that, it acquired NuWorld in November 2017, the third largest color cosmetics ODM company in the United States. Through the acquisition of NuWorld, COSMAX is operating its existing Ohio factory as a skin care factory and enhancing efficiency by utilizing the Nuworld factory as a color factory. In addition, it has secured a new customer base so that it can continue to grow in the US market.

In addition to China and the US, it also expanded into Southeast Asian markets. COSMAX Indonesia, which was established in Jakarta in 2012, started its operations in 2014, while the Jakarta plant is pioneering Southeast Asian markets such as Indonesia and Malaysia. Furthermore, COSMAX Thailand has been established and is in operation to open up markets such as Thailand, Myanmar, and Vietnam.

COSMAX's production capacity has been greatly increased to 1150 million at the end of 2016 from 750 million at the end of 2015. Furthermore, in 2021, it reports more than 1850 million production volumes.

At the heart of COSMAX's ascent to global dominance is its unwavering commitment to research and innovation. With over 720 researchers across its R&I centers in five countries, COSMAX dedicates more than a quarter of its total workforce to R&D activities. This dedication is evident in its innovative approach to product development, where it blends skincare and makeup technologies to create novel products. The company's R&I centers are not just laboratories but hubs of creativity and exploration, where traditional boundaries between skincare and makeup are blurred to meet the evolving demands of the beauty industry. The Pangyo R&I center in Korea exemplifies this philosophy, having restructured in 2015 to promote synergy between skincare and makeup categories. This innovative mindset is critical for COSMAX to stay ahead in an industry where the demand for new and unique products is ever-present.

3.2 Embracing Industry 4.0: COSMAX's Digital Strategy in ODM

COSMAX's embrace of the Fourth Industrial Revolution reflects its foresight in leveraging emerging digital technologies like IoT and AI to innovate and stay competitive. The company's strategic focus is on preemption, connection, and concentration, aiming to outpace competitors through innovation and organizational agility. This strategy involves forging strong linkages with partners and academia, fostering a culture that values creativity, and simplifying processes to deliver value effectively. COSMAX's Chairman, Kyung-soo Lee, emphasizes the importance of enthusiasm and creativity in driving innovation, fostering a work environment where communication is open, and failure is seen as a stepping stone to success. This approach aligns with the company's aspiration to simplify and streamline the commercialization process, ensuring that its products not only meet but exceed consumer expectations.

COSMAX's business model showcases versatility, catering to both traditional cosmetics brands through its ODM services and emerging venture firms through its Original Brand Manufacturing (OBM) model. In the OBM model, COSMAX provides comprehensive support, from R&D to packaging design, helping new ventures establish their brand in the market. This multi-faceted approach allows COSMAX to offer a range of services to a diverse client base, including small and medium-sized firms in emerging economies, thereby reinforcing its position as a global leader in the cosmetics ODM industry.

As a leading global cosmetics firm, COSMAX pays close attention to the innovative opportunities associated with the Fourth Industrial Revolution, utilizing IoT and AI technologies. The company's strategy centers around three key principles: preemption, connection, and concentration. COSMAX aims to enhance its speed and flexibility to stay ahead of its competitors (Kim & Lee, 2018). It fosters innovation through forward linkages with affiliated companies, partners, and academia. The company implements organizational innovation for selection and concentration, building a system that can deliver value to customers. In light of the opportunities presented by the Fourth Industrial Revolution, COSMAX initiated a cultural shift in 2014, embodying the values of "Be innovative," "Stay simple," and "Aspire to be Industry No. 1" through various pilot projects (Kim & Lee, 2018). Chairman Kyung-soo Lee believes that new technologies are essential for COSMAX to be recognized for its innovation, offering new experiences to consumers. He emphasizes that enthusiasm and creativity are crucial for COSMAX. Efforts have been made to remove communication barriers; for example, project participants are encouraged to share their opinions during meetings. A culture of active engagement and interaction is promoted, where teams have the freedom to experiment and potentially fail in pilot projects. The company also recognizes that innovation requires simplicity in concept and boldness in action, aspiring to develop and market products that achieve their original purpose while simplifying the commercialization and market introduction process.

Figure 2 illustrates two distinct business models employed by COSMAX. In the first model, COSMAX operates as an Original Design Manufacturer (ODM), collaborating with traditional cosmetics brand Original Equipment Manufacturers (OEMs) that already possess established brand names. COSMAX assists these OEMs in overcoming their vertical integration bottlenecks by providing specific functional services as needed. This includes developing new products based on the OEM customers' proposals and delivering these products as branded items under the OEM's name. In the second model, COSMAX acts as an Original Brand Manufacturer (OBM), partnering with venture firms that lack established brand names. This model offers a customized service for venture firms that have innovative concepts and business ideas but are inexperienced in value proposition and marketing activities. COSMAX not only engages in research and development, manufacturing, and technological functions in both models but also assists in packaging design for the OBM model, catering to the needs of venture firms without established brands. As an OBM, COSMAX provides comprehensive functional support to customers aiming to create and market their own new brand value. It specifically supports small and medium-sized firms from emerging economies that do not have established brands. In summary, COSMAX collaborates with venture firms that bring innovative ideas to the table but lack the capabilities in manufacturing and marketing.

Speed is essential in the era of the Fourth Industrial Revolution. Chairman Kyung Soo Lee uses the catchphrase to "Be the First Mover". The current competitive market environment is characterized by high volatility and great uncertainty (Kim & Lee, 2018). COSMAX's reputation among global OEMs (e.g., L'Oréal) is in its quality control capability and successful fast-cycle product delivery. COSMAX also conducts quality inspections (through an open network development system) to ensure product stability, brand compatibility, and micro-organism innovativeness that meet or exceed the standards of the L'Oréal Institute. Considering the high customer-sensitive characteristics and competitive market requirements of the

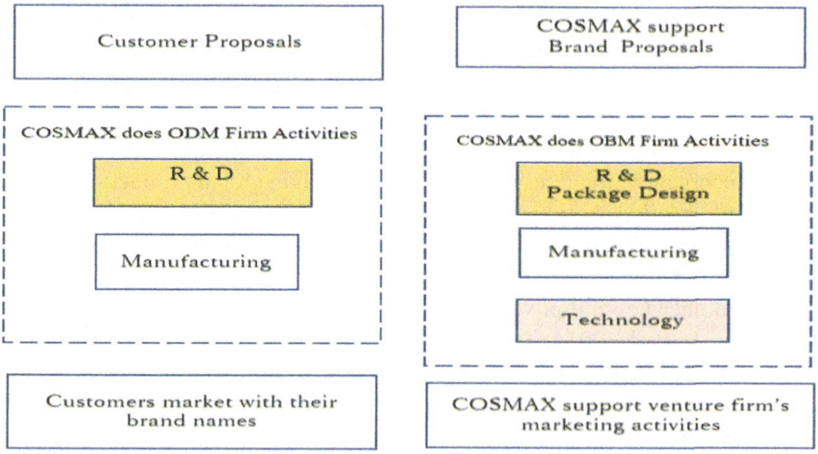

Fig. 2 ODM/OBM business model of COSMAX

cosmetic industry, COSMAX aims to excel in quality, flexibility, and fashionability. Still, the key differentiator is doing it all in a short product cycle time. COSMAX utilizes IoT technology to shorten the product development cycle from 18–24 months to 6–9 months.

COSMAX also implements the SAP as an Enterprise Resource Planning (ERP) system to fulfill the speed requirements. The SAP standardizes the business processes among subsidiaries in Korea, China, and the United States. Furthermore, it builds IT infrastructure to support reliable information flows for real-time business development among each business unit. Once the SAP system is adopted, it provides profit and loss information for each product, since the total profit and loss statement can be aggregated every five days on a monthly basis. Multi-dimensional sales, cost, and profit analysis become possible, and online based business will enable various management information to be shared, allowing for a preemptive response to future environmental changes.

Third, flexibility is crucial in the era of the Fourth Industrial Revolution. COSMAX is responding flexibly from the perspective of brand companies, not to that of producers (Kim & Lee, 2018). COSMAX cooperates with customers for this goal. Customers from emerging economies like China appreciate the speed and flexibility performance of COSMAX. Since COSMAX entered China in 2004, it operated as a customized ODM, not an OEM. It was fundamentally different from the way Japanese companies and Italian companies operated in China. These firms made product offerings in China in the minimum delivery period of three months. In contrast, COSMAX supplied its products in 1.5–2 months while satisfying the quality requirements of customers. This has become a big success factor in the Chinese market. The Chinese local cosmetics brand firms were very impressed with COSMAX that there was a huge increase in their order volumes. Soon COSMAX China became the No. 1 ODM company in China.

COSMAX also used the concept of functional headquarters (FHs) for product production, quality control, logistics, and purchasing. By integrating these FHs into ERP, they actively respond to real-time requests with their client firms on various fronts. Naturally, process productivity and functional efficiency showed drastic improvement. COSMAX has demonstrated high communication flexibility and real-time organizational responsiveness by building global production networks, improving information sharing systems, and integrating strategic planning with operational executions. Such is the mark of COSMAX being one of the outstanding hidden champions in the global cosmetic industry.

Fourth, another key initiative is to enhance linkage competence (network capability) (Hong & Park, 2014; Park, 2017; Park & Hong, 2012). The connectivity is in line with the analog and digital convergence in the Fourth Industrial Revolution (Kim & Lee, 2018). COSMAX has cooperative partnerships with more than 600 strategic customers in Korea and overseas with whom it pursues open innovation network practices. It also develops proprietary raw materials and new products through collaboration with more than 200 raw material component providers and carries out joint development projects with prominent global cosmetics companies. It shares customer progress with orders, enhancement status, and production schedule with customers, and holds meetings to share the vision with partner companies and build a mutual growth base to strengthen cooperation management.

The COSMAX R&I Center operates a variety of industry-university cooperation programs for its competitiveness as a research-oriented company where speed and flexibility are important. It is responsible for the future technology strategy of COSMAX. It continues to develop new efficacy evaluation technology, new material and process development, fusion between heterogeneous industries, and existing products through external collaboration. The COSMAX R&I Center has promoted exchanges between two fundamentally different foundation and color groups. It composes a fusion complex lab organization that goes beyond existing cosmetic research organizations. It maximizes convergence technology performance using formulation similarity. It develops new cosmetics products combining the concept of skincare and makeup.

Cosmax celebrated its 30th anniversary in 2022. The company formed technical alliances with external companies to secure cosmetic manufacturing technology at the time of establishment. However, in order to develop the technology necessary for corporate growth and development rather than just accepting the technology, an independent research institute has also been established and a large amount of money is being invested in research and development. By deploying a large number of researchers (25–30% of the total number of employees), the company is demonstrating its competitive edge by gradually improving its technology.

Cosmax has grown as an ODM company and has accumulated technological prowess in line with the growth of Korea's unique distribution channel called the One Brand Shop by manufacturing and providing a wide range of products from makeup products to basic cosmetics with high technology and product development capabilities. It is transforming into an OBM company by focusing more on R&D and product development.

4 Catalyzing Cosmax's Ascension: Key Growth Drivers

Cosmax's ascent in the beauty industry can be attributed to four pivotal growth drivers (Park, 2022; Park et al., 2023). Firstly, its diverse product portfolio has been instrumental in sustaining stable growth, particularly during the Covid-19 crisis. Cosmax successfully navigated this period by focusing on online customers, developing consumer-centric products, and investing in corporate digitalization to stay adaptable to future market shifts. Furthermore, Cosmax's commitment to clean beauty is evidenced by various certifications and participation in the UN Global Compact. This aligns with principles of human rights, labor, environmental sustainability, and anti-corruption, enhancing its position in eco-friendly sustainability through transparency platforms like EcoVadis, CDP and UNGC.

Secondly, Cosmax's growth has been bolstered by fostering mutually beneficial partnerships with both domestic (mass brand companies, ventures) and global entities (large brands, local Chinese companies). These partnerships have created synergies through close cooperation. The trust Cosmax garnered during challenges like the Asian currency crisis, by freezing supply prices and ensuring timely supply even during loss periods, led to an improvement in market share and collaborations on single-brand shops.

Another factor contributing to Cosmax's growth is its focus on enhancing management and technological capabilities and innovations. Collaborations with various companies, technical cooperation, and substantial investments in R&D have yielded innovative products and technologies, solidifying Cosmax's global market expertise.

Finally, Cosmax's strategic global expansion has been a crucial factor in its growth trajectory. Establishing a strong presence in China, Southeast Asia, the United States, and other key regions has enabled Cosmax to cater to diverse markets and compete effectively with global conglomerates. By entering new markets and addressing specific regional needs, Cosmax has fortified its global production bases, creating significant entry barriers for competitors.

5 Mastering the Market: Cosmax's Strategic Path to Dominance

Cosmax employs three core strategies to secure its market dominance (Park, 2022; Park et al., 2023). The first strategy emphasizes significant investment in R&D to uphold high technological standards and robust global manufacturing infrastructure. This investment facilitates manufacturing flexibility and enables Cosmax to quickly enter markets, even in the absence of dedicated factories, by providing versatile regional manufacturing solutions. In addition to enhancing production capabilities, Cosmax's commitment to R&D paves the way for groundbreaking product innovations and advancements in cosmetic technology. This strategic focus not only keeps

Cosmax at the forefront of industry trends but also allows for the continuous development of cutting-edge products that meet the evolving preferences and needs of consumers globally. Furthermore, this investment in R&D and manufacturing infrastructure positions Cosmax as a key player in the global cosmetics market, capable of adapting to changing market conditions and consumer trends with agility and foresight.

Secondly, Cosmax is committed to maintaining stringent manufacturing and quality control systems that align with international standards. By acquiring certifications in various countries and regions, Cosmax strengthens customer trust and lays a solid foundation for sustained business growth. This approach to quality assurance not only ensures product safety and reliability but also bolsters Cosmax's reputation as a dependable and responsible manufacturer in the global cosmetics arena. The company's adherence to international standards and certifications is a key differentiator, setting them apart from competitors and reassuring clients and consumers of the exceptional quality of their products. Additionally, this commitment to high standards in manufacturing and quality control has been instrumental in opening new market opportunities, allowing Cosmax to expand its global footprint and establish strong relationships with international clients.

The third strategic pillar is the company's adaptability to customer needs, characterized by speed and flexibility. By leveraging its accumulated expertise, Cosmax swiftly responds to market shifts, nurturing a culture of agility and innovation. The company's plans to implement Robotic Process Automation (RPA) systems are aimed at boosting automation, increasing productivity, and efficiently meeting the diverse demands of its clientele. This focus on customer-centric adaptability allows Cosmax to stay ahead of industry trends and cater to the evolving preferences of a diverse global customer base. The integration of RPA and other advanced technologies into their operations exemplifies their commitment to continuous improvement and operational excellence. Furthermore, this strategy of responsive innovation positions Cosmax as a forward-thinking leader in the cosmetics industry, capable of rapidly developing and delivering products that resonate with consumers' current and future needs. This proactive approach not only enhances customer satisfaction but also drives sustainable growth and market competitiveness for Cosmax.

Additionally, Cosmax stays ahead of industry trends by focusing on personalized products and is poised to integrate AI-based solutions into its product development process. This integration ensures accurate and rapid responses to evolving consumer needs. Cosmax's ambition extends to transitioning from an Original Design Manufacturer (ODM) to an Original Brand Manufacturer (OBM) model. This shift entails offering comprehensive services ranging from brand concept development to marketing, primarily through online channels, thereby solidifying its status as a holistic provider in the dynamic world of cosmetics. Cosmax's strategic pivot towards the OBM model represents a significant advancement in its business approach, aligning with the modern consumer's preference for brands that offer unique identities and stories. By harnessing AI technology, Cosmax aims to personalize the beauty experience, tailoring products to individual consumer preferences and behaviors, thus revolutionizing the way beauty products are developed and marketed. This strategic move is not just about product innovation; it's also about transforming the customer experience, making Cosmax a trendsetter in creating bespoke beauty solutions. This transition underscores Cosmax's commitment to staying at the forefront of the beauty industry, continuously adapting to changing market landscapes and consumer expectations.

6 Reshaping the Future: COSMAX's Path in the Digital Era and Beyond

This chapter explores post-pandemic business opportunities using the COSMAX case study and investigates the influence of IoT technologies on the ODM business model. Through field interviews and examining its response to Fourth Industrial Revolution opportunities, COSMAX's strategic initiatives demonstrate innovativeness, simplicity, and industry leadership across its business units.

The research framework, encompassing sensing customer needs, IoT technologies, and manufacturing capabilities, defines and validates the ODM/OBM business model. The lessons drawn from this case study hold implications beyond the cosmetic industry, emphasizing cross-functional creativity, operational speed, and flexibility for global market expansion. The COSMAX case study exemplifies how companies can thrive in the post-pandemic era by embracing technological advancements and adapting their business models accordingly. This approach highlights the importance of agility in responding to evolving consumer preferences and market dynamics, ensuring resilience and sustained growth. The integration of IoT technologies into COSMAX's operations demonstrates a forward-thinking approach to leveraging digital transformations for competitive advantage.

Furthermore, the case of COSMAX serves as a blueprint for other industries looking to navigate the challenges of the digital age. It underscores the significance of customer-centric innovation and the strategic use of technology in enhancing product offerings and operational efficiency. By examining COSMAX's journey, other companies can gain insights into developing robust strategies that align with the rapidly changing business landscape. This chapter, therefore, contributes not only to academic discourse but also provides practical guidance for businesses seeking to capitalize on the opportunities presented in a post-pandemic world, particularly in the realm of digitization and customer-focused innovation.

References

Alexandri, G., & Janoschka, M. (2020). Post-pandemic transnational gentrifications: A critical outlook. *Urban Studies, 57*(15), 3202–3214.

Baines, T., & Lightfoot, H. (2013). Servitization of the manufacturing firm: Exploring the operations practices and technologies that deliver advanced services. *International Journal of Operations & Production Management, 34*(1), 2–35.

Beane, M., & Brynjolfsson, E. (2020). Working with robots in a post-pandemic world. *MIT Sloan Management Review, 62*(1), 1–5.

Byun, J. H., & Shin, J. S. (2017). *From cosmetic companies without faces to beauty and health groups: Kolmar Korea.* Asan Entrepreneurship Review. The Asan Nanum Foundation. (In Korean).

Chang, L.-C., Wang, X., Zhang, S.-Q., Chen, C.-B., Yuan, Z.-H., Zeng, X.-J., Chu, J.-Q., & Tsai, S.-B. (2021). User-driven business model innovation: An ethnographic inquiry into Toutiao in the Chinese context. *Asia Pacific Business Review, 27*(3), 359–377.

Chouhan, N., Vig, H., & Deshmukh, R. (2021, February). *Cosmetics market by category (skin and sun care products, hair care products, deodorants & fragrances, and makeup & color cosmetics), gender (men, women, and unisex), and distribution channel (hypermarkets/supermarkets, specialty stores, pharmacies, online sales channels, and others): Global opportunity analysis and industry forecast, 2021–2027.* Allied Market Research.

Čirjevskis, A. (2020). Managing competence-based synergy in acquisition processes: Empirical evidence from the ICT and global cosmetic industries. *Knowledge Management Research & Practice, 18*(4), 1–10.

Coronado Mondragon, A. E., & Coronado Mondragon, C. E. (2018). Managing complex, modular products: How technological uncertainty affects the role of systems integrators in the automotive supply chain. *International Journal of Production Research, 56*(20), 6628–6643.

Demil, B., & Lecocq, X. (2010). Business model evolution: In search of dynamic consistency. *Long Range Planning, 43*, 227–246.

Dharmani, P., Das, S., & Prashar, S. (2021). A bibliometric analysis of creative industries: Current trends and future directions. *Journal of Business Research, 135*, 252–267.

Dieppe, A. (Ed.). (2021). *Global productivity: Trends, drivers, and policies.* World Bank Publications.

Faria-Silva, C., Ascenso, A., Costa, A. M., Marto, J., Carvalheiro, M., Ribeiro, H. M., & Simoes, S. (2020). Feeding the skin: A new trend in food and cosmetics convergence. *Trends in Food Science & Technology, 95*, 21–32.

Foster, C., Graham, M., Mann, L., Waema, T., & Friederici, N. (2018). Digital control in value chains: Challenges of connectivity for East African firms. *Economic Geography, 94*(1), 68–86.

Foster, C., & Graham, M. (2017). Reconsidering the role of the digital in global production networks. *Global Networks, 17*(1), 68–88.

Frederick, S., Bamber, P., Brun, L., Cho, J., Gereffi, G., Lee, J., Cho, J. (2017, September). *Korea in global value chains: Pathways for industrial transformation.* Duke GVCC.

Frederick, S., Bamber, P., & Cho, J. (2018, December). *The digital economy, global value chains in Asia.* Duke GVCC.

Fujimoto, T., & Park, Y. W. (2012). Complexity and control: Benchmarking of automobiles and electronic products. *Benchmarking: An International Journal, 19*(4–5), 502–516.

Gardner, K. (2021). *Beauty during a pandemic: The impact of COVID-19 on the cosmetic industry.* Doctoral dissertation: University Honors College Middle Tennessee State University.

Gereffi, G., & Fernandez-Stark, K. (2016). *Global value chain analysis: A primer* (2nd ed.). Duke University Center on Globalization, Governance & Competitiveness (Duke CGGC). http://www.cggc.duke.edu/pdfs/Duke_CGGC_Global_Value_Chain_GVC_Analysis_Primer_2nd_Ed_2016.pdf

Goldberg, P. K., & Reed, T. (2020). The effects of the coronavirus pandemic in emerging market and developing economies: An optimistic preliminary account. *Brookings Papers on Economic Activity, 2020*(2), 161–235.

Hong, P., & Park, Y. W. (2014). *Building network capabilities in turbulent competitive environments: Practices of global firms from Korea and Japan.* CRC Press.

Hong, P., & Park, Y. W. (2020). *Rising Asia and American hegemony: Case of competitive firms from Japan, Korea, China, and India.* Springer. ISBN 978-981-13-7634-4.

Jacobides, M. G., & Reeves, M. (2020). Adapt your business to the new reality. *Harvard Business Review, 98*(5), 74–81.

Jarvenpaa, S. L., & Leidner, D. E. (1999). Communication and trust in global virtual teams. *Organization Science, 10*(6), 791–815.

Kaiser, M., Goldson, S., Buklijas, T., Gluckman, P., Allen, K., Bardsley, A., & Lam, M. E. (2021). Towards post-pandemic sustainable and ethical food systems. *Food Ethics, 6*(1), 1–19.

Kano, L. (2018). Global value chain governance: A relational perspective. *Journal of International Business Studies, 49*, 684–705.

Kano, L., Tsang, E. W. K., & Yeung, H. W. (2020). Global value chains: A review of the multi-disciplinary literature. *Journal of International Business Studies, 51*, 577–622.

Kim, J. H., & Lee, K. S. (2018). *COSMAX story 2*. Maeil Economic Newspaper Publishing. (In Korean).

Kochhar, R. (2020). A global middle class is more promise than reality. In *The middle class in world society* (pp. 15–48). Routledge India.

Kwon, D. (2020, December). *2020 cosmetic industry analysis report*. Korea Health Industry Development Institute. (In Korean).

Laplume, A. O., Petersen, B., & Pearce, J. M. (2016). Global value chains from a 3D printing perspective. *Journal of International Business Studies, 47*(5), 595–609.

Leach, M., MacGregor, H., Scoones, I., & Wilkinson, A. (2021). Post-pandemic transformations: How and why COVID-19 requires us to rethink development. *World Development, 138*, 105–233.

Li, F. (2020). The digital transformation of business models in the creative industries: A holistic framework and emerging trends. *Technovation, 92*, 102–112.

Li, F., Frederick, S., & Gereffi, G. (2019a). E-commerce and industrial upgrading in the Chinese apparel value chain. *Journal of Contemporary Asia, 49*(1), 24–53.

Li, J., Chen, L., Yi, J., Mao, J., & Liao, J. (2019b). Ecosystem-specific advantages in international digital commerce. *Journal of International Business Studies, 50*(9), 1448–1463.

Lim, C., & Fujimoto, T. (2019). Frugal innovation and design changes expanding the cost-performance frontier: A Schumpeterian approach. *Research Policy, 48*(4), 1016–1029.

Liu, J., Tong, T. W., & Sinfield, J. V. (2021). Toward a resilient complex adaptive system view of business models. *Long Range Planning, 54*(3), 1020–1030.

Low, P., & Pasadilla, G. (Eds.). (2016). *Services in global value chains: Manufacturing-related services*. World Scientific Publishing for Asia-Pacific Economic Cooperation Secretariat.

Maliszewska, M., Mattoo, A., Van Der Mensbrugghe, D. (2020). *The potential impact of COVID-19 on GDP and trade: A preliminary assessment*. World Bank Policy Research Working Paper 9211.

Morea, D., Fortunati, S., & Martiniello, L. (2021). Circular economy and corporate social responsibility: Towards an integrated strategic approach in the multinational cosmetics industry. *Journal of Cleaner Production, 315*, 128–232.

Nguyen, J. K., Masub, N., & Jagdeo, J. (2020). Bioactive ingredients in Korean cosmeceuticals: Trends and research evidence. *Journal of Cosmetic Dermatology, 19*(7), 1555–1569.

Park, H. S. (2022, February 7). DNA analysis of Global Firm COSMAX, Joint venture business.

Park, Y. W., Hong, P., & Shin, G. C. (2023). Rising and thriving in the post COVID-19 era: A case study of COSMAX, a leader of the Korean cosmetic industry. *Asia Pacific Business Review, 29*(4), 1105–1124.

Park, Y. W. (2017). *Business architecture strategy and platform-based ecosystems*. Springer.

Park, Y. W. (2020). Data driven innovation: A business strategy serving the digital transformation era. In *MMRC discussion paper* (Vol. 531, pp. 1–22). (In Japanese).

Park, Y. W., Hong, P., Shin, G. C. (2019). Internet of Things and original design manufacturing business model: Case study of COSMAX. In *2019 Portland international conference on management of engineering and technology (PICMET)* (pp. 1–5).

Park, Y. W., & Hong, P. (2012). *Building network capabilities in turbulent competitive environments: Practices of global firms from Korea and Japan*. Taylor & Francis.

Reeves, M., Levin, S., Fink, T., & Levina, A. (2020). Taming complexity. *Harvard Business Review, 98*(1), 112–121.

Seyoum, B. (2021). Product modularity and performance in the global auto industry in China: The mediating roles of supply chain integration and firm relative positional advantage. *Asia Pacific Business Review, 27*(5), 651–676.
Spieth, P., Schneider, S., Clauß, T., & Eichenberg, D. (2019). Value drivers of social businesses: A business model perspective. *Long Range Planning, 52*(3), 427–444.

Chapter 8
The Art of Allure: Inside Shiseido's Groundbreaking Marketing Mastery

Abstract This chapter examines the exceptional marketing strategies of Shiseido, Japan's trailblazing cosmetics company with a heritage dating back to 1872. Shiseido's historical pivot from pharmaceuticals to cosmetics under the leadership of Fukuhara Shinzo marked the brand's rise as a cosmetics powerhouse. The company's commitment to aesthetic excellence is evident in its innovative product line, which has included pioneering offerings like non-lead face powders and early forays into floral perfumes. It also highlights Shiseido's early adoption of the chain store model and direct sales system, which became pivotal to its robust sales infrastructure. With a strong foundation rooted in tradition and innovation, Shiseido not only mastered the art of beauty but also skillfully crafted a brand identity that seamlessly wove together Eastern philosophy and Western innovation. In the realm of brand identity, Shiseido stands out with a philosophy that merges inner beauty and well-being, encapsulated in its concept of "Graceful Aging." The brand's mission, "Beautiful Moments, Beautiful Lifetimes," underscores its commitment to deliver beauty through a spectrum of products and services globally. Shiseido's expansion beyond cosmetics into restaurants and pharmaceuticals reflects its 3H policy—High Quality, High Image, High Service. The global marketing strategy, including the shift to e-commerce in China, is part of Shiseido's adaptive approach to global trends and consumer behaviors. In the digital age, Shiseido has embraced DX to reinvent its business model, aiming to lead as a Data-Driven Personal Skin Beauty & Wellness Company. This strategy marks Shiseido's dedication to innovation, customer satisfaction, and a vision that harmonizes with the evolving digital landscape.

1 Introduction: Enabling Knowledge Creation

The book "Enabling Knowledge Creation: How to Unlock the Mystery of Tacit Knowledge and Release the Power of Innovation" by Von Krogh et al. (2000), offers insights that are highly applicable to understanding its innovation dynamics. It provides valuable perspectives on the dynamics of innovation, especially in

Y. W. Park and P. Hong, *Cosmetics Marketing Strategy in the Era of the Digital Ecosystem*, https://doi.org/10.1007/978-981-97-3674-4_8

relation to the Japanese cosmetic industry. A key idea presented is the crucial role of tacit knowledge, which refers to the intuitive, often unexpressed expertise individuals possess. This form of knowledge is a cornerstone for the industry, enabling the development of innovative products that not only meet but also anticipate consumer trends. The industry's ability to harness the silent, profound understandings of its workforce, from researchers to sales teams, showcases its skill in transforming internal knowledge into market success.

Furthermore, the importance of fostering a culture that emphasizes knowledge sharing and collaboration is highlighted as essential for innovation. The Japanese cosmetic industry thrives on creating an environment where open communication and teamwork are encouraged, extending beyond internal operations to include partnerships with external entities. This collaborative atmosphere facilitates the integration of diverse insights and research, driving the creation of products that are not only innovative but also deeply attuned to consumer expectations. Such a strategy underscores the industry's commitment to staying at the cutting edge of beauty and cosmetics.

Lastly, the discussion on optimizing organizational structures to support knowledge dissemination underscores another strategy employed by the Japanese cosmetic industry. By adopting flexible and dynamic frameworks that encourage employee empowerment and risk-taking, the industry has positioned itself to quickly respond to market changes and integrate new technologies. This approach not only fosters a culture of continuous learning and innovation but also sets a standard for other sectors looking to enhance their innovative capabilities through effective knowledge management. The book's exploration of these themes offers a blueprint for leveraging tacit knowledge and collaboration to drive innovation, illustrating practices that have propelled the Japanese cosmetic industry to global prominence.

2 The Legacy and Evolution of Shiseido

Shiseido, established in 1872 in Tokyo by Arinobu Fukuhara, began as a small Western-style pharmacy in the Ginza district. Initially selling Western pharmaceuticals and imported medicines, Shiseido reflected the Meiji era's societal changes, merging Eastern herbal remedies with Western techniques. In 1897, Shiseido's pioneering introduction of its cosmetics line marked its entry into the beauty industry, offering products like face powders and lotions. Influenced by Western culture, founder Fukuhara's approach in product development, packaging, and marketing distinctively set Shiseido apart from traditional Japanese cosmetic practices.

In 1897, Shiseido took a ground-breaking step by introducing its own line of cosmetics, marking its official foray into the beauty industry. The company's early cosmetics consisted of face powders and skin lotions, catering to the evolving beauty preferences of Japanese women. The brand's founder, Arinobu Fukuhara, was deeply influenced by Western culture and innovations. This influence was evident in the company's approach to product development, packaging, and marketing, setting Shiseido apart from traditional Japanese cosmetic practices.

2.1 *Shiseido: A Journey from East to West in Beauty Innovation*

Transitioning from pharmaceuticals to cosmetics in 1915 under Fukuda Arinobu's son, Fukuhara Shinzo, represented a pivotal moment for Shiseido. Its diverse product range included skin toners, hair styling balms, toothpaste, face powders, perfumes, vanishing and cold creams, and soaps. Emphasizing quality, Shiseido's allure extended beyond its products, encompassing its Ginza locale and elegant packaging.

Innovative product launches characterized Shiseido's growth. Notably, the introduction of Japan's first skin-colored powder, Hana Oshiroi (later renamed Yayoi Oshiroi) in 1906, signaled a shift towards healthier cosmetics. The company's early tinted face powders, such as the Poudre de Riz line, were groundbreaking. The creation of perfumes like "Hanatsubaki" in 1917 and other floral fragrances underscored Shiseido's commitment to aesthetics.

Shiseido's journey through the twentieth century was marked by several pivotal milestones that shaped its strategic evolution. In 1923, the company adopted a chain store system, which significantly expanded its business reach. This expansion continued in 1927 when Shiseido became a joint-stock company. Further strengthening its position in the beauty industry, Shiseido established the Shiseido Chemical Research Laboratory in 1939, followed by the founding of a beauty school in 1959. These developments not only solidified Shiseido's presence in the cosmetics sector but also emphasized its commitment to innovation and quality.

2.2 *Shiseido's Artistic Essence: Merging Culture and Cosmetics*

Parallel to its business growth, Shiseido evolved into a cultural and artistic hub, intertwining beauty, art, and culture in a unique way that significantly enhanced its brand image and appeal. This cultural integration was particularly evident in the early twentieth century as Shiseido expanded its product range, catering to a diverse and growing consumer base both within Japan and on international fronts. The iconic camellia flower logo, introduced in 1916, became a symbol of the company's global ambitions and its dedication to beauty and elegance. Shiseido's global expansion initially targeted Asian markets and gradually extended to the United States, Europe, and beyond. The brand's commitment to research and innovation was further demonstrated through the establishment of research laboratories and collaborations with medical institutions. Embracing a holistic approach, Shiseido's philosophy evolved to encompass nature, art, culture, and personal well-being, with a focus on "Graceful Aging" and eco-friendly practices. Moreover, Shiseido diversified its business operations to include pharmaceuticals, beauty services, dining, and health foods. In the digital age, Shiseido embraced technological advancements, leveraging digital marketing and technology to offer enhanced customer experiences, thus remaining at the forefront of the beauty industry in an increasingly digital world.

2.3 *The Timeless Saga of Shiseido: Embracing Modernity and Tradition*

Shiseido's history is marked by continuous innovation and adaptation. From its establishment as a Western-style pharmacy to its evolution into a global cosmetics brand, Shiseido has maintained a focus on blending Western technology with Eastern philosophy. Its commitment to scientific research, artistic collaborations, and cultural engagement has cemented its position as a brand that transcends traditional beauty ideals. As Shiseido continues to innovate and adapt to modern trends, it remains a leader in the beauty industry, drawing on its rich heritage while embracing modernity and global trends.

Shiseido was not just a cosmetics company. Namely, it also became a hub for artistic and cultural exchange. It supported various artists and designers, fostering a unique connection between beauty, art, and culture. This association with the arts contributed significantly to its brand image and appeal.

In the early twentieth century, Shiseido expanded its product range, introducing new lines of skincare, haircare, and fragrances. This diversification allowed the brand to cater to a broader consumer base, both within Japan and internationally.

The iconic Shiseido logo, resembling a camellia flower, was created in 1916 by Fukuhara's son, Shinzo Fukuhara. Inspired by French Art Nouveau design, this logo symbolized the company's ambition to expand globally and represented its commitment to beauty and elegance. Shiseido's global expansion began in the early twentieth century, initially targeting Asian markets. By the mid-twentieth century, the brand had established a presence in the United States, Europe, and other parts of the world. Its international success was propelled by its innovative products and dedication to quality.

Throughout its history, Shiseido has been committed to research and innovation. It established research laboratories and institutes to delve into skincare, beauty science, and product development. Collaborations with medical institutions and universities bolstered its scientific approach to beauty.

Shiseido's brand philosophy evolved beyond superficial beauty. It embraced a holistic approach that encompassed nature, art, culture, and personal well-being. The brand emphasized the concept of "Graceful Aging," promoting healthy and happy aging as an integral part of beauty.

In response to global environmental concerns, Shiseido adopted eco-friendly practices. It was among the first cosmetics companies to address environmental issues, obtaining certifications for environmental management and launching initiatives to minimize its ecological footprint.

Shiseido expanded its business beyond cosmetics into pharmaceuticals, beauty services, dining, and health foods. This diversification aimed to cater to diverse consumer segments and leverage its brand image in different sectors.

In recent years, Shiseido has embraced digital transformation. The brand leverages digital marketing, e-commerce, and technology, offering virtual try-ons and personalized experiences to engage customers in an increasingly digital landscape.

Shiseido has adopted a customer-centric approach, focusing on enhancing customer experiences, understanding consumer preferences, and engaging with customers through various touchpoints. The brand continually innovates to meet evolving consumer needs.

The company's historical journey can be outlined:

1872–1915: Establishment of Shiseido as a Western-style pharmacy

1916–1926: Transition from pharmaceuticals to cosmetics

1927–1948: Creation of new value as Shiseido Co., Ltd.

1949–1956: Progress amidst economic growth

1957–1976: Expansion into global markets post-war

1977–1986: Promotion of new lifestyles through fashion

1987–1995: Merging beauty and health in the industry

1996–1999: Further globalization endeavors

2000–2011: Embracing CSR and environmental efforts

2012–2019: Embracing an Internet-based business style

2020 onward: Continual commitment to holistic beauty research and consistent brand identity.

Shiseido's ethos, blending Western technology with Eastern philosophy, places a premium on inner beauty. Its relentless scientific pursuit spans cosmetics, skin, and health over 140 years, upholding a steadfast brand identity. Shiseido's journey from a small pharmacy in Tokyo to a global beauty giant is a testament to its pioneering spirit, innovation, and adaptability. Its commitment to quality, scientific research, artistic collaborations, and cultural engagement has shaped its legacy as a brand that transcends traditional beauty ideals, embracing a more holistic definition of beauty. As it continues to evolve and innovate, Shiseido remains a leader in the beauty industry, drawing on its rich heritage while embracing modernity and global trends.

3 Shiseido's Branding Strategy

Shiseido's branding strategy is a meticulously crafted approach that interweaves its rich heritage with modern innovation, aiming to create a global identity that resonates with a diverse customer base. Central to this strategy is the harmonization of traditional Japanese aesthetics with contemporary beauty trends, which allows Shiseido to offer products that are both culturally authentic and globally appealing. The brand emphasizes quality, innovation, and a holistic approach to beauty, integrating elements of nature, art, and well-being into its products and marketing. This multifaceted strategy is not only about selling cosmetics but also about promoting a lifestyle and philosophy that appeals to the customer's sense of beauty and wellness. Shiseido's branding extends beyond product offerings to include immersive experiences, such as high-end dining and cultural engagements, further solidifying its image as a luxury brand that transcends the conventional boundaries of the cosmetics industry.

3.1 Define Brand Identity

Shiseido, established in 1872 in Tokyo by Arinobu Fukuhara, started as a small Western-style pharmacy, initially selling Western pharmaceuticals and imported medicines. Embracing the societal changes during Japan's Meiji era, Fukuhara aimed to blend Eastern herbal remedies with Western pharmaceutical techniques. In 1897, Shiseido made a significant shift into the beauty industry by introducing its own line of cosmetics, including face powders and skin lotions, catering to the changing beauty preferences of Japanese women. Influenced by Western culture, the brand's approach to product development, packaging, and marketing distinguished it from traditional Japanese cosmetic practices.

Shiseido's transition from pharmaceuticals to cosmetics under Shinzo Fukuhara, Arinobu's son, in 1915, marked a pivotal moment in its history. The company offered a diverse range of products such as skin toners, hair styling balms, toothpaste, perfumes, and soaps, all emphasizing quality. The introduction of Japan's first skin-colored powder in 1906 and the creation of perfumes like "Hanatsubaki" in 1917 were among its innovative product launches. In the 1920s and 1930s, Shiseido further solidified its market presence by adopting a chain store system, becoming a joint-stock company, and establishing a chemical research laboratory and a beauty school. These advancements not only expanded its business but also entrenched its position as a leader in the cosmetic industry.

Shiseido's expansion was not just limited to cosmetics; it also became a cultural and artistic hub, fostering a unique connection between beauty, art, and culture. This association significantly contributed to its brand image and appeal. The company's global expansion began in the early twentieth century, initially targeting Asian markets and eventually establishing a presence in the United States, Europe, and other parts of the world. Shiseido's commitment to research and innovation led to the establishment of research laboratories and collaborations with medical institutions, emphasizing a scientific approach to beauty. The brand's philosophy evolved to encompass nature, art, culture, and personal well-being, with a focus on "Graceful Aging" and eco-friendly practices. The company diversified its business to include pharmaceuticals, beauty services, dining, and health foods, embracing digital transformation to engage customers in an increasingly digital world. Adopting a customer-centric approach, Shiseido continually innovated to meet evolving consumer needs, maintaining its position as a leader in the global beauty industry.

3.2 Develop Brand Identity

In 1934, Shiseido recruited beauty consultants, training 9 Miss Shiseido candidates for seven months in beauty techniques, scientific knowledge, speech, fashion, and culture, presenting a cultured image. "Beauty Staff," renamed in 1959, evolved to include sales consultation, embodying "Omotenashi" (serving with sincerity). With societal shifts, they became "Shiseido BC (Beauty Consultants)" operating globally.

Shiseido's commitment to research led to the establishment of the "Life Science Research Laboratories" in Yokohama in 1939, focusing on molecular biology and sharing information globally. The "Institute of Beauty Science" founded in 1953 studies cosmetics from physiological, psychological, and philosophical perspectives. Shiseido's emphasis on education saw the creation of the Shiseido Beauty Fashion & Art Academy in 1985.

Shiseido's global research expanded with the "Cutaneous Biology Research Center (CBRC)" established with Harvard Medical School in 1989, focusing on health sciences. Since 1992, Shiseido pioneered environmental policies, earning ISO14001 certification for its factories in 2000, intensifying environmental protection with the "Shiseido Earth Care Project" in 2009, and launching eco-friendly products in 2014.

3.3 Determine Its Brand Frontiers

Shiseido's expansion into diverse segments illustrates its commitment to continuous innovation and adaptation. The company's foray into the culinary world began with the introduction of Western cuisine at the "Shiseido Parlour" in 1928, originally an extension of the "Soda Fountain" at the Shiseido Pharmacy. Its dedication to culinary excellence further manifested in the establishment of "L'Osier," an authentic French restaurant in 1973. Earning global recognition, "L'Osier" was awarded three Michelin stars in 2008, cementing its status as a culinary icon. Shiseido's re-entry into the pharmaceutical industry in 1987 marked another strategic diversification. By 1993, the company expanded its pharmaceutical portfolio to over 40 products, including prescription medications, showcasing its versatility and scientific expertise.

In the 1990s and 2000s, Shiseido continued to align its brand with global trends and sustainability efforts. "Royal Shiseido," established in Paris in 1992, was an embodiment of a unique fusion of French and Eastern aesthetics in perfumery, attracting tourists and fragrance enthusiasts alike. The new millennium saw Shiseido branching into men's cosmetics, health foods, and proactive responses to climate change, demonstrating its responsiveness to evolving market demands and societal concerns. This period of exploration and expansion into new domains not only broadened Shiseido's consumer base but also reinforced its reputation as a versatile and forward-thinking brand, committed to addressing the diverse needs and preferences of its global audience.

The time-intensive nature of developing and implementing such a comprehensive branding strategy stems from the need to balance tradition with innovation while also adapting to dynamic global markets. Crafting a brand identity that encapsulates the essence of a company with over a century of history requires careful consideration of its legacy, values, and vision for the future. Moreover, as Shiseido expands its reach globally, it must ensure that its brand messaging remains consistent yet adaptable to different cultural contexts and consumer preferences. This involves extensive research, market analysis, and creative development to ensure that the brand resonates in various regions without losing its core identity. Additionally, Shiseido's commitment to innovation and sustainability adds layers of complexity to its branding strategy, as it continuously evolves to incorporate new technologies, sustainable practices, and respond to changing consumer behaviors and environmental concerns. Such a multifaceted and dynamic branding approach naturally demands significant time and resources to develop and maintain effectively.

4 Unveiling Shiseido's Global Marketing Mastery

Shiseido, a titan in the beauty industry, has not just adapted to the changing tides of global commerce but has also been a trendsetter, shaping the very landscape of beauty and skincare. This transition from a broad overview to a more focused examination of their global strategy reveals the depth and breadth of Shiseido's market acumen. Their approach is not merely about expanding reach but about deepening connections with diverse markets, understanding unique cultural landscapes, and leveraging technological advancements. This strategic shift from a macro to a micro perspective in their global marketing strategy exemplifies Shiseido's commitment to marrying tradition with innovation, ensuring that each step in their global journey is as informed as it is bold.

4.1 Charting New Horizons: Shiseido's Global Expansion Blueprint

Shiseido, a renowned name in the global beauty industry, stands as a symbol of innovation, quality, and longevity in cosmetics. The company's global marketing strategy showcases its dedication to evolving and expanding into diverse markets, striking a balance between traditional expertise and cutting-edge innovation.

Shiseido's ascendancy in the global cosmetics industry is underpinned by a meticulously crafted global marketing strategy. The company's strategic vision is multifaceted, encompassing a blend of product diversification, market penetration, technological innovation, and consumer-centric approaches. Shiseido's trajectory towards global prominence has been guided by a profound understanding of cultural nuances, consumer preferences, and technological advancements across diverse geographies.

The foundation of Shiseido's global success is rooted in its rich heritage that dates back to the late nineteenth century. Established in 1872 in Ginza, Tokyo, Shiseido was founded by Fukuhara Arinobu, a visionary entrepreneur who laid the groundwork for the company's enduring legacy. Since its inception, Shiseido has consistently embodied a fusion of Eastern philosophy and Western technology, a guiding principle that still reverberates through its brand identity and marketing endeavors.

The core tenets of Shiseido's global marketing strategy include:

- Innovation and Product Development: Shiseido's relentless pursuit of innovation and product development stands as a cornerstone of its global marketing strategy. The company's commitment to R&D and cutting-edge technologies fuels the creation of skincare, makeup, fragrance, and hair care products that resonate with diverse consumer segments worldwide. Shiseido's product portfolio boasts a wide spectrum of offerings, catering to various skin types, cultural preferences, and lifestyle choices.
- Cultural Sensitivity and Localization: Shiseido's astute understanding of cultural nuances and its adeptness in localizing marketing strategies have been instrumental in its global success. The company's approach involves tailoring products, marketing campaigns, and brand experiences to resonate with the unique tastes and preferences of each market. This cultural sensitivity has enabled Shiseido to establish an emotional connection with consumers, transcending geographical boundaries.
- Digital Transformation and E-commerce Prowess: Embracing the digital era, Shiseido has spearheaded a transformative journey into the realm of e-commerce and digital marketing. The company's digital initiatives span omnichannel retailing, personalized online consultations, and leveraging data analytics to comprehend consumer behavior. This comprehensive digital footprint enables Shiseido to engage consumers on multiple platforms, delivering personalized experiences while amplifying its global reach.
- Brand Identity and Aesthetic Excellence: Shiseido's brand identity is intricately tied to aesthetic excellence and a commitment to beauty beyond external appearances. The company's philosophy of "Graceful Aging" transcends conventional

beauty standards, promoting a holistic approach to well-being and happiness. This philosophy resonates across its products, marketing endeavors, and brand ethos, fostering a loyal consumer base globally.

4.2 Tailoring Success: Market-Specific Strategies Unfolded

Shiseido's strategic focus on China marks a key element of its global marketing efforts, acknowledging China's significant role in the cosmetics market. Comprehensive strategies for this region include e-commerce expansion and product localization. In the Asia–Pacific, Shiseido customizes its approach to cater to the region's diverse markets, while in Western markets, the company adapts its strategies to fit unique consumer needs, successfully establishing its brand in these areas.

- China Focus Strategy: Shiseido's strategic focus on China represents a pivotal component of its global marketing strategy. Recognizing China's exponential growth in the cosmetics market, Shiseido has outlined comprehensive strategies, encompassing e-commerce expansion, product localization, and capitalizing on the burgeoning demand for beauty and wellness products among the Chinese demographic.
- Asia–Pacific Expansion: The Asia–Pacific region remains a strategic priority for Shiseido's global expansion efforts. The company's tailored approach to diverse markets within the region involves leveraging cultural insights, understanding local beauty preferences, and capitalizing on emerging trends to drive growth and market penetration.
- Western Market Penetration: Shiseido's presence in Western markets underscores its commitment to global diversity and expansion. By adapting marketing strategies to cater to the distinctive needs and preferences of Western consumers, Shiseido has successfully carved a niche in these markets, leveraging its brand heritage and innovative product offerings.

4.3 Conquering the Dragon: Shiseido's Chinese Market Game Plan

Shiseido's global marketing strategy, particularly in China, is a blend of sustained growth, market expansion, and innovative customer-centric approaches. The company's focus on China as a growth catalyst is evident in its three-year plan and four growth pillars—Global Mega Brands, Asia Breakthrough, New Frontier, and Customer-First. In China, Shiseido's strategies include expanding e-commerce, introducing the 'Pure Mild Soa' series, expanding 'Bare Essentials' in Hong Kong, launching 'Tsubaki,' and testing collagen drinks. These initiatives showcase Shiseido's adaptability and innovative strength in a dynamic market.

Shiseido, renowned in the cosmetics industry for its innovation and quality, has a robust Global Marketing Strategy focusing on sustained growth, market expansion, and customer-centric innovation. Central to this strategy is the emphasis on the Chinese market, identified as a significant growth catalyst. The company's three-year plan initiated in 2022, anchored by four growth pillars announced in April 2023—Global Mega Brands, Asia Breakthrough, New Frontier, and Customer-First—reflects Shiseido's commitment to fortifying its market position and leveraging China's thriving cosmetics industry.

- E-commerce Expansion in China: A Pillar of the New Frontier Strategy. Shiseido's foray into China's e-commerce landscape underscores its dynamic approach to market penetration. The introduction of the 'Pure Mild Soa' series tailored for China's post-80s demographic epitomizes Shiseido's customized consumer approach. Moreover, the brand's eco-friendly packaging initiatives, utilizing non-wood paper sourced from sugar cane, align with evolving sustainability norms, resonating strongly with environmentally conscious consumers. However, Shiseido's e-commerce venture transcends mere transactional platforms. It integrates sophisticated algorithms and customer data to offer personalized beauty recommendations. With call center support and online counseling, Shiseido aims not just to sell products but to foster lasting customer relationships, emphasizing satisfaction and loyalty.
- Expanding Bare Essentials in Hong Kong: A Core Tenet of the Global Mega Brands Strategy. Shiseido's commitment to developing multi-billion-yen brands, focusing on 'SHISEIDO,' 'Clé de Peau Beauté,' and 'Bare Essentials 'Bare Minerals,' is pivotal to its Global Mega Brands Strategy. Leveraging the synergy with Bare Essentials, acquired in March 2010, Shiseido initiated product sales in two department stores in Hong Kong via its subsidiary Shiseido Hong Kong in October 2023. Preceded by a product launch event in Hong Kong, this move reflects Shiseido's concerted effort to strengthen its presence in crucial markets.
- Introduction of Tsubaki, a Global Mega Brand, in China. Under the Mass + Prestige brands initiative within the Global Mega Brands Strategy, Shiseido is introducing 'Tsubaki,' a popular Japanese hair care brand, to China. This localized adaptation caters to the unique preferences of Chinese women. The planned launch across approximately 10,000 sales outlets, primarily hypermarkets and drugstores, is complemented by infrastructure expansion at the Shanghai factory (Shanghai Zotos Citic Cosmetics Co., Ltd.) to accommodate increased 'Tsubaki' production.
- Testing Collagen Drinks: Pioneering Healthcare in China. Amidst significant growth in China's health food market, Shiseido is venturing into collagen drinks as part of its healthcare business expansion. The company is test-launching collagen-containing beauty drinks under the "Pure Mild" brand in Japan, targeting customers seeking high-quality beauty solutions. This strategic move aligns with the "Asia Breakthrough Strategy," aiming to bolster growth in this domain by introducing these products in approximately 1,600 key Pure Mild outlets. Shiseido plans to enhance its presence in China, bolster its prestige in department store

channels, and introduce dedicated brands like "Urara" in over 5,000 cosmetics specialty store channels.

In essence, Shiseido's multi-faceted initiatives in China epitomize its adaptability and innovative prowess. These strategies not only cater to diverse market segments but also underscore Shiseido's commitment to staying ahead in an ever-evolving market landscape.

4.4 Blueprint for the Future: Shiseido's Four Pillars of Growth

Shiseido's blueprint for the future is built on four key pillars of growth: the Global Mega Brands Strategy, the Asia Breakthrough Strategy, the New Frontier Strategy, and the Customer-First Strategy.

- Shiseido's Global Mega Brands Strategy aims to nurture key brands to achieve multi-billion-yen sales, focusing on prestige brands, SHISEIDO, Clé de Peau Beauté, and Bare Essentials' Bare Mineral.
- Asia Breakthrough Strategy: Shiseido has designated Asia as its central region, with a focus on Japan, which is expected to become the world's largest market by 2020. They are pursuing activities to address specific challenges in each country, including China, which has strengths.
- New Frontier Strategy: Shiseido is actively deploying web marketing to expand contact points with customers in new areas. In Japan, they have established a new business model that integrates web and existing stores and have been deploying it since April 2012. They plan to create new growth engines by pioneering emerging markets.
- Customer-First Strategy: Shiseido places the customer as the top priority in all business processes and aims for fundamental reform by thoroughly refining product manufacturing, sales, and customer service activities.

The Global Mega Brands Strategy, in particular, is set to elevate Shiseido's position in the luxury beauty segment, capitalizing on the growing demand for premium cosmetics. The Asia Breakthrough Strategy targets the dynamic and diverse Asian markets, where beauty trends are rapidly evolving and influencing global beauty standards. With the New Frontier and Customer-First strategies, Shiseido is set to redefine the cosmetics industry, emphasizing digital innovation and customer-centric approaches to create a more personalized and satisfying consumer experience. These strategies collectively aim to propel Shiseido to new heights of global success and customer engagement.

5 Recent Digital Marketing Strategy

With over 150 years of history, Shiseido primarily relied on offline sales before the era of COVID-19. Especially in Japan's distribution structure, cosmetics sales through online channels were relatively weak compared to other products. However, with the demand for a transformation in cosmetics sales methods due to COVID-19, Shiseido is actively pursuing a DX (Digital Transformation) strategy. In January 2021, they hired Angelica Munson as their CDO (Chief Digital Officer) and established a DX promotion department. Under the long-term vision called "Win2023 and Beyond," they have reorganized their business portfolio, strengthened their skincare and beauty capabilities, and positioned DX as a core element of business reconstruction. Specifically, they are accelerating e-commerce sales and omnichannel initiatives, enhancing data analysis and digital marketing expertise, transitioning to digital business models, and building organizations. As a result, the e-commerce ratio has increased to 33% by 2022 and continues to grow in 2023. Shiseido aims to become the global No. 1 Data-Driven Personal Skin Beauty & Wellness Company by further promoting a digital marketing strategy based on DX. They plan to increase the e-commerce sales ratio to 40% and the digital media ratio to 90% by 2025, while also focusing on enhancing customer experiences as a beauty tech company, including expanding personalized service offerings based on customer data and utilizing AI for skin diagnosis.

Shiseido's digital marketing strategy is a holistic approach that leverages various digital channels to create personalized experiences and engage with customers to drive sales. Central to this strategy is their omnichannel approach, which integrates different digital platforms to offer a consistent and unified brand experience. This includes their website, social media, mobile applications, and in-store experiences. Additionally, Shiseido understands the power of social media and likely maintains a strong presence on platforms such as Instagram, Facebook, Twitter, and YouTube, focusing on community building, customer engagement, and influencer partnerships. Their content marketing efforts, crucial in the digital landscape, probably involve creating engaging and informative content like tutorials, behind-the-scenes glimpses, beauty tips, and user-generated content.

The company also places a high emphasis on personalization and customer experience. They employ data-driven strategies to provide personalized recommendations and targeted advertising based on user behavior, ensuring a more engaging and relevant experience for each customer. In tandem with this, Shiseido's e-commerce and mobile strategy are likely optimized for a seamless shopping experience, acknowledging the increasing use of mobile devices for shopping. Their influencer marketing strategy, involving collaborations with influencers and beauty experts, plays a significant role in their digital marketing. This helps them create content, promote products, and reach a wider audience, leveraging the influencers' credibility and reach in the beauty industry.

Shiseido's approach to data analytics and AI is an integral component of their marketing efforts. They use these tools to gain insights into customer behavior, preferences, and market trends, which assist in making informed marketing decisions and optimizing campaigns. The incorporation of virtual try-on features and augmented reality (AR) technology is another innovative aspect, enhancing the online shopping experience by allowing customers to virtually try products. Furthermore, acknowledging the increasing emphasis on sustainability, Shiseido likely highlights its commitment to eco-friendly practices through digital campaigns, engaging with a customer base that values sustainability. Lastly, customer feedback and engagement are crucial to Shiseido; they actively engage with customers through surveys, reviews, and social media interactions to understand their preferences, address concerns, and build stronger relationships.

6 Navigating Global Trends with Local Sensibilities

Japanese cosmetic firms, characterized by their innovative approaches and global marketing strategies, have consistently adapted to meet both domestic and international consumer needs. The exploration of international cosmetics advertising in Japan reveals the nuanced marketing strategies that these firms employ. They are tailored to resonate with a diverse consumer base, all the while maintaining a deep appreciation for Japanese aesthetic values. This blend of global appeal and cultural authenticity has been pivotal in the industry's success (Barnes & Yamamoto, 2008). Moreover, the integration of advanced research methodologies, as discussed by Clithero et al., underscores the industry's commitment to leveraging cutting-edge science and technology to deeply understand consumer psychology and preferences. This dedication to innovation, grounded in a profound understanding of both market trends and scientific advancement, has enabled Japanese cosmetic firms to lead in product development and customer engagement (Clithero et al., 2024).

Shiseido embodies these industry characteristics while also carving out a distinct identity that has contributed to its longstanding success. Shiseido's journey from a small pharmacy to a global cosmetics powerhouse is a testament to its strategic growth, adaptability, and visionary leadership (Shiseido Homepage; Umemura & Slater, 2017). The company's focus on research and development, highlighted by Sasson, Silva, and Ratledge's work on biotechnological advancements, has positioned Shiseido at the forefront of utilizing plant cell cultures and other innovations to create products that are both effective and environmentally sustainable (Sasson et al., 1992). Furthermore, Shiseido's ability to harness tacit knowledge and cultivate a culture of continuous learning and innovation, as suggested by Von Krogh, Ichijo, and Nonaka, has been crucial in its efforts to not just respond to consumer needs but to anticipate and shape them (Von Krogh et al., 2000). This blend of heritage, innovation, and global strategic vision continues to drive Shiseido's success, setting a benchmark for excellence within the Japanese cosmetics industry and beyond.

7 Conclusion: Shiseido's Odyssey: Pioneering Beauty Across Centuries

In concluding our exploration of Shiseido's remarkable journey, we witness a narrative that transcends the story of a mere company to become an emblem of innovation, elegance, and cultural depth within the beauty industry. Shiseido's evolution is a testament to a brand that has adeptly blended its rich heritage with forward-thinking strategies, seamlessly navigating the changing landscapes of consumer trends and preferences across different eras and regions. From its inception as a modest pharmacy in Tokyo to its rise as a global beauty powerhouse, Shiseido's story is marked by strategic innovation and expansion, each phase signifying a crucial era in its storied history.

Legacy of Innovation and Adaptability: Shiseido's transition from a Western-style pharmacy founded in 1872 by Arinobu Fukuhara into a leading global beauty brand showcases its commitment to innovation and adaptability. The brand's unique fusion of Eastern herbal wisdom with Western scientific practices carved a niche for Shiseido, further solidified when it expanded into cosmetics in 1897. This not only affirmed its dedication to quality and elegance but also positioned Shiseido as a cultural and artistic beacon, deepening consumer connections and enhancing its brand image.

Strategic Growth and Global Expansion: Shiseido's trajectory is highlighted by key milestones and strategic decisions that underscore its growth and global outreach. The creation of the Shiseido Chemical Research Laboratory in 1939 and its expansion into international markets exemplify its resilience and visionary ethos. The brand's iconic camellia logo symbolizes its aesthetic and global ambitions, while its embrace of the "Graceful Aging" philosophy has innovatively shifted beauty paradigms towards holistic well-being. Through diversification into sectors like pharmaceuticals, beauty services, and health foods, Shiseido demonstrates an unparalleled adaptability to consumer trends and a robust brand presence across industries.

Embracing the Future with Digital Innovation: In the face of the digital revolution, Shiseido has pivoted towards embracing technological advancements and digital marketing strategies, particularly focusing on market diversification in regions such as China. Its strategic digital transformation, encompassing omnichannel marketing, social media, and e-commerce optimization, reflects Shiseido's agility and commitment to innovation. This blend of legacy and forward-looking strategies underscores Shiseido's enduring mission to redefine beauty standards, marrying its historical essence with contemporary trends to navigate the future landscape of the beauty industry.

As Shiseido forges ahead, it invites further scholarly inquiry into its business and marketing strategies, offering a fertile ground for research into its sustainability efforts, digital transformation, consumer behavior in key markets, and response to global challenges. Such studies would not only enrich our understanding of Shiseido's strategic directions but also illuminate the broader implications for the beauty industry's future, showcasing the enduring impact of a brand that continues to inspire with its legacy of beauty, innovation, and cultural significance.

References

Barnes, B., & Yamamoto, M. (2008). Exploring international cosmetics advertising in Japan. *Journal of Marketing Management, 24*(3–4), 299–316.

Clithero, J. A., Karmarkar, U. R., Nave, G., & Plassmann, H. (2024). Reconsidering the path for neural and physiological methods in consumer psychology. *Journal of Consumer Psychology, 34*(1), 196–213.

Shiseido Homepage. https://corp.shiseido.com/en/

Sasson, A., Silva, E., & Ratledge, C. (1992). Production of useful biochemicals by higher-plant cell cultures: Biotechnological and economic aspects. *Biotechnology-Economic and Social Aspects: Issues for Developing Countries*, 81–109.

Umemura, M., & Slater, S. (2017). Reaching for global in the Japanese cosmetics industry, 1951 to 2015: The case of Shiseido. *Business History, 59*(6), 877–903.

Von Krogh, G., Ichijo, K., & Nonaka, I. (2000). *Enabling knowledge creation: How to unlock the mystery of tacit knowledge and release the power of innovation.* Oxford University Press.

Williamson, P. J. (2007). From a national to a metanational ecosystem: Harnessing the value of global knowledge diversity. *The Digital Business Ecosystem*, 82–100.

Chapter 9
Transformation in Beauty: LG Life and Health's Bold Marketing Evolution

Abstract This chapter "Transformation in Beauty," explores the dynamic evolution of LG Life and Health (LG H&H) in the global cosmetic industry, emphasizing its innovative strategies and growth. It traces LG H&H's journey from its beginnings in 1947 as Lucky Chemical Industry, highlighting milestones like South Korea's first tube toothpaste and the launch of key cosmetic brands. The narrative describes how LG H&H, under effective leadership, grew to dominate the domestic household goods market, venturing into various sectors and continuously innovating. The study illustrates LG H&H's resilience in navigating market changes, including the COVID-19 pandemic, and its ability to maintain growth through strategic leadership transitions and market adaptations. It further delves into LG H&H's branding and global expansion strategies, detailing its re-entry into the cosmetics market and the development of diverse cosmetic brands catering to different market segments. LG H&H's approach to overcoming challenges in the Chinese market, its shift towards color cosmetics, and its strategic acquisition of the premium brand 'Hince' are highlighted. This move aims to capture the Japanese market and the MZ generation, demonstrating LG H&H's adaptability and foresight. The discussion covers LG H&H's unique digital marketing strategies, including its foray into NFTs with the 'belif Universe' collection and collaborations with influencers, showcasing the company's innovative approach to engaging the digital-savvy younger generation. The narrative concludes with a look at LG H&H's future strategies, focusing on improving profitability, restructuring operations, and exploring new markets and digital trends, positioning it for sustained growth and market leadership.

1 Introduction

The global cosmetic industry is renowned for its intense competition and ever-evolving nature, with Korean cosmetic firms emerging as key players in this challenging landscape. These firms are gaining recognition for their innovative products and successful global market expansion. This chapter aims to delve into the strategic landscape of the Korean cosmetic industry, focusing specifically on LG Life and

Y. W. Park and P. Hong, *Cosmetics Marketing Strategy in the Era of the Digital Ecosystem*, https://doi.org/10.1007/978-981-97-3674-4_9

Health (LG H&H). Korean companies, including LG H&H, have managed to blend tradition with modernity, creating products that draw from ancient beauty wisdom while incorporating advanced technology. This approach has not only garnered them a global following but also set new industry benchmarks. Despite fierce competition, LG H&H exemplifies Korean excellence, making significant impacts in the global cosmetic market.

Tracing back its legacy to 1947, LG H&H, originally known as "Lucky Chemical Industry," was established by Mr. Gu In-hoe in Busan. Starting with the production of 'Lucky Cream,' the company laid the foundation for its future endeavors. Key milestones include the development of South Korea's first tube toothpaste in 1954, expansion into soap production, and the introduction of the country's first cosmetics soap in 1960 and shampoo in 1967. The company's commitment to diversification led to the construction of a synthetic detergent factory in 1966. The pivotal restructuring in 1968 and subsequent changes, including strategic partnerships and brand introductions, marked significant phases in the company's evolution.

Korean global firms, particularly in the cosmetic industry, have showcased a remarkable journey of growth and resilience that serves as a testament to their ability to rise from modest beginnings (Rugman & Oh, 2008). These companies, including giants like LG Household & Health Care (LG H&H), have demonstrated an exceptional capacity to innovate and expand on a global scale, despite starting from situations that could metaphorically be described as 'out of nothing or ashes.' This ability to emerge and thrive can be attributed to their strategic approach to blending traditional wisdom with cutting-edge technology, setting new benchmarks in the highly competitive cosmetic industry. The narrative of these firms emphasizes the significance of necessity-based innovation and adaptability in navigating the complexities of global markets (Park, Oh & Fujimoto, 2012; Kim, 2013).

The rapid transition of Korean firms, driven by necessity-based innovation, has been a key factor in their growth and global expansion. LG H&H's evolution from its early days as "Lucky Chemical Industry" showcases how these firms have capitalized on crisis moments to foster growth and strengthen their market position. By continuously adapting their product lines and embracing technological advancements, they have managed to not only survive but also excel in the face of global challenges. This growth out of crisis is exemplified by LG H&H's strategic decisions during pivotal restructuring phases and its expansion into diverse product offerings (Kim, 2010). Furthermore, their excellence in supply chain integration highlights the importance of efficient operations and international partnerships in maintaining competitiveness (Hong & Kim, 2012; Park, Shintaku & Hong, 2015a, 2015b). Korean firms' ability to navigate through crises, coupled with their supply chain expertise, has cemented their status as leaders in the global business landscape, particularly within the dynamic cosmetic industry.

The transformation into LG H&H in 2001, following LG Chemical's corporate split, marked a new era of growth and expansion. Since 2005, strategic mergers and acquisitions have been instrumental in its international outreach. This included joint ventures, acquisitions of companies like The Face Shop, and expansions into the derma cosmetics sector. Presently, LG H&H operates across household goods, cosmetics, and food and beverage sectors, demonstrating a strong market presence. Leadership changes, including the appointment of the first female CEO, and the achievement of significant sales milestones, such as the success of its 'Megabrand' household goods, reflect the company's resilience and adaptability.

This journey of LG H&H, from a modest beginning to a dominant force in the global cosmetic industry, serves as an inspiring case study. It shows how dedication, innovation, and a consumer-focused approach can lead to remarkable achievements in skincare and beauty. As LG H&H continues to navigate the complexities of the global market, its story remains a beacon of inspiration and a testament to the dynamic nature of the cosmetic industry. Future research could delve deeper into LG H&H's strategies, exploring how they continue to innovate and adapt in an ever-changing global landscape.

2 Navigating Change: LG H&H's Brand Strategy

The brand strategy of Korean firms like LG Household & Health (LG H&H) has been pivotal in their ascendance on the global stage, a strategy deeply rooted in the consistent improvement of products and services through firm-level independent efforts. This approach has allowed Korean companies to not only adapt to but also shape consumer preferences and trends worldwide. Korean firms have developed their international brand strategies, emphasizing the importance of innovation, quality enhancement, and brand localization to meet diverse consumer needs (Cheng et al., 2005; Jeong et al., 2019; Lee et al., 2008). This dedication to excellence and adaptability to local tastes and preference has enabled LG H&H to distinguish itself in the competitive cosmetics market, reflecting a broader trend among Korean firms to leverage brand strength as a key component of their international success (Jeong et al., 2019).

Furthermore, the growth of Korea's national brand has been significantly influenced by the global popularity of its cultural products, such as K-pop, which has played a crucial role in enhancing the country's image and the appeal of its products and services worldwide. The Korean Wave, or "Hallyu" has contributed to a favorable perception of Korean brands, creating a strong foundation for companies like LG H&H to expand their reach (Kim & Hong, 2017; Kim and Park, 2020). This cultural phenomenon has allowed Korean companies to integrate cultural affinity into their branding strategies, making their products not just commodities but also carriers of cultural value. LG H&H, leveraging the halo effect of Korea's national brand growth, has effectively utilized the allure of Korean culture to appeal to consumers globally, illustrating the powerful synergy between national branding and corporate success in the international market (Kim and Lee, 2018).

LG Household & Health (LG H&H) has cemented its position as a leader in South Korea's cosmetics industry since 2018, overtaking Amorepacific in market share. The company's journey began in 1947 with the introduction of 'Lucky Cream' by Lucky Chemical Industry. Initially focusing on cosmetics, the company temporarily halted its cosmetics research in 1949, only to re-enter the industry in 1982 through a partnership with Germany's Beiersdorf, leading to the creation of 'Nivea Cream.' The launch of the 'Debon' brand in 1984 marked a significant resurgence in LG H&H's cosmetic ventures.

2.1 Evolving Sales Strategies and Brand Growth

LG H&H initially adopted door-to-door sales, a popular approach in the domestic cosmetics market, later shifting to discount corners, now known as cosmetics specialty stores. By its fifth-year post-launch in 1989, LG H&H had surged to second place in the industry. The launch of the 'Lacvert' brand in 1996, featuring a memorable advertisement with Kim Nam-joo, further solidified its market position. The introduction of the 'LG H&H' brand in 1997 during the Lifelong CU era propelled 'Isanox' to fame and laid the groundwork for the success of other brands, with LG H&H gaining recognition for refraining from animal testing.

LG H&H's portfolio includes premium brands like 'The History of Whoo,' 'OHUI,' 'Sulwhasoo,' 'Belif,' as well as mid-priced and lower-priced brands. Strategic mergers and acquisitions until 2020 propelled LG H&H from the 7th global company to the top spot in South Korea. However, since 2020, the company faced challenges in the cosmetics business due to its heavy reliance on the Chinese market, significantly impacted by COVID-19.

To counteract the setback, LG H&H refocused its strategy in 2021, concentrating on bolstering its color cosmetics portfolio. The heavy reliance on the luxury cosmetics brand 'Whoo' posed challenges amidst China's economic downturn. To address this, LG H&H diversified its international presence, shifting focus from basic products to color cosmetics targeting the MZ generation.

2.2 Acquisition of Viva Wave and Focus on the MZ Generation

In 2023, LG H&H acquired a 75% stake in Viva Wave, owner of the premium color cosmetics brand 'Hince,' launched in 2019. 'Hince' emphasizes emotion and mood concepts, resonating with the MZ generation. Its notable products like 'Second Skin Foundation' and 'True Dimension Radiance Balm' have garnered a dedicated fan base among younger consumers.

Despite facing challenges, LG H&H has established various sales channels, including online malls and H&B stores like Olive Young. However, the company's efforts in the North American market have yet to produce visible results. In early 2023, LG H&H initiated a restructuring of its North American business, focusing on operational efficiency under the leadership of Vice President Moon Hye-young.

In 2023, LG H&H's Refreshment business continued to grow, but the Beauty division faced recovery challenges post-COVID-19. Despite declining sales in major channels like duty-free and Chinese domestic markets, domestic sales in South Korea showed growth. LG H&H also conducted rebranding activities for its luxury brand 'Whoo' and introduced new products in its premium brand portfolio.

The beverage business witnessed revenue growth, driven by non-carbonated and energy drinks. LG H&H bolstered its product lineup with launches aligning with health trends and engaged in marketing activities to connect with consumers. Despite the challenges, LG H&H remains focused on nurturing its premium brands and expanding its market reach, demonstrating resilience and adaptability in a constantly evolving industry.

3 Expanding Horizons

As LG Household & Health (LG H&H) embarked on this transformative journey, the goal was clear: to create a diversified conglomerate capable of weathering market fluctuations and capturing new opportunities. This shift in strategy represented a significant departure from LG H&H's earlier focus, demonstrating a keen understanding of the dynamic nature of the global market. The company recognized that to maintain and expand its market presence, it needed to diversify its portfolio and enter new sectors. This realization set the stage for the series of strategic decisions and acquisitions that followed, reshaping LG H&H into a multifaceted powerhouse. The integration of these diverse businesses not only broadened LG H&H's market reach but also provided a balanced portfolio that could leverage cross-sectoral strengths and offset potential risks in specific markets.

3.1 Strategic Initiatives and Key Acquisitions

LG H&H sets itself apart from competitors like Amorepacific by expanding beyond the cosmetics realm. Starting around 2005, under Vice Chairman Cha Seok-yong's leadership, LG H&H embarked on an aggressive merger and acquisition (M&A) strategy, diversifying its business across consumer goods, cosmetics, and beverages. The company's M&A approach aimed to strengthen each business division, establishing LG H&H as a dominant player in these sectors.

Key acquisitions began in 2007 with Coca-Cola beverages, followed by the acquisition of Diamond Sammul in 2009. Subsequent significant purchases included The Face Shop, Haitai Beverages, Violet Dream Cosmetics, Ginza Stephanie, Everlife, Fruits & Passion, and Youngjin Pharmaceutical's drink division. In 2014, the acquisition of CNP Cosmetics, under the Cha and Park brand, marked LG H&H's entry into the cosmeceutical market. This strategy helped counteract seasonal risks in the cosmetics sector, providing balance with the beverage division's performance.

3.2 Business Expansion and International Growth

LG H&H's successful M&A strategy has led to a robust portfolio across three main divisions: consumer goods (featuring brands like Perio, Jukyeom, Tech, Safran, Elastin), cosmetics (including OHUI, Whoo, Sulwhasoo, Belif, Prostin, Dabi, Cashé, The Face Shop, VDL), and beverages (such as Coca-Cola, Sprite, Fanta, Minute Maid, Powerade).

In the consumer goods division, LG H&H enhanced its product offerings with innovative items like 'Han-Ip Laundry Detergent,' 'Elastin Perfume Shampoo,' 'Perio Total 7' toothpaste, and 'Safran Flower Mint.' These products helped drive market engagement. Additionally, LG H&H's M&A initiatives aimed at expanding its global presence, reaching over 20 countries, including the UK, Canada, Australia, Russia, and the Middle East. This expansion was part of a broader strategy to proliferate K-beauty's influence worldwide, with overseas cosmetics sales surpassing 20% since 2015.

In China, the 'Whoo' brand saw rapid growth by leveraging its identity as 'Korean royal court herbal cosmetics.' Belif expanded its global footprint, entering Sephora stores in the United States in 2015 and becoming the first Korean prestige cosmetics brand to target the U.S. market. Despite the challenges posed by COVID-19, especially in the Chinese market, the potential for further growth in high-end cosmetics remains substantial.

LG H&H's global M&A strategy has been a critical driver of its expansion and dominance in the consumer goods and cosmetics sectors. By strategically acquiring and integrating diverse brands, the company has not only fortified its market position but also established a significant international presence, showcasing the power and potential of Korean beauty and consumer products on the global stage.

4 LG H&H's Digital Marketing Initiatives in the Post-COVID Era

Recognizing the dramatic shift in consumer behavior and market dynamics during the post-COVID era, LG Household & Health (LG H&H) has strategically realigned its marketing approach to harness the potential of digital platforms. This realignment signifies a proactive response to the increasing digitalization of consumer interactions and the growing importance of online presence in the beauty industry. LG H&H's foray into innovative digital marketing techniques and online sales channels is not just a reaction to the pandemic's challenges but a visionary step towards future-proofing the brand in an increasingly digital world. By integrating cutting-edge digital initiatives such as NFTs with traditional marketing strategies, LG H&H is poised to offer a more immersive and engaging brand experience to consumers worldwide.

4.1 NFT Ventures and Digital Marketing Innovations

In response to market changes brought about by the COVID-19 pandemic, LG Household & Health (LG H&H) has embraced a robust digital marketing strategy, focusing on online sales to adapt to the evolving post-COVID era. A key part of this strategy involved venturing into the issuance of Non-Fungible Tokens (NFTs) in early 2022, marking a pioneering move in South Korea's beauty industry.

The launch of the 'belif Universe Collection' and related NFTs in 2022 signifies this new direction. The 'belif Universe' brings to life a world of imaginative characters, including the hub shop clerks 'Beli' and 'Eli,' and others like 'Doctor Duncan' and 'Brownie,' interlinked with the belif product line. The NFTs feature characters like 'Beli' and 'Roy,' aligning with LG H&H's premium beauty brands and targeting the MZ generation with a focus on brand loyalty and digital engagement rather than investment.

LG H&H's digital marketing strategy has extended to other brands as well, with the introduction of the 'Doctor Groot Universe Collection' NFT in July 2022. This collection explores the world of the hair loss care brand 'Doctor Groot,' offering consumers a unique blend of character-driven narrative and product value. Emphasizing generative art, this approach caters to both NFT collectors and brand enthusiasts.

4.2 Influencer Collaboration and International Market Engagement

LG H&H has also leveraged influencer-based product development as a key component of its digital marketing strategy. A notable example is the collaboration between the makeup brand 'VDL' and beauty influencer 'Office Worker A.' This partnership led to the creation of the 'Perfecting Silky Fit Cover Cushion Foundation' and 'Perfecting Silky Fit Powder,' products that resonated strongly in the Japanese market.

The development process involved extensive consumer research and adaptation to the unique makeup habits of Japanese women. This collaboration resulted in a significant surge in VDL's online sales in Japan and plans for further expansion into Japanese offline stores. The successful launch of the Perfecting Silky Fit line exemplifies LG H&H's commitment to understanding and catering to diverse consumer preferences, marking a strategic shift in the company's approach to international markets.

LG H&H's digital marketing strategy, characterized by innovative ventures into NFTs and influencer collaborations, demonstrates the company's agility in adapting to the digital landscape and its commitment to engaging with consumers in meaningful and technologically advanced ways. As LG H&H continues to explore these new frontiers, it solidifies its position as a leader in the beauty industry, capable of navigating the complexities of the digital age while expanding its global influence.

5 Charting the Future: LG H&H's Strategic Vision

At the heart of LG Household & Health's (LG H&H) new direction lies a comprehensive re-evaluation of its global strategy, aligning with the evolving demands of the modern consumer and the shifting landscapes of the cosmetics industry. This strategic pivot is not merely a reaction to the challenges brought about by the pandemic but a proactive move to stay ahead in a highly competitive and rapidly changing market. In 2023, LG H&H's decision to restructure its business model, particularly its approach to retail and distribution, exemplifies a bold step towards embracing more digital and flexible operations. This move reflects a broader industry trend where traditional retail is increasingly giving way to innovative, digitally-driven business models. As LG H&H prepares to delve into the details of its redefined strategy, it is poised to illustrate how adaptive measures can lead to sustained growth and greater market relevance in a post-COVID world.

5.1 Redefining the Game: LG H&H's Blueprint

In 2023, LG Household & Health (LG H&H) embarked on a transformative journey, reshaping its operations to enhance profitability and adapt to the rapidly changing cosmetics industry. This strategic pivot involved withdrawing from offline franchise stores, notably 'The Face Shop,' and transitioning to simplified supply contracts with 406 franchise stores, a significant change reported by the Seoul Newspaper on November 23, 2023. This decision was influenced by dramatic shifts in South Korea's cosmetics distribution landscape, characterized by a rise in multi-brand concept stores like 'CJ Olive Young' and a growing preference for online shopping.

Simultaneously, LG H&H began phasing out high-cost stores in Southeast Asia and certain offline outlets in China, indicating a strategic refocus on operational efficiency. However, challenges remain, particularly in diversifying market strategies and reviving sluggish sales in the Chinese market, where dependency on duty-free channels has been significant. Despite the renewal of 'The History of Whoo' products in China, LG H&H's largest overseas market, sales have been underwhelming. Nevertheless, the 2023 acquisition of the color cosmetics brand 'HINCE' signals a strategic move into the competitive Japanese market.

5.2 Adapting to Change: LG H&H's Strategic Responses

The restructuring of LG H&H's domestic franchise operations marks a crucial adaptation to South Korea's evolving cosmetics sector. Moving away from physical franchise stores like 'The Face Shop' to more flexible supply contracts reflects a shift in consumer behavior towards multi-brand concept stores and online shopping. This strategic realignment positions LG H&H to respond more effectively to market demands.

Yet, LG H&H's gradual withdrawal from high-cost stores in Southeast Asia and China has sparked criticism regarding its pace in diversifying market approaches, particularly in light of the protracted recovery in the Chinese market and heavy reliance on duty-free channels. Despite attempts to rejuvenate its brand presence in China, LG H&H faces ongoing sales challenges. The acquisition of 'HINCE' represents a proactive step towards expanding LG H&H's presence into new markets, particularly targeting the distinct consumer base of Japan. This move could provide a crucial foothold in the Japanese beauty sector, renowned for its discerning customers and competitive environment.

5.3 Embracing Opportunities Amidst Challenges

LG H&H's 2023 restructuring initiatives signify a strategic pivot towards more adaptive and cost-efficient business models. Aligning with changing consumer preferences, the company is focusing on multi-brand concept stores and online platforms, while recalibrating its overseas presence.

Navigating through these transformative changes, LG H&H confronts several challenges. The slow recovery in the Chinese market and a high dependence on duty-free sales present hurdles in the company's international expansion plans.

Furthermore, LG H&H needs to swiftly adapt its market strategies to rebound in key overseas markets. The strategic entry into the Japanese market with 'HINCE' offers promising growth prospects. However, success in this new venture will require a deep understanding of Japanese consumer behaviors and an effective market penetration strategy. LG H&H's restructuring and strategic shifts position it to navigate the complexities of the global cosmetics industry effectively. Overcoming challenges in key markets while leveraging new opportunities will be crucial for LG H&H to maintain its leadership and continue its legacy in the ever-evolving beauty industry.

6 LG H&H's Journey of Resilience and Innovation in the Beauty Industry

Amidst these strategic shifts and market adaptations, LG Household & Health (LG H&H) stands at a crucial juncture, poised to redefine its approach to the global beauty industry. This period of transformation is characterized not just by reactive changes but by a proactive vision that seeks to anticipate and shape future trends. As LG H&H pivots from traditional retail models to embrace more digital and flexible operations, it exemplifies a broader industry trend where innovation and adaptability are key to success. The company's ability to recognize and respond to these shifts, especially in a post-pandemic world, sets the stage for the strategic initiatives and market expansions detailed in the sections to follow. LG H&H's journey, therefore, is not just about overcoming challenges but also about seizing opportunities to innovate and grow in a rapidly evolving beauty landscape.

6.1 Navigating Industry Shifts and Expanding Horizons

LG Household & Health (LG H&H) has long been a beacon of innovation and adaptability in South Korea's cosmetics realm. From its humble beginnings as 'Lucky Chemical Industry' in 1947, the company has charted a course marked by pioneering products and strategic growth, encompassing consumer goods, cosmetics, and beverages. LG H&H's response to the COVID-19 pandemic in 2023 epitomizes its agile approach, as seen in the decision to move away from offline franchise stores, including the notable 'The Face Shop.' This move, a reflection of changing consumer preferences favoring multi-brand stores and online shopping, signifies LG H&H's adaptability to evolving market trends. However, the company faced criticism for its slower pace in diversifying its market strategy, especially in the sluggish recovery of key markets like China, even as it strove to rejuvenate flagship products such as 'The History of Whoo.'

In response to these challenges and as part of its strategy to tap into new markets, LG H&H acquired the Japanese color cosmetics brand 'HINCE.' This move represents a strategic shift, demonstrating LG H&H's ambition to explore new territories and cater to a wider range of consumer demographics. This acquisition not only diversifies LG H&H's portfolio but also opens doors to new opportunities in the competitive Japanese market.

6.2 Embracing Digital Innovation and Consumer-Centric Approaches

LG H&H's venture into the digital realm, particularly with the introduction of the 'belif Universe' and related NFTs, highlights the company's commitment to staying ahead in the digital age. Targeting the MZ generation, this initiative reflects LG H&H's focus on creating immersive and engaging brand experiences. By embracing digital marketing strategies like NFTs, LG H&H is not only adapting to the preferences of a digitally savvy consumer base but also setting new standards in the beauty industry.

As LG H&H continues to navigate the complexities of the beauty industry, its focus on digital engagement, adaptive strategies, and consumer-centric approaches distinguishes it from its peers. The company's shift towards online retail and embracing multi-brand concepts indicates a keen understanding of the changing consumer landscape. LG H&H's resilience in the face of industry challenges underscores its dedication to redefining beauty standards and making lasting contributions to the global cosmetics sphere. This dynamic evolution, balancing tradition with innovation, cements LG H&H's position as a trailblazer in the beauty industry, poised to shape its future with pioneering initiatives and a forward-thinking mindset.

6.3 Future Research Directions in LG H&H's Digital and Consumer-Centric Strategies

As LG Household & Health (LG H&H) continues to break new ground in the beauty industry with its digital innovations and consumer-focused strategies, several areas emerge as key topics for future research. Firstly, a comprehensive analysis of consumer behavior in response to LG H&H's digital initiatives, such as the 'belif Universe' NFTs, would offer valuable insights. Investigating how these digital tools influence customer engagement, brand loyalty, and purchasing decisions could provide a deeper understanding of the effectiveness of NFTs and similar digital assets in marketing. Additionally, research into how different demographics, particularly the MZ generation, interact with and perceive these digital strategies would be beneficial. This could include studies on consumer attitudes towards digital collectibles and their impact on brand perception and value.

Another important area for future research is the assessment of LG H&H's shift towards online retail and multi-brand concepts. This could involve exploring the operational challenges and opportunities of transitioning from traditional retail models to digital platforms. In-depth case studies on the performance of LG H&H's online channels versus traditional stores, especially in the context of changing consumer shopping behaviors post-pandemic, would be enlightening. Furthermore, evaluating the success of LG H&H's multi-brand strategies in various international markets could uncover best practices and areas for improvement. This research could also delve into how LG H&H manages brand identity and customer experience across different digital platforms and physical outlets.

In essence, future research in these areas would not only enhance the understanding of LG H&H's current strategies but also provide strategic insights for other companies in the beauty industry looking to navigate the digital landscape effectively. This research could contribute significantly to the broader discussion on digital transformation in the retail sector and the evolving relationship between brands and consumers in the digital era.

References

Cheng, J. M. S., Blankson, C., Wu, P. C., & Chen, S. S. (2005). A stage model of international brand development: The perspectives of manufacturers from two newly industrialized economies—South Korea and Taiwan. *Industrial Marketing Management, 34*(5), 504–514.

Hong, P., & Kim, S. C. (2012). Business network excellence for competitive advantage: Case of Korean firms. *International Journal of Business Excellence, 5*(5), 448–462.

Jeong, I., Lee, J. H., & Kim, E. (2019). Determinants of brand localization in international markets. *Service Business, 13*, 75–100.

Kim, J. N. (2010). Korean Firms Come out Winners from Global Crisis. *SERI Quarterly, 3*(3), 30–39.

Kim, J., & Lee, M. (2018). Nation branding or marketization? K-Classic and Korean classical musicians in an era of globalization. *International journal of cultural policy, 24*(6), 756–772.

Kim, N., & Hong, L. (2017). The power of culture in branding: How the Korean Wave can help global brands thrive in Asia. *Journal of Brand Strategy, 6*(3), 293–307.

Kim, S. Y. (2013). The rise of East Asia's global companies. *Global Policy, 4*(2), 184–193.

Kim, S. M., & Park, M. J. (2020). Evaluation of cross-national global market segmentation and strategy: The case of Korean Wave for ASEAN countries. *Asia Pacific Management Review, 25*(4), 207–215.

Lee, M. Y., Knight, D., & Kim, Y. K. (2008). Brand analysis of a US global brand in comparison with domestic brands in Mexico, Korea, and Japan. *Journal of Product & Brand Management, 17*(3), 163–174.

LG Household & Health Hompage. https://www.lghnh.com/global/

Park, Y., Oh, J., & Fujimoto, T. (2012). Global expansion and supply chain integration: Case study of Korean firms. *International Journal of Procurement Management, 4*, 5(4), 470–485.

Park, Y. W., Shintaku, J., & Hong, P. (2015a). Effective supply chain integration: Case studies for Korean global firms in China. *International Journal of Manufacturing Technology and Management, 29*(3–4), 161–179.

Park, Y. R., Song, S., Choe, S., & Baik, Y. (2015b). Corporate social responsibility in international business: Illustrations from Korean and Japanese electronics MNEs in Indonesia. *Journal of Business Ethics, 129*, 747–761.

Rugman, A. M., & Oh, C. H. (2008). Korea's multinationals in a regional world. *Journal of World Business, 43*(1), 5–15.

Chapter 10
Crafting Elegance: Amorepacific's Innovative Approach to Cosmetic Marketing

Abstract This chapter, "Crafting Elegance: Amorepacific's Innovative Approach to Cosmetic Marketing," highlights the journey and strategies of Amorepacific, a leading Korean cosmetic company renowned for its innovation and global influence in promoting K-beauty. The company, which originated as Pacific before rebranding, has played a pivotal role in shaping the global cosmetics industry. With a workforce of over 5,000 and significant annual revenues, the company's primary income stems from its cosmetic products, contributing to 88.63% of its sales. The historical evolution of Amorepacific is marked by its expansion into various cosmetic and non-cosmetic ventures, significant restructuring in the 1990s, and strategic focus on digital and global marketing. The construction of their headquarters in 2017 and the development of Amorepacific Group in 2011 underscore their commitment to growth and innovation. The brand strategy centers around a diverse range of cosmetic and household products, with a special focus on Asian Beauty. The company's wordmark symbolizes the harmony of contrasts, encompassing the philosophy of blending outer and inner beauty, tradition and innovation, reason and emotion, nature and science. Its marketing strategies have been customer-centric since its inception, with significant developments like the first beauty counseling room in South Korea and the pioneering of door-to-door sales system. Despite recent challenges in the Chinese market and duty-free sales due to the COVID-19 pandemic, Amorepacific continues to explore new growth engines and diversify its brand sales channels. The company's focus is now on premium brands and expanding in various overseas markets. The commitment to digital transformation and customer-centric approaches is evident in its latest digital marketing strategies and innovative ventures, including explorations into the metaverse and Web3 projects. Despite facing operational challenges, Amorepacific remains focused on recovering growth and maintaining its stature in the global beauty industry.

The history of Korean global firms is a compelling narrative of rapid transformation and resilience, beginning in the aftermath of Korea's independence from Japan in 1945 (Park et al., 2023). This period marked the inception of Korea's journey towards becoming a global economic powerhouse, despite its relatively short history in the

Y. W. Park and P. Hong, *Cosmetics Marketing Strategy in the Era of the Digital Ecosystem*, https://doi.org/10.1007/978-981-97-3674-4_10

global business arena. Initially, the Korean economy was heavily reliant on light and simple manufacturing products, a strategic choice that laid the groundwork for future industrialization and economic development. This focus on light industries such as essential life necessities and hygiene products such as soup, toothpastes and food was pivotal for Korea, providing a foundation upon which more complex and technologically advanced industries could build.

As the Korean economy evolved, it gradually shifted towards more foundational manufacturing cores, such as basic chemical components, and steel. These sectors were instrumental in propelling the country's industrial capabilities and economic growth, serving as the backbone of Korea's manufacturing industry. The strategic emphasis on these core industries facilitated Korea's transition from a primarily agrarian economy to an industrial powerhouse, renowned for its technological innovation and manufacturing excellence that has expanded to more complex areas such as automotive, shipbuilding and defense industries (Hong et al., 2024).

However, the history of the cosmetics industry in Korea presents a contrast to the rapid development seen in other sectors. The onset of the Korean War in the 1950s significantly impeded the growth of non-essential industries, including cosmetics. During this tumultuous period, the national priorities were focused on reconstruction and survival, leaving little room for the luxury of cosmetics. This historical context contributed to a relatively slow start for the Korean cosmetics industry, which would only begin to flourish decades later.

Despite these initial challenges, the Korean cosmetics industry eventually emerged as a global leader, driven by innovation and a keen understanding of global consumer trends. AmorePacific's cushion foundation, which revolutionized the global beauty market, represents a prime example of peripheral innovation where the focus on non-core components opened up new avenues for product development (Lee & Kang, 2016). The resilience and capacity for growth was evident even in the post-COVID-19 era.

The trajectory of Korean global firms, from their humble beginnings in light manufacturing to their current status as leaders in various high-tech and consumer industries, reflects a remarkable journey of economic development and global integration. The cosmetics industry, in particular, showcases Korea's ability to overcome initial hurdles and leverage its strengths in innovation and manufacturing to capture global markets, establishing Korea as a formidable player in the international business landscape.

1 Amorepacific: The Trailblazer in Global Beauty from Korea

As Amorepacific stands today as a leading force in the global beauty industry, it's important to recognize the strategic journey and visionary approach that have been instrumental in shaping its success. The story of Amorepacific is not just about a company's growth but about the transformation of an entire industry and the introduction of Korean beauty (K-beauty) to the world. This journey, marked by a dedication to innovation and an unwavering commitment to quality, has seen the company evolve from its modest beginnings into a global powerhouse. Amorepacific's path has been paved with bold decisions and pioneering initiatives that have not only contributed to its growth but have also influenced beauty trends and standards globally. As we delve into the details of Amorepacific's remarkable journey, we uncover the pivotal moments and strategic decisions that have defined its role as a trailblazer in the beauty industry.

1.1 A Journey of Innovation and Global Expansion

Amorepacific, a luminary in the realm of Korean cosmetics, has carved a significant niche in the global beauty industry. Established initially as the 'Lucky Chemical Industry' in 1947, the company's evolution has been characterized by a relentless pursuit of innovation and a pioneering spirit in taking K-beauty to the international stage. By December 2022, Amorepacific had grown to a formidable workforce of 5,194 employees, boasting impressive annual revenues of KRW 4.1 trillion. The company's financial health is further underscored by its substantial net profit and total assets, with cosmetics being the primary revenue driver, accounting for 88.63% of its sales composition.

The essence of the Amorepacific brand, blending 'Amore' and 'Pacific,' reflects a harmonious balance of softness, sophistication, strength, and intelligence. This brand identity was a strategic move during its transition from 'Pacific' to 'Amore,' marking its dominance in the domestic cosmetics landscape. Amorepacific's journey, marked by its recognition in prestigious global rankings and its iconic headquarters, is underpinned by fundamental values emphasizing human service, dignity, and future creation.

1.2 Overcoming Challenges and Charting New Paths

Despite its storied history and market leadership, Amorepacific has navigated periods of intense competition, notably the rivalry with LG H&H and market challenges post the THAAD crisis. The company's foundations can be traced back to the humble origins of 'ChangSung,' where Yun Dok-jeong began producing camellia oil in 1932. The subsequent establishment of 'Pacific Chemical Industry' by Jang Won-seok laid the groundwork for iconic products like 'Melody Cream' and 'ABC Pomade,' culminating in significant partnerships and product launches that revolutionized women's beauty routines. Amorepacific's foray into international markets, marked by its first exports under the brand 'Oscar,' has been complemented by diversification into various product categories. The construction of the Anseong Factory and expansion into international territories, including Tokyo and New York, set the stage for the company's global presence. Going public on the Korea Stock Exchange and diversifying into construction and finance further exemplified its conglomerate status.

However, the company faced hurdles as it expanded into non-cosmetic businesses, leading to a surge in debt and a downturn in its core cosmetics business. The comprehensive restructuring initiated in 1991, with Seo Gyeong-bae's strategic leadership, aimed to revitalize Amorepacific's core focus. This transition was marked by organizational changes, divestments, and the emergence of 'Amorepacific Group,' reflecting a renewed commitment to the cosmetics sector.

Amorepacific's remarkable growth trajectory in international markets, particularly in China, has contributed significantly to its revenue (Oh & Rugman, 2007). The establishment of local subsidiaries across Asia, Europe, and the Middle East, and partnerships like the one with Alshaya Group, have solidified its global footprint. By 2023, Amorepacific's pioneering efforts in registering new materials in China further showcased its innovative edge and commitment to global beauty standards. Amorepacific's legacy, encapsulating resilience, innovation, and a vision for global influence, mirrors the rise of Korean beauty on the world stage. From a small shop producing camellia oil to becoming a global beauty conglomerate, Amorepacific's journey is not just a corporate success story; it is a testament to the transformative power of vision, innovation, and adaptability in the ever-evolving beauty industry.

2 Amorepacific: Mastering Brand Strategy in the Evolving Beauty Landscape

At the heart of Amorepacific's brand strategy is a deep understanding of its heritage and a clear vision for its future. The company's identity, intricately woven into its logo, goes beyond mere aesthetics; it encapsulates Amorepacific's journey and philosophy. This blend of history, culture, and innovation serves as a foundation for the company's customer-centric approach and its strategies for market engagement. As Amorepacific evolved, so did its methods of connecting with customers—from the establishment of beauty counseling rooms to pioneering personalized beauty services. This evolution reflects Amorepacific's commitment to staying relevant and resonant in an industry that is constantly influenced by changing consumer preferences, technological advancements, and global trends. As we delve into the specifics of Amorepacific's brand strategy, we see how these elements come together to shape a company that is not only a leader in the beauty industry but also a trendsetter and innovator.

2.1 *Crafting a Symbolic Identity and Customer-Centric Beginnings*

Amorepacific's emblematic logo, ingeniously incorporating the alphabet 'ABC' from its roots in Pacific Chemical Industry's production of ABC foam, embodies the essence of 'Asian Beauty Creator.' This alignment with the company's vision is reflected in the logo's green color, symbolizing respect for life, nature, and harmonious business practices. The square in the logo represents the group's diverse business sectors, while the circle signifies human society, where Amorepacific predominantly focuses. The recent transformation of the logo into a simplified circular form on product packaging signifies the company's continuous evolution.

The customer-centric ethos of Amorepacific has been a cornerstone since its early days, evidenced by the opening of South Korea's first beauty counseling room in 1961. This initiative was a response to the increasing interest in beauty, sparked by the publication of 'Hwajanggye,' the first monthly beauty information magazine. Unlike many contemporaries that prioritized production, Amorepacific's establishment of a beauty counseling room was a significant step in prioritizing customer satisfaction and engagement.

2.2 *Navigating Distribution Channels and Responding to Market Challenges*

Amorepacific's innovative approach to distribution transformed the cosmetics industry. The introduction of the Amore brand and the pioneering door-to-door sales system in 1964 created a new distribution channel, breaking the norms of traditional retail. The brand's success in door-to-door sales, driven by its focus on high-quality products and personalized service, became a model for competitors.

This distribution revolution began with the internal selection of the 'Amore' brand name and the recruitment of door-to-door sales representatives. Amorepacific's strategy of dividing the country into special agency areas ensured consistent pricing, augmented after-sales services, and built customer trust. Despite a decline in the door-to-door sales system's prominence from the 1980s, Amorepacific adapted by innovating its sales strategies and rebranding its sales representatives as 'Amore Counselors.'

Recent years, however, brought new challenges, especially in the Chinese market, due to political tensions and the COVID-19 pandemic. In response, Amorepacific pivoted its brand strategy towards premium brands and diversified its sales channels. Notably, while sales through duty-free and global e-commerce channels declined in 2023, there was substantial growth in the multi-brand shop (MBS) channel and domestic e-commerce. The company also saw success in its luxury brands, while facing competition in the mass brand sector. To address these challenges, Amorepacific is exploring new growth avenues, including entering the professional skin care and hair care sectors, expanding in overseas markets, and leveraging M&A opportunities. With a focus on innovation and diversification, Amorepacific is poised to strengthen its presence in both domestic and international markets.

The journey of Amorepacific, from its symbolic logo to its innovative brand strategies, narrates a story of evolution, resilience, and commitment to excellence. This history, marked by pioneering customer-centric approaches and adaptability, continues to drive the company's growth and prominence in the ever-changing global beauty industry.

3 Amorepacific's Global Expansion: Charting the Path in International Beauty Markets

Amorepacific's approach to global expansion has been marked by a strategic and well-orchestrated blend of traditional market entry and modern digital transformation. This strategy has enabled the company to not only capture but also to create demand in various regions, adapting to local preferences while maintaining its core values and identity. At the heart of Amorepacific's global expansion lies a deep understanding of cultural nuances and consumer behaviors, allowing the company to tailor its offerings to meet diverse beauty ideals and practices across the globe. The company's global journey, while rooted in its dedication to "Asian Beauty," showcases its agility in navigating different market landscapes, from establishing production facilities abroad to forming strategic alliances with major e-commerce players. This comprehensive approach to global expansion, balancing physical presence with digital innovation, sets the stage for the detailed exploration of Amorepacific's expansion strategies in the East and West, highlighting its adaptability and foresight in the international beauty market.

3.1 Laying the Global Foundation and Expanding Eastward

Since its establishment in 1945, Amorepacific has been passionately dedicated to promoting "Asian Beauty" globally. This pursuit began with its first overseas export in 1964, signifying the start of a mission to establish a profound global presence. This expansion strategy led to the establishment of production facilities in strategic locations like China and France, which played a crucial role in the company's growth, particularly from the early 2000s.

Amorepacific's focus areas for expansion included the Greater China region, ASEAN countries, and North America. The allure of China's cosmetics market, with its vast user base and significant growth rate, was a key driver for Amorepacific's strategic endeavors. The company's journey in China began with a branch in 1992 and evolved into a full-fledged local corporation in Shanghai by 2000, culminating in the inauguration of a Shanghai factory in 2002.

The 2014 opening of the Shanghai Beauty Plant marked a milestone in Amorepacific's commitment to the Chinese market. This facility, with its advanced production and environmental standards, reflected the company's dedication to excellence. The groundbreaking alliance with Alibaba Group in 2021 further solidified Amorepacific's position in China, enhancing its digital presence and brand reach.

3.2 Venturing Westward and Embracing Digitalization

Amorepacific's global strategy extended beyond China into ASEAN markets, with Laneige entering premium Singaporean department stores in 2003 and gaining popularity across Thailand, Malaysia, Indonesia, and Vietnam. The company embraced digital marketing and expanded through various channels, ensuring sustained growth in Asia. The company's expansion into the United States began with its New York entry in 2003. Subsequently, brands like Sulwhasoo, Laneige, and Innisfree established a strong presence in the U.S., with Innisfree opening a Manhattan store in 2017. The 2020 debut of AMOREPACIFIC and Mamonde on Amazon in the U.S. highlighted Amorepacific's strategy to cater to a clientele seeking premium skincare rooted in natural ingredients.

Amorepacific's outreach extends to Australia, India, the Middle East, Japan, and Europe, with Laneige's entry into Sephora stores across Europe in 2019 being a notable milestone. Post-COVID-19, the company sharpened its focus on digital marketing, especially in China, revamping its organizational structure to enhance global e-commerce capabilities and live commerce. With ambitious growth targets for 2022, Amorepacific concentrated on premium brands and restructuring efforts in China. Strategies varied across platforms, focusing on brand image on Tmall, profitability on Jingdong, and expansion through video platforms. In Korea, the company adapted product and brand differentiation for specific platforms, capitalizing on the surge in online channels and robust North American growth, despite challenges in Asia due to COVID-19.

Amorepacific's global marketing strategy reflects a journey of strategic expansion, innovation, and adaptation to changing market dynamics. From its early forays into China to its digital transformation and expansion into diverse global markets, Amorepacific's narrative is one of a visionary company redefining the contours of the international beauty industry.

4 Amorepacific's Digital Transformation in Beauty Marketing

Amorepacific's journey into the digital era has been marked by a strategic focus on integrating cutting-edge technology into its core operations. Recognizing the transformative potential of the digital world, the company has positioned itself at the forefront of the beauty industry's digital revolution. This strategic focus on digital innovation is not just about adopting new technologies; it's about reimagining how beauty products are marketed, experienced, and consumed in an increasingly digital-centric world.

The company's progressive steps towards digitalization have been evident through its targeted collaborations and expansions in online channels, as highlighted in its 2021 Whitepaper. These efforts represent a deeper understanding of the changing landscape of consumer behavior and market dynamics, driven by digital technology. Amorepacific's commitment to this digital transformation underscores its recognition of the importance of staying relevant and competitive in a rapidly evolving digital landscape.

4.1 Accelerating Digital Initiatives and Executive Appointments

Amorepacific's commitment to robust brand cultivation and digital transformation has been unwavering, both domestically and globally. The company's focused collaboration with digital platforms and growth in online channels was emphasized in its December 2021 Whitepaper.

The beginning of 2022 marked a strategic shift in Amorepacific's leadership, with the promotion of Mr. Park Jong-man, the former Head of the Digital Strategy Unit, and Mr. Lee Dong-soon, the Head of the SCM Unit, to Vice President roles. This shift underscores Amorepacific's dedication to evolving into a customer-centric organization and its pursuit of continual growth.

Mr. Park Jong-man, with his extensive background in digital strategy and technology development, has been pivotal in integrating advanced technologies such as AI, big data, and blockchain into Amorepacific's operations. His leadership in e-commerce and digital marketing is expected to drive further innovation and global expansion for the brand.

4.2 Embracing the Metaverse and Web3 Innovations

As part of its digital transformation, Amorepacific has been keen to explore emerging platforms and technologies that redefine customer engagement and brand experience.

The company's entry into the metaverse and its involvement in the 2023 Metaverse Fashion Week mark significant steps in this direction (Kakao Story, March 24). Amorepacific's New Beauty Land in Decentraland exemplifies this innovative approach, offering a unique blend of fashion, beauty, and digital art in a virtual space that mirrors the creativity and vision of its physical headquarters.

A significant milestone occurred on March 28, 2023, when Amorepacific orchestrated the New Beauty Land event on the metaverse platform Decentraland, drawing inspiration from its Yongsan headquarters. As an official partner of the 2023 Metaverse Fashion Week, Amorepacific unveiled a groundbreaking virtual space alongside global fashion and beauty entities. The three themed sections within New Beauty Land catered to visitors, offering photo zones and new beauty quests on the first floor, providing an immersive exploration of major Amorepacific brands like Sulwhasoo, Laneige, and Innisfree on the second floor, and showcasing 12 NFT artworks that triumphed in the Colors of New Beauty contest on the third floor. Visitors traversing this innovative space were entitled to receive NFTs issued by Amorepacific. An executive from the Digital Strategy Division at Amorepacific affirmed, "Decentraland New Beauty Land serves as a platform to present Amorepacific's vision and introduce a novel brand experience to global customers." He further emphasized that "The launch of New Beauty Land is just the beginning, with Amorepacific set to unveil various Web3 projects in the foreseeable future" (Sul, 2023).

This venture into the metaverse is more than just a digital marketing tactic; it represents Amorepacific's understanding of the evolving digital landscape where consumer interactions and experiences are being transformed. By embracing Web3 technologies and integrating them into its brand strategy, Amorepacific is not only reaching out to a wider, tech-savvy audience but also setting new standards in digital engagement within the beauty industry. The issuance of NFTs and the creation of interactive, immersive experiences in a virtual world demonstrate the company's ability to innovate and adapt to the digital era's demands. As Amorepacific continues to explore these new frontiers, it cements its position as a visionary leader in the global beauty market, ready to embrace the future of digital marketing and consumer interaction.

5 Amorepacific's Challenges and Resilience in a Shifting Landscape

As Amorepacific looks back on its journey since the COVID-19 pandemic, it faces the dual challenge of adapting to a rapidly evolving global market while addressing internal franchise dynamics. The company's strategic agility will be tested as it seeks to balance market demands with the needs of its franchise partners, a crucial aspect of its business model.

5.1 *Facing Market Realities and Franchise Dynamics*

Amorepacific's journey has been marked by resilience, as it faced the uphill challenge of recuperating its growth trajectory following the slump in sales triggered by the profound disruptions of the COVID-19 pandemic in 2020.

In 2023, Amorepacific faced significant challenges in regaining its market position post-pandemic. Despite strides in international markets, the company encountered setbacks in key areas such as duty-free, global e-commerce, and the crucial Chinese market. These issues contributed to an overall decline in revenue, indicating a need for strategic recalibration. A notable incident that exemplifies these challenges occurred when proprietors of the 'Aritaum' franchise protested at Amorepacific's headquarters. This protest highlighted the impact of product discontinuations on their businesses and underscored the complex interplay between corporate strategy and its implications for franchisees, compelling Amorepacific to address the grievances with a commitment to open dialogue and cooperation.

Despite struggling to reclaim the heights it once occupied among the top global brands, Amorepacific has shown signs of progress in diverse international markets such as the Americas, EMEA (Europe, the Middle East and Africa), and Japan throughout 2023. However, this glimmer of success has been tempered by a decline in crucial segments like duty-free, global e-commerce, and the pivotal Chinese market, leading to an overarching descent in the group's revenue (Kim, 2023a).

5.2 *Strategic Responses and Future Outlook*

In response to these challenges, Amorepacific has reaffirmed its commitment to cooperative engagement with franchisees, emphasizing the need for a balance between strategic brand decisions and the realities of franchise operations. As the company moves forward, it is poised to navigate these evolving dynamics while upholding its core values and commitments to its partners.

The winds of change have brought forth significant challenges for Amorepacific, especially evident in the turmoil surrounding the preservation of its domestic franchise stores (Kim, 2023b). This situation came to a head when over a hundred proprietors affiliated with the 'Aritaum' road shop franchise rallied in front of Amorepacific's headquarters in Yongsan-gu, Seoul. Their chants of "Save Aritaum" echoed a collective plea against the substantial discontinuation of products they had stocked, voicing concerns that their livelihoods were under threat. They passionately called for proactive intervention from the headquarters, reminding them of Chairman Seo Kyung-bae's commitment to collaborative engagement with franchisees during the 2020 parliamentary audit.

In its statement, Amorepacific acknowledged that the decision to discontinue certain products was made at the brand level and was not directly associated with franchisees. While recognizing the challenges arising from the evolving distribution landscape, the company underscored its steadfast commitment to honoring cooperative agreements with franchise owners. Amorepacific also reiterated its unwavering dedication to bridging gaps and fostering dialogue as a means to mitigate disparities.

The vocal outcry from the franchise owners and Amorepacific's responsive stance highlight the delicate balance the company must maintain. This situation is illustrative of the intricate interplay between brand evolution, market demands, and the crucial symbiotic relationship between corporate entities and their franchise partners in the ever-evolving beauty landscape.

6 Amorepacific's Evolution and Future Prospects

As Amorepacific embarks on a new chapter, it carries the legacy of its past achievements and lessons learned. The company's ability to navigate market shifts and technological advancements will play a pivotal role in shaping its future trajectory in the competitive beauty industry.

6.1 A Legacy of Resilience and Global Expansion

Amorepacific's journey from a modest producer to a global cosmetic giant showcases its resilience and adaptability in a dynamic industry. The company's fiscal performance in 2022, with revenues totaling KRW 4.1 trillion (4.1 billion USD), underscores its significant impact on the beauty landscape. However, as it navigates the 2020s, Amorepacific is encountering a mix of successes and challenges. These primarily revolve around balancing traditional sales channels with strategies focused on digital platforms and premium brands.

Standing as a vanguard in the realm of Korean cosmetics, Amorepacific is recognized as an emblem of innovation and a torchbearer for introducing Korean beauty to the world. Its evolution from a small-scale operation to a global powerhouse reflects the overall resilience and adaptability of the K-beauty industry. Despite facing recent challenges due to market shifts and strategic repositioning, Amorepacific's legacy continues to resonate across international borders. Its substantial revenue in 2022 attests to its enduring presence and significance in the global beauty landscape. Nevertheless, the company is currently navigating a period marked by a complex blend of successes and setbacks. The recent protests by Aritaum franchise owners stand as a pivotal moment for the company. They highlight the delicate balance between corporate brand decisions and their impact on the livelihoods of franchisees. Amorepacific's response, which emphasizes open dialogue and commitment to cooperative agreements, demonstrates the company's dedication to addressing these complexities thoughtfully and collaboratively.

6.2 Embracing Innovation and Digital Transformation

As Amorepacific looks ahead, it remains committed to fostering innovation and adaptability. The company's proactive strategy encompasses several key elements, including the exploration of new product sectors, the implementation of digital marketing strategies, and strategic mergers and acquisitions aimed at strengthening its market position. Moreover, recent executive appointments in the fields of digital and supply chain management underscore Amorepacific's unwavering dedication to a digital-first approach, ensuring its preparedness to meet the future demands of the beauty industry.

Amorepacific's journey, from its humble beginnings rooted in camellia oil production to its pivotal partnerships and global expansions, serves as a testament to its commitment to innovation and adaptation. The company's expansion into international markets and strategic collaborations, particularly in regions like China, ASEAN, and the United States, reflect its adaptability and unwavering dedication to cultivating a global brand presence. Despite facing challenges in traditional sales channels, Amorepacific's pivot toward premium brands and digital initiatives mirrors its ability to adapt. Notably, its focus on live commerce, e-commerce expansion, and strategic mergers underscores its proactive approach to future growth. Furthermore, recent executive appointments in digital and supply chain management reaffirm Amorepacific's dedication to digital transformation and sustained growth. The company's innovative ventures into the metaverse exemplify its forward-looking stance in exploring new marketing frontiers.

As Amorepacific ventures into the future, its capacity to seamlessly integrate brand evolution with evolving market demands while maintaining strong relationships with franchise partners will be of paramount importance. The company's enduring legacy in the beauty industry is defined by its ongoing pursuit of excellence, commitment to innovation, and a profound understanding of global beauty trends.

7 Conclusion

As the Korean cosmetics industry mirrors the transformative journey of the nation's other leading sectors, such as electronics, automobiles, chemicals, steel, and shipbuilding, it stands at a pivotal crossroads (Hong et al., 2024; Park et al., 2023). Just as these Korean industries have established global competitiveness through consistent transitions, the cosmetics sector has also evolved from establishing a robust domestic foundation to entering the global arena and reaching a stage where it competes on an international scale. This evolution is significantly propelled by the global fascination with Korean culture, often referred to as the "Korean Wave" or Hallyu. The industry has adeptly leveraged this cultural export, giving rise to the global phenomenon of K-beauty. This concept not only showcases Korea's innovative beauty products and routines but also imbues them with a distinct cultural identity that resonates worldwide. As a result, K-beauty has become synonymous with quality, innovation, and a unique approach to cosmetics that appeals to diverse audiences across the globe.

Moving forward, the expansion and sustained global influence of Korean cosmetic firms will hinge on their continuous drive for creativity and innovation. These attributes must be deeply intertwined with Korean sensibilities, offering products that not only cater to global beauty standards but also carry the essence of Korean culture. In this endeavor, companies like Amorepacific are at the forefront, pioneering the globalization of the Korean cosmetic industry. Amorepacific's journey from its humble origins to becoming a global cosmetics leader underscores the importance of innovation, digital transformation, and strategic global expansion. The company's ability to adapt to changing market dynamics, coupled with its commitment to research and development, positions it as a model for how Korean cosmetic firms can navigate the challenges and opportunities of the global market. By continuing to push the boundaries of innovation and leveraging the unique appeal of K-beauty, Amorepacific and its counterparts are well-placed to further extend Korea's influence in the global beauty landscape.

References

Hong, P. C., Park, Y. S., Hwang, D. W., & Sepehr, M. J. (2024). A growth theory perspective on the competitive landscape of shipbuilding: a comparative study of Japan, Korea, and China. *Maritime Economics & Logistics*, 1–28

Kim, H. (2023b). 'K-beauty' two-top pain: LG Household & Health Care-late in leaving China, Amore in conflict with franchisees, Seoul Newspaper, November 23. https://v.daum.net/v/20231123050220370.

Kim, J. (2023a). Amore Pacific Group continues to show poor 3Q performance: Simultaneous decline in operating profit and sales, News 1, Oct 31. https://v.daum.net/v/20231031085451423.

Lee, B., & Kang, J. (2016). The power of peripheral innovation: A case study of AmorePacific's cushion foundation: Shifting attention from a product's core to its peripheral components can open up new possibilities for innovation. *Research-Technology Management, 59*(4), 21–29.

Oh, C. H., & Rugman, A. M. (2007). Regional multinationals and the Korean cosmetics industry. *Asia Pacific Journal of Management, 24*, 27–42.

Park, Y. W., Hong, P., & Shin, G. C. (2023). Rising and thriving in the post COVID-19 era: A case study of COSMAX, a leader of the Korean cosmetic industry. *Asia Pacific Business Review, 29*(4), 1105–1124.

Sul, Y. (2023). Amore Pacific Decentraland K-Beauty Virtual Space New Beauty Land, Kookmin Biz TV

Kakao Story, March 24. https://story.kakao.com/_INWgn0/hS4ZMl5nBaa.

Chapter 11
Innovative Synergies in the Cosmetic Industry

Abstract In the dynamic landscape of the global cosmetics industry, the intersection of the sharing economy and globalization offers unique opportunities for innovation and growth. This study explores the potential synergy between these two distinct concepts, with a specific focus on the cosmetics industry. Both sharing economy platforms and globalization-driven cosmetic enterprises share a common need for adaptability and responsiveness. The study reveals how the agility of the sharing economy, in aligning supply and demand and establishing trust mechanisms, can mirror the strategies of global cosmetics firms in areas such as supply chain management and international partnerships. Insights from the sharing economy can help cosmetic companies optimize resource allocation, enhance user experiences, and build global trust. The exchange of ideas and practices between sharing economy platforms and globalization-focused cosmetic businesses holds significant potential. It investigates how innovative practices from the sharing economy, like dynamic pricing algorithms and user review systems, can inspire global cosmetic enterprises. Conversely, it considers how the approaches of global cosmetics firms to sustainability, supply chain optimization, and international market entry can benefit sharing economy platforms expanding globally. This fusion of ideas could lead to innovative business strategies in the cosmetics sector, leveraging the strengths of both models to propel organizations toward success in an interconnected, globalized world.

1 Introduction

In today's rapidly evolving global marketplace, the cosmetics industry stands at a crossroads of opportunity and challenge. With globalization reshaping market dynamics and the sharing economy revolutionizing business models, there is a pressing need to understand how these forces can synergistically transform the cosmetics sector. The ability of cosmetic organizations to adapt to these changes is not just a matter of competitive advantage, but a crucial factor for sustainable

Y. W. Park and P. Hong, *Cosmetics Marketing Strategy in the Era of the Digital Ecosystem*, https://doi.org/10.1007/978-981-97-3674-4_11

success in an increasingly interconnected world. As such, exploring the convergence of strategies from the sharing economy and globalization-driven practices within the cosmetics industry is not only timely but essential. This exploration is particularly vital in addressing the industry's needs for adaptability, responsiveness, and innovative approaches to resource allocation, user experience, and trust-building mechanisms.

This chapter aims to explore in depth how the integration of sharing economy strategies and globalization-driven practices can foster innovative synergies in the cosmetics industry. The focus is on understanding how these synergies can optimize resource allocation, enhance user experiences, and strengthen trust-building mechanisms. By investigating the interplay between the agility of the sharing economy and the strategic global positioning of cosmetic enterprises, the study seeks to uncover actionable insights and practical strategies. These strategies are aimed at helping cosmetic organizations navigate the complexities of a globalized market and harness the potential of the sharing economy for sustainable growth and competitive advantage.

2 Theoretical Foundation: Sharing Economy and Cosmetic Industry

As the global cosmetic industry navigates the complexities of modern consumer demands and environmental responsibilities, the principles of the sharing economy emerge as a beacon of innovation and adaptation. This section explores the intersection of the sharing economy and the cosmetic industry, unveiling how the core ideas of the former—resource optimization, community-centric engagement, and technology-enabled platforms—can significantly address the latter's evolving challenges. The cosmetic industry is currently grappling with three primary needs: sustainable resource management, enhanced customer engagement and personalization, and the integration of advanced technology for expanded market reach (Kolling et al., 2022). These needs echo the foundational elements of the sharing economy, suggesting a fertile ground for cross-industry synergy (Rathod et al., 2020). By examining these parallels, this section lays the groundwork for a comprehensive understanding of how the sharing economy's flexible, community-focused, and technologically savvy approaches can be harnessed to propel the cosmetic industry forward, addressing both its immediate challenges and long-term sustainability goals.

2.1 Core Ideas of the Sharing Economy

The sharing economy is anchored in three core ideas: resource optimization, community-centric engagement, and technology-enabled platforms (Mackelprang et al., 2023). Firstly, it emphasizes the efficient use of resources, promoting the idea that goods and services can be shared among users, thereby reducing waste and maximizing utility. This principle challenges traditional ownership models, favoring access over ownership. Secondly, the sharing economy is fundamentally community-centric, fostering a sense of collaboration and mutual benefit among participants. This approach leverages trust and shared values within communities to facilitate exchanges. Finally, technology plays a pivotal role in the sharing economy, with digital platforms enabling easy and efficient connections between providers and users of goods and services (Kolling et al., 2022). These platforms not only facilitate transactions but also help in building and maintaining trust among users.

The concept of resource optimization in the sharing economy goes beyond mere cost-saving; it represents a paradigm shift in how we view consumption and production. In this model, the focus is on maximizing the use of existing resources rather than continually producing new ones. This approach is environmentally sustainable and economically efficient, as it minimizes waste and promotes the reuse and recycling of products. By extending the lifespan of products and resources, the sharing economy contributes to a more sustainable and less extractive economic model. This principle is particularly relevant in industries like cosmetics, where product lifecycle and environmental impact are of growing concern to both consumers and manufacturers.

Community-centric engagement in the sharing economy is another key aspect that transforms traditional business models. By building networks of trust and mutual support, the sharing economy fosters a sense of belonging and community among its participants. This aspect is crucial in today's market, where consumers are increasingly seeking authentic connections and meaningful interactions with brands. In the sharing economy, transactions are not just economic; they are also social exchanges that strengthen community bonds. This approach can be particularly impactful in the cosmetics industry, where brand loyalty and customer engagement are vital. The community-centric model can help cosmetic brands build a loyal customer base that values not only the products but also the experience and community that come with them.

2.2 Emerging Needs of the Cosmetic Industry

In the context of the cosmetic industry, there are three emerging needs that can greatly benefit from the integration of sharing economy ideas. The first is the need for sustainable resource management, as the industry faces increasing pressure to reduce waste and embrace eco-friendly practices. This involves rethinking packaging, product formulations, and the overall product lifecycle. The second need is enhancing customer engagement and personalization. Today's consumers expect more than just products; they seek experiences and personal connections with brands, emphasizing the need for community-focused marketing and customer relations. The third need is the adoption of advanced technology for better market reach and efficiency. This includes leveraging data analytics for consumer insights, employing artificial intelligence for personalized product recommendations, and utilizing e-commerce platforms for broader market access.

Cosmetic companies are increasingly relying on data analytics for consumer insights, artificial intelligence for personalized product recommendations, and e-commerce platforms for expanding their market reach. The sharing economy's reliance on technology-enabled platforms offers valuable lessons in effectively connecting providers and users. Cosmetic brands can benefit from this by leveraging digital platforms to reach a global audience, offer personalized experiences, and streamline their operations for greater efficiency. In essence, the integration of sharing economy technology practices can empower cosmetic companies to stay competitive and responsive to the demands of the modern market.

Furthermore, the adoption of sharing economy practices can help the cosmetic industry address the challenge of sustainability in the supply chain. As consumers become more environmentally conscious, cosmetic companies are under pressure to source ingredients and materials responsibly. The sharing economy's emphasis on community and collaboration can extend to partnerships with sustainable suppliers and ethical sourcing practices. Cosmetic brands can explore alliances with small-scale farmers, cooperatives, and eco-friendly suppliers to ensure the ethical and sustainable sourcing of ingredients. This approach not only aligns with consumer values but also contributes to the broader social and environmental sustainability objectives. By integrating sharing economy principles into their supply chain management, cosmetic companies can demonstrate their commitment to sustainability and build trust with consumers who prioritize ethical and eco-conscious brands (Iwao et al., 2023).

2.3 Converging Synergy Practices in the Cosmetic Industry

The convergence of sharing economy principles with the emerging needs of the cosmetic industry leads to synergistic practices that can reshape the sector. Firstly, sustainable resource management in cosmetics can be enhanced through sharing economy models like product refills, community-based recycling programs, and shared production facilities. These practices not only reduce environmental impact but also resonate with eco-conscious consumers. Secondly, community-centric engagement can be leveraged through platforms that allow consumers to share feedback, participate in product development, and engage in peer-to-peer product recommendations. This fosters a sense of community and enhances brand loyalty. Lastly, the adoption of technology-driven solutions from the sharing economy, like AI-driven customization tools and digital marketplaces, can significantly improve market reach and operational efficiency. These technologies enable cosmetic brands to offer personalized experiences at scale, catering to the diverse needs of a global customer base. Together, these converging practices offer a roadmap for the cosmetic industry to innovate and thrive in a rapidly changing market landscape.

The integration of sharing economy models like product refills and community-based recycling programs in cosmetics can significantly reduce the environmental impact of the industry. By promoting the reuse of containers and the recycling of product components, cosmetic brands can contribute to a reduction in plastic waste and resource consumption. These practices not only resonate with eco-conscious consumers but also showcase the industry's commitment to sustainability. In an era where environmental concerns are paramount, such initiatives can enhance brand reputation and customer loyalty.

The community-centric engagement approach derived from the sharing economy fosters stronger connections between cosmetic brands and their customers. Platforms that allow consumers to actively participate in product development, share feedback, and engage in peer-to-peer product recommendations create a sense of community and belonging. This enhances brand loyalty and trust, as consumers feel valued and heard. It also enables cosmetic companies to co-create products that align with the preferences and needs of their community, resulting in a more customer-centric approach. This sense of involvement can extend beyond products to social and environmental initiatives, further solidifying the bond between cosmetic brands and their consumers.

Lastly, the adoption of technology-driven solutions from the sharing economy, such as AI-driven customization tools and digital marketplaces, can revolutionize the cosmetic industry's market reach and operational efficiency. By harnessing the power of data and AI, cosmetic brands can offer personalized product recommendations at scale, meeting the diverse preferences of a global customer base (Elder et al., 2021). Digital marketplaces expand access to a wider audience, breaking geographical barriers and enabling brands to cater to a global market. These technology-driven solutions not only enhance the customer experience but also optimize internal operations, making the industry more agile and responsive to market dynamics. In this digital era, the integration of sharing economy technologies positions the cosmetic industry for sustainable growth and innovation. Together, these converging practices offer a promising roadmap for the cosmetic industry, where sustainability, community engagement, and technological advancement converge to drive success in an ever-evolving market landscape.

The adoption of technology-driven solutions from the sharing economy, such as AI-driven customization tools and digital marketplaces, can revolutionize the cosmetic industry's market reach and operational efficiency. By harnessing the power of data and AI, cosmetic brands can offer personalized product recommendations at scale, meeting the diverse preferences of a global customer base. Digital marketplaces expand access to a wider audience, breaking geographical barriers and enabling brands to cater to a global market. These technology-driven solutions not only enhance the customer experience but also optimize internal operations, making the industry more agile and responsive to market dynamics. In this digital era, the integration of sharing economy technologies positions the cosmetic industry for sustainable growth and innovation. Together, these converging practices offer a promising roadmap for the cosmetic industry, where sustainability, community engagement, and technological advancement converge to drive success in an ever-evolving market landscape.

3 A Conceptual Framework: SAUSE Model

In collaboration with the Mitsubishi Research Institute, Mercari introduced the purchase model "SAUSE," which encompasses the following stages: Search, Action, Use, Share, and Evaluation. This innovative approach to consumer behavior signifies a shift in perception from "ownership" to "usage" during the era of sharing. To delve deeper into these dynamics, surveys were conducted among users, primarily focusing on the Prima app that facilitates cosmetic transactions.

The findings from this study shed light on various intriguing trends. Firstly, it was discovered that a significant portion of consumers, especially when purchasing cosmetics or clothing, consciously consider the potential resale value of their items at the time of purchase. This awareness, in turn, influences their decisions, leading to increased purchases and a propensity for higher-priced products. The presence of sharing services like Mercari has played a pivotal role in shaping these new purchasing and consumption behaviors.

The implications of "SAUSE" extend beyond Mercari's user base, hinting at a broader shift in consumer mentality. While "SAUSE" was developed based on research conducted among Mercari users, it highlights a trend that transcends the platform. In various industries, including cosmetics, the concept of considering the resale value and evaluating purchases from a sharing perspective holds significance. To stay relevant in this evolving landscape, individuals and businesses seeking to create new products or services must be mindful of the "Share" element. Embracing this trend is crucial, as it aligns with the prevailing direction of consumer behavior—a recognition that, when an item can be resold, it adds value to the overall purchase. As such, understanding and assessing these purchasing models, whether "SAUSE," "AIDMA(Attention → Interest → Desire → Memory → Action)," or "AISAS(Attention → Interest → Search → Action → Share)," can aid in comprehending the dynamics of the modern consumer landscape and contribute to making informed business decisions.

Figure 1 depicts a dynamic, interconnected flow chart that visually represents the SAUSE (Search, Action, Use, Share, and Evaluation) model in the context of the sharing economy. Each stage—Search, Action, Use, Share, and Evaluation—will be symbolized by distinct, yet interconnected, icons or scenes. For instance, the Search stage might be represented by a magnifying glass over a digital marketplace, Action by a transaction or exchange, Use by consumers enjoying a product, Share by a person

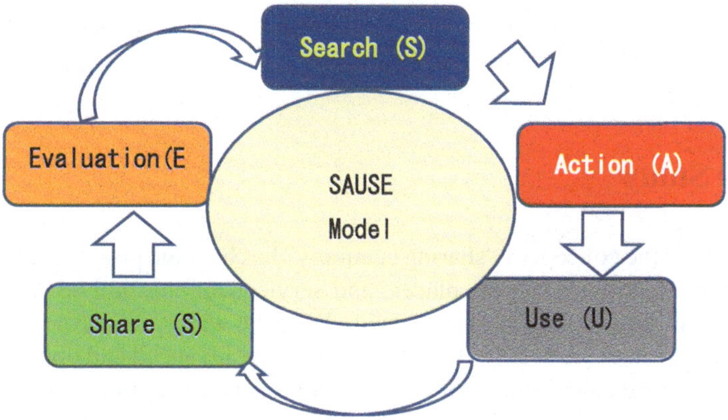

Fig. 1 Consumer behavior in the sharing economy: the SAUSE model approach

passing the product to another, and Evaluation by a thoughtful consumer leaving feedback. The background will reflect the modern, digital world, with subtle references to industries like cosmetics, automotive, real estate, and logistics. This illustration aims to capture the transformative shift from ownership to utility in consumer behavior, emphasizing the resale value consideration in purchases.

The SAUSE (Search, Action, Use, Share, and Evaluation) model presents a comprehensive framework that mirrors the evolving consumer journey in the digital era. At its core, the model highlights key stages of consumer interaction, beginning with 'Search', where consumers explore options in digital marketplaces, symbolizing the expanding role of online platforms in modern shopping. The 'Action' stage, represented by the act of pressing a button, encapsulates the ease and immediacy of digital transactions. This is followed by 'Use', emphasizing the practical experience and utility derived from products, shifting focus from ownership to actual usage. The 'Share' stage reflects the increasing trend of considering the resale value of items, propelling consumers towards more sustainable and higher-quality purchases. Finally, 'Evaluation' involves consumers assessing their satisfaction and the product's performance, influencing their future buying decisions. This model emphasizes the interconnectedness of these stages, suggesting a dynamic and continuous cycle of consumer behavior.

In the context of the sharing economy, particularly for products like cosmetics, the SAUSE model is pivotal. It underscores the transformative shift in consumer behavior from merely owning products to valuing their utility and potential for reuse. Platforms like Mercari and apps like Prima, which facilitate cosmetic transactions, play a crucial role in this landscape, driving the trend toward considering resale value in purchasing decisions. This shift not only aligns with the principles of sustainability and higher quality but also broadens the model's relevance across various industries, including cosmetics, automotive, real estate, and logistics. The SAUSE model serves as a lens to comprehend and navigate the changing dynamics of consumer behavior, emphasizing the importance of each stage in enhancing the overall value of purchase in the sharing economy (Park et al., 2022).

4 Case Study

In recent years, the concept of "sharing economy" has become popular as the internet facilitates the sharing of goods, places, and services among individuals. This has led to a shift in the perception of ownership. With the widespread availability of the internet, there is now the potential for the provision of advanced and diverse services, leading to the emergence and evolution of various services in the form of B to B, B to C, and C to C. Gradually, this has evolved into the "sharing economy." Here we introduce Japanese and Chinese sharing cases of cosmetics. In Japan, in particular, the Sharing Economy Association defines the sharing economy as an economic model that involves buying and renting goods, places, and services between individuals and businesses by leveraging the Internet. They aim to promote the development of this emerging economy, where sharing becomes an industry in itself. Currently, the sharing market size in Japan reached 2.4198 trillion yen in 2021, marking a record high. It is predicted to expand to 14.2799 trillion yen by 2030.

4.1 Mercari's Study: Shifting Consumer Behaviors

Mercari, in collaboration with the Mitsubishi Research Institute, conducted a joint study on the sharing economy (Mitsubishi Research Institute, 2019). In the era of sharing, a new consumer model called 'SAUSE' has emerged. To analyze the changes in behavior and purchasing patterns before and after using the Prima app, which facilitates cosmetic transactions, surveys were conducted among users. The results revealed that consumers who engage in the 'sharing' of goods through the Prima app exhibit different consumption behaviors, influenced by a shift in their perception of the value of items from 'ownership' to 'usage.'

After using the Prima app, 50% of respondents consciously considered reselling when purchasing new cosmetics. This awareness significantly influenced their product choices when buying new cosmetics. Following the use of the Prima app, 28% of users reported a change in the frequency of purchasing cosmetics, with 14% indicating an increase and 14% reporting a decrease. Users who experienced a decrease in purchasing frequency had different motivations beyond the conventional idea of 'saving.' The increased frequency of purchasing new cosmetics was attributed to the perception that 'sales through the Prima app are good' and 'earning pocket money through the Prima app.' This suggests that the psychological hurdle to making purchases is lowered due to the belief that items can be resold in the future."

The shift in the price range of purchased products was observed, with 33% of cosmetic buyers reporting changes in the price range after using the Prima app, including an 18% shift to higher price ranges and a 15% shift to lower price ranges. In particular, among individuals aged 20–30, 36% shifted towards higher-priced cosmetics. The tendency to purchase higher-priced products, influenced by the potential for resale value, has resulted in an increased budget for product purchases, leading to a preference for higher-priced items compared to traditional consumption patterns. This trend is particularly evident among individuals in their 20s and 30s who frequently use sharing services in their daily lives."

4.2 *Emerging Sharing Trends in Personal Care: Insights from Panasonic's Survey*

In 2022, Panasonic Corporation conducted a survey focusing on the sharing awareness of intimate daily necessities among 200 men and women in Japan (Panasonic, 2022). Key findings from the survey include an increase in the sharing of daily necessities due to the stay-at-home situation. Particularly, within the age group of 18 to 29 years, about half reported an increase in sharing, and nearly 40% expressed a strong desire to actively share. The most commonly shared items were skincare products, such as lotions, indicating a trend toward popular beauty items.

The survey also uncovered that the rise in sharing consciousness is partly due to the growth of the men's beauty market. After the stay-at-home period, approximately 30% of respondents felt that their awareness of beauty had increased. Among males aged 18 to 29, 60% reported heightened beauty consciousness and about 50% were more proactive in seeking information and purchasing beauty items. Specifically, there was a notable increase in the sharing of various daily necessities like lotions, especially among those aged 18 to 29, with nearly half of them engaging in this trend. This shift suggests a growing inclination towards sharing intimate and personal items within families or between partners, reflecting changing consumer behaviors and attitudes.

The results of a survey question posed to individuals aged 18 to 29 regarding their sharing habits of daily necessities like lotions during and after a stay-at-home period. The question aims to gauge whether there has been an increase in the sharing of personal care items among this age group, with nearly half of the respondents indicating a rise in such behavior, suggesting a notable trend towards communal usage within this demographic.

Additionally, regarding the sharing of daily necessities such as cosmetics and suits between men and women (partners or family), 39.0% of all respondents indicated that they are "actively interested in sharing and trying out" or "want to share what they can." Among those aged 18 to 29, the figure is 40.0%, and notably, it rises to 60% among people in their 30s, demonstrating that the younger generation, particularly those under 30, has a stronger inclination towards sharing. Additionally, regarding the sharing of daily necessities such as cosmetics and suits between men and women (partners or family), 39.0% of all respondents indicated that they are "actively interested in sharing and trying out" or "want to share what they can." Among those aged 18 to 29, the figure is 40.0%, and notably, it rises to 60% among people in their 30s, demonstrating that the younger generation, particularly those under 30, has a stronger inclination towards sharing.

Specifically, the items most commonly shared are skincare products, like lotions, which top the list at 61.0%. Following closely are fashion items such as suits and bags, along with beauty products like foundation and suncream. Beauty electronics, including facial steamers and cleansing devices, also rank highly among the beauty-related items that are being shared. This data showcases a significant trend where personal care and fashion products are increasingly becoming communal, with a special emphasis on beauty and skincare leading the charge in shared usage.

The survey revealed that 60% of men aged 18 to 29 have become more conscious about their appearance and beauty routines, with roughly half of them taking initiative in seeking information on and purchasing beauty items. This increasing trend of sharing beauty-related items among this demographic has a strong connection to the burgeoning men's beauty market. When asked whether their beauty consciousness, including concerns and considerations, has increased after stay-at-home measures, 26.5% of all respondents felt it had significantly or slightly increased. A closer look at the responses shows a slight difference between genders, with 29.0% of women acknowledging a heightened sense of beauty consciousness compared to 24.0% of men. However, among the male respondents in the 18 to 29 age group, there was a notable increase, matching the level of their female counterparts at 60.0%. This suggests that young men are equally engaged in the beauty conversation and practices, reflecting a shift towards gender parity in beauty and grooming habits.

Moreover, when asked whether the procurement of beauty items such as cosmetics had increased after experiencing a period of stay-at-home, 22.5% of all respondents affirmed a significant or slight increase in their self-directed information gathering and purchasing activities. Notably, among males aged 18 to 29, the percentage reached 45.0%, showing no difference from females in the same age bracket. This indicates a clear rise in interest in male grooming, underscoring that young men are actively participating in the beauty and cosmetics market to the same extent as their female counterparts, highlighting a trend of increasing engagement with beauty products among young men following the stay-at-home period.

4.3 Survey Summary

A comprehensive survey was conducted across the regions of Tokyo, Kanagawa, Chiba, and Saitama, engaging a diverse group of 200 individuals ranging from 18 to 69 years of age. The survey spanned five days, starting on February 10 and concluding on February 14, 2022, utilizing an online platform to gather data. This initiative aimed to delve into the behaviors and attitudes towards shared beauty and grooming practices among both men and women in these prefectures.

The findings indicate a cultural shift towards "Shared Beauty," a trend where not only women but also men are actively participating in beauty and grooming rituals. While sharing items like hair dryers has been common among families and partners, there's now a noticeable pivot towards sharing more personal beauty products. The survey highlights an increasing trend among men to engage in beauty routines, likely fueled by heightened self-awareness during online interactions and a modern emphasis on looking good and feeling comfortable. Men are not just more conscious of their skincare and grooming needs but are also more willing to share related products, such as lotions, with others.

Panasonic's observations corroborate these survey results, particularly in the purchasing trends for their beauty products (Panasonic, 2022). Their "Light Esthetic" hair removal device, on the market since 2009, has experienced a shift in its customer demographics and usage patterns. Initially, male customers accounted for a mere 7% of the product's buyers. However, after the product was adapted for facial hair use in 2019, there was a significant increase in male patronage, with their numbers surging to 31% and then 39% by 2021. Moreover, about 60% of the product's consumers, irrespective of gender, share it within their household. Customer feedback has shed light on a new trend: a robust uptick in proactive purchases by men and a commonality of sharing these products among friends and family.

5 Sharing Beauty Company Case

Leveraging expertise in producing content that simplifies complex information and utilizing unique user data, Sharing Beauty Company engaged in brand consulting for major cosmetic manufacturers and growing companies in the health food industry, focusing on product distribution. Operating one of the largest hair style-focused media platforms, "HAIR," Sharing Beauty Company not only provides stylists with a space to showcase their skills and styles to users but also uses this platform as a digital advertising venture that connects brand development with product distribution. Through various business ventures, Sharing Beauty Company has actively built relationships with numerous professionals and influencers. By accumulating expertise in meeting the needs of all stakeholders and utilizing its influencer network, the firm is creating a new concept of advertising that blends real and digital experiences. This innovative approach allows the firm to offer unique and effective advertising solutions that leverage both online and offline channels, catering to a diverse range of audiences and industries.

5.1 MCN Solution Business

Recognizing the importance of both online and offline presence for stylists, Sharing Beauty Company currently operates seven direct-owned hair salons in the region as of January 2022. These establishments include brand-centric salons and shared salons that create new employment environments for stylists, achieving a remarkable 130% growth compared to the previous year. Its future plans involve expanding beyond the local region to establish a national presence. By integrating real-world hair salons with digital services, Sharing Beauty Company aims to create optimal matching opportunities between users and stylists, thereby invigorating the beauty industry.

The beauty industry possesses enormous potential for the distribution of "information" and "products." The reach, both offline and online, coupled with the credibility and influence of information disseminated by stylists, has been largely untapped until now. The goal of Sharing Beauty Company is to update the beauty industry, traditionally confined to the provision of services, into a new, evolving sector. In the midst of accelerating digital transformation (DX) across various economic sectors, the firm provides platforms and content aimed at digitalizing hair salons. Additionally, Sharing Beauty Company is developing stylist-collaborated products, focusing on the beauty sector. These products are scientifically backed and developed based on effective ingredients. The firm is also progressing in developing new products and establishing unique distribution channels, catering to consumer needs with its innovative beauty offerings.

5.2 The Case of Share Salons

The term "Share Salon" has become increasingly familiar recently, giving off a relatively new vibe. Along with this, terms like "business consignment" and "booth renting" are also being heard more often. These terms represent a shift in the working methods and employment choices for hairstylists over the past decade, signifying the emergence of new operational models in the industry.

"Share Salons," "booth renting," and "business consignment" all refer to systems where, typically, the hairstylist is not in an employment relationship with the salon or store. Instead, the stylist rents space from the owner or operating company, paying either a rental fee or a percentage of their sales to the salon. One of the primary benefits of this system is the lack of initial investment required to use the facilities. While starting an independent salon can be a significant financial barrier due to startup costs, share salons and similar services eliminate this need, allowing stylists to offer services to their clients without substantial upfront investment.

This model is particularly valuable for stylists contemplating independence but still accumulating capital, as well as for those balancing work with childcare. It offers the flexibility to work part-time or during specific hours. However, for traditional salon owners who employ staff, this trend has led to concerns about staff turnover. The increase in options for stylists signifies a new dimension emerging due to industry changes. A salon owner who manages multiple locations and traditionally employs staff, hiring new graduates annually, is now considering the adoption of "business consignment" or "booth renting" as new operational models. Accepting the changes of the times and making judicious decisions without bias towards traditional methods, salon owners are now assessing which approach will be more accepted in the current era, making strategic choices based on their judgment of the evolving industry landscape.

6 Case in China

Following the trend of shared bicycles, cars, and chargers, "Shared makeup booths" designed for women's convenience in makeup application are quietly emerging as a trend in major Chinese cities like Beijing, Shanghai, and Guangzhou. These facilities offer the first 15 min of use for free, gradually gaining popularity among women. However, amid a declining sharing economy boom, there is speculation about the potential rise of these shared beauty booths (People's Daily Online, 2019).

Let us introduce two cases. First, the target demographic of 17 Beauty makeup booths is 25- to 35-year-old students and white-collar workers (Takizawa, 2019). These booths are equipped with a wide range of brand cosmetics, from makeup removers to foundations and coloring cosmetics, and can be used for as long as the customer desires, with a pay-by-the-hour system. With no staff present, customers can freely try the makeup products to their heart's content. The 17 Beauty booth was set up inside a shopping mall in Shanghai. Customers use the WeChat smartphone app to register, pay, and configure other details before entering the booth. After scanning the QR code affixed to the door, customers launch the custom mini-program within WeChat, and a screen appears where they can select the amount of time they want to spend in the booth. The shortest usage time is 15 min, which is regularly priced at US$4.20 (the first time is free).

Once payment is made via smartphone, customers enter the booth, and the usage time begins immediately. They can check the remaining time on their smartphones. The enclosed 3-square-meter space contains a glass case that houses the cosmetics. The booth door is made of frosted glass, providing privacy away from the public eye, which is essential in a shopping mall setting with many passersby. The cosmetics available include luxury brands such as Lancôme and Dior, which are popular with younger generations. The ability to freely try these mid to high-end brands, which are typically hard to access, and at a reasonable usage fee, is perhaps the greatest advantage that 17 Beauty offers. To deter theft, the booths feature surveillance cameras, and all cosmetics are securely fixed to the table to prevent them from being taken. 17 Beauty's main sources of revenue come from usage fees and advertising from cosmetics makers and brands. The company partners with several popular brands in China, and featuring their products in the booths serves as a form of advertising. Customer touchpoints are created similarly to distributing samples.

Second, PlusBeauty launched almost simultaneously with 17 Beauty, opening its first branch in Shanghai at the end of July 2018 (Takizawa, 2019). It has since expanded to ten locations within the city. As of 2020, shared makeup booths are installed in only six cities nationwide: Beijing, Shanghai, Guangzhou, Nanjing, Hangzhou, and Wuhan. For example, in Wuhan, a pink Beauty Booth located in the basement of a commercial facility is stocked with various cosmetics from major brands, valued at around 4,000 yuan, available for free use by patrons. The usage fee, after the initial 15 free minutes, is capped at 58 yuan for a maximum of 45 min. According to customer service staff, while many first-time users take advantage of the free 15 min, only about 10% return as paying repeat customers. Similar to 17 Beauty, PlusBeauty booths are also located inside shopping malls. These booths are not only equipped with branded cosmetics but also staffed with a beauty stylist to provide makeup services. Reservations and payments are made through WeChat, similar to 17 Beauty. When it's time for a reservation, customers enter the booth.

Although relatively expensive for China, the appeal lies in having a professional do makeup. The booths feature a wide range of skincare products and cosmetics; from Western brands such as Lancome and Clinique, to Japanese goods by brands such as Muji. The in-booth stylist creates a friendly, conversational atmosphere while working, asking which color or style customers prefer for aspects such as eye makeup or blusher. Their work comes across more as makeup for a special occasion rather than everyday makeup, but it is thorough, of high quality and brings a high level of satisfaction.

The founder and CEO of PlusBeauty has up to 12 years' experience working in the wedding and fashion industries. She says the idea for PlusBeauty came from thinking about how women can look their best on occasions other than weddings, by giving them access to professional makeup services. Adopting the smaller booth format allowed PlusBeauty to expand in different locations and to take advantage of cheap rentals. Looking at both franchises, it is clear that 17 Beauty is aimed at savvy users comfortable with applying their own makeup, while PlusBeauty targets makeup novices. Compared to 17 Beauty's privacy-oriented setup, the design of PlusBeauty's booths is also more bare bones, as if to showcase the makeup experience to passers-by.

China's cosmetics market has boomed in recent years. More women apply makeup every day, at least among the younger generation. The growing presence of shared makeup booths could bring about even more widespread use of makeup in the country. Yet, increased competition will likely result in a race to the bottom, with cheaper services in turn leading to a drop in quality. Then there's the issue of upkeep. Unstaffed shared makeup booths, including those of 17 Beauty, are reportedly poorly maintained. Bottles aren't replenished often enough, period-after-opening dates on product packaging are unclear, and garbage is strewn on the floor. This has led to concerns about the booths' hygiene levels and potential risks of contagious diseases. Solving these issues will be key to ensuring the stability of these makeup booth businesses.

7 Implications

The research on the implications of the sharing economy and globalization in the cosmetics industry holds significant importance. Primarily, it enhances the understanding of shifting consumer behaviors, spotlighting the transition from traditional ownership to a preference for utility, convenience, and experiences. This insight is crucial for businesses to align their strategies with evolving market trends. Moreover, the research serves as a strategic guide for cosmetic companies, aiding in the innovation of product offerings, marketing, and operational models, crucial for maintaining competitiveness in a dynamic industry. It also emphasizes the growing importance of sustainability and ethical consumption, aligning with the increasing consumer emphasis on environmentally conscious practices. Additionally, the focus on globalization presents opportunities for market expansion and diversification, encouraging cosmetic companies to tailor their products to diverse cultural contexts and involving small and medium enterprises in emerging economies , thereby expanding their customer base and enhancing market resilience (Yeon et al., 2022).

However, the case study approach used in this research also presents certain limitations. The findings' limited generalizability, being specific to the contexts and demographics studied, might not apply universally across different regions or consumer groups in the cosmetics industry. The contextual and cultural specificity, especially in studies like the "share beauty booth" in China, may not be replicable in other cultural or economic settings. Moreover, the rapidly changing nature of the cosmetics industry means these findings could quickly become outdated. Potential biases in data collection and the focus on specific aspects might have led to overlooking other influential variables such as regulatory changes, technological advancements, and economic fluctuations. These factors could also significantly affect consumer behavior and market dynamics, pointing to the need for a more comprehensive and continually updated approach to research in this field.

7.1 Theoretical Implications

Theoretical implications represent the ways in which a study's findings extend, refine, challenge, or provide new perspectives on established theories or conceptual frameworks. Theoretical implications can shape how scholars and practitioners understand particular phenomena, lead to the development of new theories, or suggest modifications to existing ones. In essence, they are the broader, often more abstract, outcomes of research that contribute to the overall advancement of academic disciplines and inform future research directions.

First, relevance of sharing economy theory. The cosmetic industry is increasingly influenced by the sharing economy theory, which emphasizes the value of utility and convenience over ownership and individual self-interest. This shift is particularly evident in consumer behavior, where a growing number of customers, especially in the cosmetics sector, are more interested in the practicality and accessibility of products rather than owning them. This trend is showcased in innovative business models like "Share Beauty Booth" in major Chinese cities, where makeup and personal care facilities are provided in public spaces. These shared spaces, offering high-end cosmetic products for temporary use, align with the sharing economy's principles of maximizing resource utilization and enhancing user convenience. This approach reflects a significant change in consumer preferences, where easy access to quality products, even in a shared environment, is becoming more appealing than the traditional notion of personal ownership.

Second, globalization orientation of the cosmetics industry. The cosmetics industry is actively expanding its horizons beyond domestic and regional markets to capture global opportunities. This global orientation is driven by the need to explore new growth engines and expand organizational capabilities to cover both advanced and emerging markets (Fujimoto et al., 2022; Hong et al., 2023). The case studies of 17 Beauty and PlusBeauty in China illustrate this trend, where companies are innovating to meet the diverse needs of a global customer base. These businesses leverage the widespread use of the internet and digital platforms to offer unique services like makeup booths and professional styling assistance, catering to a wide range of consumers from different cultural backgrounds. The globalization of the cosmetics industry is not just about expanding market boundaries but also about adapting to various consumer preferences and cultural nuances worldwide (Abraham et al., 2022). By tapping into global markets, these companies can gather varied consumer insights, which in turn fuel innovation and help in creating products and services that resonate with a global audience.

In summary, the cosmetic industry is witnessing a paradigm shift influenced by the sharing economy and globalization. Consumers are increasingly valuing utility, convenience, and experiences over ownership, pushing companies to rethink their business models. Simultaneously, the global expansion of the industry offers new opportunities and challenges, requiring cosmetic companies to be adaptable, culturally sensitive, and innovative in their approach to cater to a diverse global market.

7.2 Practical Implications

Practical implications involve the concrete applications, recommendations, or benefits that arise from research findings for real-world situations. They encompass how the results of a study can be used to address specific problems, improve practices, inform policy-making, or guide decision-making in various fields. Practical implications are particularly important because they bridge the gap between theory and practice, translating academic research into tangible actions or changes that can be implemented in everyday contexts.

First, the expansion of sharing economy platforms in the beauty industry: One practical implication of the research is the potential expansion of sharing economy platforms within the beauty industry, moving beyond the typical domains of Uber and Airbnb. This expansion can take the form of shared beauty spaces, such as communal makeup studios or pop-up styling stations, where individuals can access high-quality beauty products and professional equipment on a pay-per-use basis. Additionally, there is an opportunity for the development of digital platforms for sharing beauty-related insights and advice, facilitating peer-to-peer learning and exchange of beauty techniques. These platforms could also enable the sharing of personal beauty products in a controlled and hygienic manner, fostering a sense of community among users. For beauty industry stakeholders, this implies a need to explore collaborative consumption models, invest in the development of such platforms, and create strategies that address health, safety, and hygiene concerns associated with shared beauty products and services.

Second, the diversity of sharing concepts in different cultural contexts. It is important to recognize and cater to the diversity of sharing concepts in different cultural contexts, particularly in individualistic versus collective societies, when applying cosmetic products in global markets. In individualistic cultures, sharing in the beauty industry might focus more on personalization and unique experiences, such as customizable product options or one-on-one beauty consultations. In contrast, in collective cultures, the emphasis might be on community experiences, like group beauty tutorials or shared beauty rituals. This cultural variation suggests that global cosmetic brands need to adopt flexible marketing strategies and product offerings that are culturally sensitive and tailored to the specific sharing preferences of different regions. This approach can help in effectively penetrating diverse global markets, ensuring that the concept of sharing in the beauty industry is respectful and appealing to various cultural norms and values.

8 Conclusion

Future research in the field of sharing economy platforms within the beauty industry should focus on addressing several key issues. One area for exploration is the development of guidelines and standards to ensure health, safety, and hygiene in shared beauty spaces. This research should investigate the best practices for maintaining cleanliness and preventing contamination, especially when personal beauty products are involved. Another important area is the economic and business model analysis for such sharing platforms, evaluating their sustainability, profitability, and scalability. Additionally, research should delve into consumer behavior and preferences regarding shared beauty services, understanding the motivations, hesitations, and expectations of users. This would provide valuable insights for tailoring services and enhancing user experiences. Future studies could also explore the environmental impact of shared beauty services, contributing to the broader understanding of sustainable practices in the beauty industry.

In conclusion, the integration of sharing economy principles into the beauty industry presents significant opportunities for innovation, sustainability, and cultural inclusivity (Park and Hong, 2022). The development of shared beauty spaces and digital platforms offers a new dimension to beauty services, catering to modern consumers' desire for convenience, community, and personalized experiences.

However, this integration must be approached thoughtfully, considering diverse cultural contexts and ensuring the safety and well-being of users. As the industry advances, it will be imperative for stakeholders to embrace these changes while remaining sensitive to the varying needs and values of consumers across different regions. Adapting to this evolving landscape with strategic and informed approaches will be key to the future success and growth of various multinational enterprises, including the beauty industry, in the dynamic post-pandemic sharing economy era (Hong et al., 2022; Mackelprang et al., 2023).

References

Abraham, J. S. E., Floreto, S. J. L., Pagkalinawan, M. I. B., & Etrata, A. E. (2022). Consumer perception on influencer marketing efforts of brands in the beauty and cosmetics industry. *International Journal of Social and Management Studies, 3*(2), 105–118.

Elder, A., Ring, C., Heitmiller, K., Gabriel, Z., & Saedi, N. (2021). The role of artificial intelligence in cosmetic dermatology—current, upcoming, and future trends. *Journal of Cosmetic Dermatology, 20*(1), 48–52.

Fujimoto, T., Mitsuhiro Fukuzawa, M., Park, Y. W., & Hong, P. (2022). Developing effective measures of organizational capability of manufacturing firms: An exploratory case study of Japanese manufacturing firms. *Sustainability, 14*, 14811. https://doi.org/10.3390/su142214811

Hong, P., Singh, N., Elangovan N., & Yeon, G. (2022). Responding to the COVID-19 pandemic challenges: Case of multinational enterprises (MNEs) in India. *Journal of Management Development, 41*(4), 205–222.

Hong, P., Jagani, S. J., Pham, P., & Jung, E. (2023). Globalization orientation, business practices and performance outcomes: An empirical investigation of B2B manufacturing firms. *Journal of Business & Industrial Marketing, 38*(10), 2259–2274. https://doi.org/10.1108/JBIM-02-2021-0098)

Iwao, S., Park, Y.C., Park, Y. W., & Hong, P. C. (2023). A new mathematical learning curve model based on the empirical analysis of Japanese sharing economy companies. *IEEE Access, 11*, 4944–4955 (2023). https://doi.org/10.1109/ACCESS.2022.3233391

Kolling, C., Ribeiro, J. L. D., & de Medeiros, J. F. (2022). Performance of the cosmetics industry from the perspective of corporate social responsibility and design for sustainability. *Sustainable Production and Consumption, 30*, 171–185.

Mackelprang, A., Modi, A., Dobtzykowski, D., & Hong, P. C. (2023). Sharing economy: An agenda for OM/SCM research. *Journal of Operations Management, 69*(9), 706–718. https://onlinelibrary.wiley.com/doi/10.1002/joom.1269

Mitsubishi Research Institute. (2019). Conducting joint research on sharing economy with Mercari, MRI news release, Feb 26, pp. 1–4.

Panasonic. (2022). Beauty awareness survey, Mar 1st.

Park, Y. W., Hong, P., & Shin, G. C. (2022). Rising and thriving in the post COVID-19 era: A case study of COSMAX, a leader of the Korean cosmetic industry. *Asia Pacific Business Review*. https://doi.org/10.1080/13602381.2022.2059955

Park, Y. C., & Hong, P. (2022). Knowledge sharing practices for corporate sustainability: An empirical investigation of sharing economy firms in Japan. *Sustainability, 14*(24), 16655. https://doi.org/10.3390/su142416655

People Daily Online. (2019). Unlimited use of cosmetics worth 4,000 yuan! Will shared makeup booth be the savior of the shared economy? (January 10). http://j.people.com.cn/n3/2019/0110/c94475-9536655.html

Rathod, S., Mali, S., Shinde, N., & Aloorkar, N. (2020). Cosmeceuticals and beauty care products: Current trends with future prospects. *Research Journal of Topical and Cosmetic Sciences, 11*(1), 45–51.

Takizawa, Y. (2019). Will China's makeup booth industry leave a mark? BeautyTech, Jul 9. https://beautytech.jp/n/n39ada2a59f23

Yeon, G., Hong, P. C., Elangovan, N., & Divakar, M. (2022). Implementing strategic responses in the COVID-19 market crisis: A study of small and medium enterprises (SMEs) in India. *Journal of Indian Business Research, 14*(3), 319–338. https://doi.org/10.1108/JIBR-04-2021-0137

Chapter 12
Beauty Reloaded: Top Cosmetic Trends Shaping the Digital Age and Beyond

Abstract This chapter, "Beauty Reloaded: Top Cosmetic Trends Shaping the Digital Age and Beyond," discusses the evolving landscape of the cosmetics industry in the digital era. It highlights the shift towards natural and organic cosmetics, driven by consumer demand for purity and sustainability. The clean beauty movement, which combines natural ingredients with safe chemicals, is gaining popularity globally, with major players like Shiseido acquiring clean beauty brands to adapt to this trend. The emergence of robust clean beauty certification systems, such as those established by Credo Beauty and adopted by Sephora, emphasizes transparency, safety, and eco-conscious practices. Additionally, the chapter explores the significant rise in male grooming, influenced by cultural phenomena like K-Pop, and the increasing acceptance of makeup as a form of self-expression beyond traditional gender norms. The industry is also moving away from promoting whitening cosmetics, aligning with a global shift towards inclusivity and diversity. This reflects a growing recognition of the multifaceted nature of beauty and the rejection of discriminatory beauty standards. The chapter also delves into the rise of femtech in cosmetics, focusing on women's health and wellness, and the growing trend of individual-created cosmetics brands by non-traditional experts, emphasizing authenticity and personal connection. The industry is adopting inclusive business models targeting lower-income groups, aligning with Sustainable Development Goals (SDGs) and promoting accessibility and affordability. Environmental sustainability and packaging innovations, such as the Loop system for reusable containers, are also examined as ways to reduce ecological impact. The chapter concludes by emphasizing the importance for cosmetics companies staying agile and adapting to these evolving trends and consumer values in the digital transformation era, ensuring continued success and relevance in the rapidly changing beauty landscape.

Y. W. Park and P. Hong, *Cosmetics Marketing Strategy in the Era of the Digital Ecosystem*, https://doi.org/10.1007/978-981-97-3674-4_12

1 Introduction

In a world where beauty knows no bounds, the cosmetics industry stands at the forefront of a dynamic transformation. With consumers seeking natural ingredients, sustainable practices, and cutting-edge technology, the beauty landscape is shifting at a remarkable pace. As sustainability and inclusivity take center stage, and digital transformation (DX) reshapes the way products are marketed and consumed, cosmetics companies find themselves at a pivotal moment. This chapter delves into the ever-evolving strategies that are shaping the future of cosmetics marketing, offering insights into the trends that are driving this exciting era of change. From the rise of clean beauty to the embrace of aging as a beautiful journey, we explore the vibrant world of cosmetics in the age of DX.

The cosmetics industry is witnessing significant shifts towards sustainability and consumer health consciousness. The growing trend towards environmental responsibility is evident in the emphasis on sustainable and eco-friendly product packaging at the point of sale, highlighting the industry's commitment to reducing its ecological footprint (Borja Guerrero et al., 2022). Concurrently, the COVID-19 pandemic has dramatically influenced consumer behavior, leading to heightened awareness and interest in cosmetic products that align with health and safety concerns. This shift has prompted changes in purchasing behavior, with a preference for products that ensure both beauty and well-being (Choi et al., 2022).

Additionally, there's a noticeable pivot towards natural ingredients and the integration of skincare benefits into cosmetic formulations. The demand for botanical ingredients in anti-aging cosmetics has surged, driven by consumers seeking natural, yet effective, solutions to combat skin aging (Ferreira et al., 2021). This trend is paralleled by the development and rising popularity of functional cosmetics, which combine makeup products with skincare benefits, catering to a more informed and health-conscious consumer base (Jang & Lee, 2021). Furthermore, advancements in biotechnology have played a crucial role in introducing bioactive ingredients into cosmeceuticals, particularly from Korean beauty trends, offering innovative skincare solutions backed by scientific research (Nguyen et al., 2020).

As we transition from the overarching themes of sustainability, digital transformation, and the pursuit of inclusivity, we now delve deeper into each trend, examining their intricacies and the impact they hold over the industry's future. This next segment examines how specific trends, such as the integration of biotechnology in product formulation, the rise of digital marketing strategies, and the consumer-driven demand for transparency and natural ingredients, are not only reshaping consumer expectations but also setting new benchmarks for innovation and responsibility in the global cosmetics sector (Kumar, 2005; Jones, 2011). By scrutinizing these trends individually, we provide a clearer understanding of how they are interwoven with the digital age's demands, laying the groundwork for a future where beauty products are not just consumed but experienced in a way that aligns with ethical values and innovative technology.

2 Top Cosmetic Trends Shaping the Digital Age and Beyond

The realm of cosmetics is continuously evolving, especially in the digital age where technology and innovation significantly influence consumer behavior and industry practices. Top cosmetic trends are those that define the current preferences, demands, and innovations within the beauty industry. These trends can range from the types of products in vogue, such as natural or organic cosmetics, to the methods of marketing and distribution, heavily influenced by digital platforms and social media. The digital age, characterized by the pervasive use of digital technology, internet, and social media, has redefined how beauty products are developed, marketed, and consumed. The interplay between consumer trends and the digital environment is intricate, as it not only reflects current consumer preferences but also shapes future demands and industry standards (Su et al., 2023).

Understanding these trends in the context of the digital age is crucial as they offer insights into the evolving nature of consumer preferences and the industry's direction (Kumar et al., 2021; Lopaciuk and Laboda, 2013). It is important to consider these trends beyond the current moment because they have long-term implications for the beauty industry, from product development to branding and consumer engagement. The decisions made today by cosmetic brands, influenced by these trends, will shape the future landscape of the industry. Moreover, in a rapidly changing world, foresight is essential for sustainability and innovation. By analyzing current trends and their potential future impact, brands can better adapt, innovate, and remain relevant in a market that is increasingly competitive and globally interconnected.

2.1 Rise of Natural and Organic Cosmetics

In recent years, the cosmetics industry has experienced an unprecedented surge in the demand for natural and organic products, fundamentally altering the landscape of beauty choices (Rawlings, 2003; Siahaan et al., 2017). Consumers are increasingly drawn to cosmetics that prioritize the use of wholesome, naturally sourced ingredients, reflecting a broader shift towards purity and sustainability in their purchasing decisions. This transformation in consumer preferences has not only reshaped product formulations but has also challenged brands to reevaluate their entire approach to beauty.

The global proliferation of the clean beauty movement has played a significant role in this transformation (McDonald et al., 2022). While the allure of natural ingredients continues to resonate with consumers, the clean beauty trend has introduced a new dimension to the beauty world. Originating in the United States, clean beauty products distinguish themselves by their active incorporation of chemical ingredients alongside natural components, harnessing the power of both worlds. This trend has transcended geographical borders, making its way into the heart of the Asian market. Major industry players, exemplified by Shiseido, have recognized the critical importance of clean beauty and responded with strategic acquisitions of clean beauty brands, positioning themselves to cater to the evolving preferences of beauty enthusiasts who seek a harmonious blend of nature and science in their cosmetic choices.

The rise of natural and organic cosmetics also signifies a deeper, more nuanced understanding of health and wellness among consumers. This shift goes beyond mere aesthetic preferences, delving into the realm of ethical consumerism. People are not just seeking products that make them look good, but also those that make them feel good about their choices, in terms of both personal health and environmental impact. This trend is reflected in the growing demand for transparency in ingredient sourcing and production processes. Consumers are more informed and more inquisitive than ever, often favoring brands that can provide clear, honest information about their products. This demand for transparency is reshaping how companies approach not only their product formulations but also their overall brand messaging and customer engagement strategies.

Moreover, the integration of digital technologies in the cosmetics industry has been instrumental in fueling the growth of the natural and organic cosmetics trend (Ngoc et al., 2019). Social media platforms, influencer marketing, and online retail channels have played pivotal roles in raising awareness and accessibility of these products to a global audience (Mu & Zhang, 2021). Digital platforms have enabled niche organic brands to reach a wider market and have facilitated a two-way conversation between brands and consumers. This digital engagement has allowed consumers to voice their preferences, concerns, and values more directly, influencing brands to adapt and innovate in response. The result is a dynamic, consumer-driven market where natural and organic products are not just a trend, but a significant, enduring segment of the cosmetics industry.

2.2 Clean Beauty Certification

In response to the rising popularity of clean beauty, the cosmetics industry has witnessed the emergence of robust certification systems designed to offer consumers peace of mind regarding product safety, sustainability, and transparency. Pioneering brands like Credo Beauty have played a pivotal role in setting exceptionally high standards for their product formulations. These standards extend beyond the mere absence of harmful ingredients; they encompass a comprehensive evaluation of the product's environmental impact throughout its lifecycle. From responsibly sourced raw materials to sustainable packaging and ethical production processes, clean beauty certification demands an all-encompassing commitment to eco-conscious practices.

Moreover, the commitment to clean beauty certification has transcended individual brands and permeated the strategies of major retailers, including industry giant Sephora. These retailers have proactively established their own clean beauty standards, marking a significant shift in the cosmetics landscape. This industry-wide dedication underscores a shared goal of meeting the demands of discerning consumers who are increasingly conscious of the products they use. In an era where consumers prioritize both the efficacy of their cosmetics and their alignment with personal values and priorities, clean beauty certification has become a vital tool in building trust and delivering products that resonate with the evolving expectations of the beauty industry.

The growing emphasis on clean beauty certification has also catalyzed innovation in the cosmetics industry. As brands strive to meet these stringent standards, there is a notable uptick in research and development focused on sustainable ingredients and technologies. This pursuit of certification is not merely about adhering to current norms but is also about pushing the boundaries of what is possible in cosmetic science. New, innovative ingredients derived from sustainable sources are being discovered and incorporated into products, enhancing their appeal to environmentally conscious consumers. Moreover, the drive for clean beauty certification has encouraged collaborations between cosmetics companies and environmental and scientific experts, fostering a holistic approach to beauty that respects both human health and the environment (Redondo et al., 2021).

Another crucial aspect of this certification trend is its impact on consumer education and awareness. As certifications become more prevalent, they serve as informative tools that guide consumers in making mindful choices. The presence of a certification label on a product not only assures quality but also educates the buyer about the standards and values the product upholds. This heightened consumer awareness has broader implications for the industry, as it elevates the overall expectations for product safety, efficacy, and ethical standards (Grappe et al., 2022). Consequently, clean beauty certification is not just transforming the products on the shelves; it is reshaping the very criteria by which consumers evaluate and select their cosmetics, leading to a more informed and conscientious market.

2.3 Rise in Male Grooming: Embracing Beauty Beyond Gender Norms

In the contemporary era of cosmetics, a noteworthy trend has emerged—the significant rise in male grooming and makeup use (Del Saz-Rubio, 2019; Liu, 2019). This phenomenon can be attributed, in part, to the global popularity of K-Pop, a South Korean music genre that has transcended boundaries and captured the hearts of millions worldwide. K-Pop not only entertains but also influences cultural perceptions, challenging traditional gender norms and promoting the idea that beauty is a universal concept. As a result, South Korea, often at the forefront of beauty innovations, has witnessed a remarkable increase in the number of men who embrace grooming and makeup as essential tools for self-expression and confidence.

The influence of the younger Z-generation, which values diversity, individuality, and inclusivity, plays a pivotal role in this shift. Unlike previous generations, the Z-generation has demonstrated a heightened awareness of and support for makeup use among men. They recognize that makeup is not confined to a single gender and that it serves as a means of artistic expression and empowerment for all. This change in mindset has fostered an environment where men feel encouraged to explore and experiment with cosmetics, challenging societal norms and redefining beauty standards. Consequently, the cosmetics industry has responded by diversifying its product offerings to cater to this growing segment of male consumers, further cementing the notion that beauty knows no gender boundaries.

This progressive trend in male grooming and makeup use is further amplified by the influential role of social media and digital influencers (Simay et al., 2023). Platforms like Instagram, YouTube, and TikTok have become powerful tools for showcasing diverse beauty standards, including those for men. Influencers and content creators, often breaking gender stereotypes, use these platforms to share their grooming routines, makeup tutorials, and beauty tips, reaching a global audience. This visibility has played a crucial role in normalizing makeup use among men and promoting a more inclusive view of beauty. It allows men to see practical demonstrations and real-life examples of grooming and makeup, making it more accessible and relatable. As a result, social media has not only been a platform for expression but also a catalyst for change in how beauty and grooming are perceived across genders.

The evolution in the male grooming market has also led to increased innovation and specialization in product development. Cosmetics brands are now creating products specifically designed for men's skin types and preferences, acknowledging the physiological and aesthetic differences. This specialization goes beyond just packaging and branding; it includes formulation changes tailored to men's skincare needs, considering factors like skin texture, facial hair, and common skin concerns among men. This targeted approach shows a keen understanding of the market and a commitment to meeting the unique needs of male consumers. As a result, the rise in male grooming is not just a trend; it is a significant and lasting change in the cosmetics industry, reflecting a broader societal shift towards inclusivity and diversity in beauty standards.

2.4 *Changing Sales Approaches: Embracing Diversity and Shifting Away from Whitening Cosmetics*

In response to the evolving landscape of consumer preferences and societal values, the cosmetics industry is undergoing a significant transformation in its sales approaches (Underhill, 2009). One notable shift is the departure from marketing and selling whitening cosmetics, a product category that has faced scrutiny for its association with elements of racial discrimination and the promotion of fairer skin as the ideal standard of beauty. This paradigm shift reflects a global movement towards inclusivity, where beauty is celebrated in its diverse forms, and the industry is taking proactive steps to eliminate products that perpetuate harmful stereotypes (Baird, 2021).

The decision to phase out whitening cosmetics is not limited to specific regions but has become a global phenomenon. Leading beauty conglomerates, such as Johnson & Johnson, took a momentous step in 2020 by discontinuing the sale of some whitening products in Asia and the Middle East. This move was a response to growing concerns about the messaging behind these products, which implied that lighter skin was superior. As a result, the cosmetics industry is reevaluating its messaging and product offerings, focusing on celebrating and enhancing natural beauty while avoiding any connection to discriminatory beauty standards. This shift aligns with the broader cultural shift towards acknowledging that beauty is multifaceted, and individuals should be able to express their unique identities without facing prejudice or discrimination based on their skin tone or appearance.

This transformative approach extends beyond product offerings to include a more inclusive and diverse representation in marketing and advertising campaigns. The cosmetics industry, historically criticized for its narrow portrayal of beauty, is now embracing a broader spectrum of models in terms of race, ethnicity, age, gender, and body type. This inclusive representation is crucial in shaping public perception and consumer behavior. By showcasing a diverse range of beauty, these campaigns challenge long-standing biases and empower individuals to feel represented and valued. This shift in marketing strategy not only aligns with the ethical responsibilities of the brands but also resonates deeply with a consumer base that is increasingly aware and appreciative of diversity.

Additionally, the industry's shift away from whitening cosmetics has paved the way for the development and promotion of products that cater to a wide variety of skin tones and types. Brands are investing in research and development to create makeup and skincare products that are truly inclusive. This includes expanding shade ranges in foundations and concealers, developing skincare products suited for different ethnicities and skin conditions, and embracing a more holistic approach to beauty that acknowledges the unique needs and preferences of a diverse customer base. These changes are not merely cosmetic; they represent a fundamental rethinking of what beauty products should be and who they are for. In doing so, the cosmetics industry is not only adapting to current societal values but also shaping a more inclusive and equitable vision of beauty for future generations.

2.5 *Exploring Sustainable Distribution Channels*

The cosmetics industry is not only focusing on evolving product offerings but also rethinking its distribution channels to align with sustainability and environmental responsibility. In an era where environmental concerns are paramount, companies are increasingly exploring alternative distribution methods to reduce waste and promote the circular economy. One significant trend in this regard is the emergence of reselling surplus cosmetic products and the creation of secondhand cosmetic trading platforms, offering consumers more eco-conscious options (Coelho et al., 2020). One approach to sustainable distribution involves companies actively repurposing and reselling surplus cosmetic products.

Instead of disposing of excess inventory, which contributes to environmental waste, brands are finding ways to extend the lifecycle of their products. This approach not only reduces waste but also allows consumers to access high-quality cosmetics at a reduced cost, making it a win–win for both the environment and budget-conscious beauty enthusiasts. By adopting these sustainable practices, cosmetics companies are demonstrating their commitment to minimizing their ecological footprint while meeting the demands of eco-conscious consumers. In addition to reselling surplus products, the cosmetics industry is witnessing the rise of secondhand cosmetic trading platforms. These platforms provide a space for consumers to buy and sell gently used or unopened cosmetics. The popularity of these platforms has been bolstered by consumers' desire to reduce waste and make environmentally responsible choices. By participating in secondhand cosmetic trading, individuals can contribute to reducing cosmetic-related waste, promoting sustainability, and supporting a circular economy. This shift in distribution channels reflects a broader commitment within the industry to embrace sustainable practices and cater to the growing consumer demand for eco-friendly options (Vecino et al., 2017).

Moreover, the development of sustainable distribution channels extends to packaging and delivery methods. Many cosmetic companies are now adopting eco-friendly packaging solutions, such as biodegradable materials, refillable containers, and minimalistic designs, to reduce their environmental impact. This initiative not only addresses the issue of packaging waste but also resonates with the values of consumers who are increasingly seeking sustainable options. In terms of delivery, brands are exploring greener logistics, such as carbon–neutral shipping and local sourcing, to minimize the carbon footprint associated with transporting their products. These changes in packaging and delivery demonstrate a comprehensive approach to sustainability, considering every aspect of the product's journey from production to the consumer, and adopting circular business models. (D'Amato et al., 2020).

Furthermore, the integration of digital technologies is playing a crucial role in enhancing the sustainability of distribution channels. E-commerce platforms and digital marketplaces have become instrumental in connecting consumers with sustainable cosmetic options, often providing detailed information about the environmental impact of products and brands. The use of digital tools also allows for more efficient inventory management, reducing the likelihood of overproduction and excess stock. Additionally, digital platforms facilitate the sharing of knowledge and best practices among brands and consumers, fostering a community committed to sustainability. By leveraging technology, the cosmetics industry is not only streamlining its distribution channels but also promoting a culture of environmental consciousness and responsibility.

2.6 Embracing Aging with Aging Care Products: A Paradigm Shift

The cosmetics industry is witnessing a significant transformation in the realm of skincare products, particularly in aging societies such as Japan. This transformation is characterized by a shift in consumer attitudes towards aging and the corresponding surge in demand for aging care products (Shanbhag et al., 2019). Unlike the traditional focus on erasing blemishes and wrinkles, the contemporary approach is centered around embracing the aging process as a positive transformation, reflecting changing perceptions of beauty and self-acceptance.

In response to this shift, cosmetics companies have introduced a wide range of aging care products designed to cater to the specific needs and desires of mature consumers. These products not only address age-related concerns such as fine lines, wrinkles, and skin elasticity but also promote overall skin health and vitality. The emphasis is on nurturing and enhancing the natural beauty that comes with age, rather than attempting to reverse the signs of time. This paradigm shift aligns with the evolving consumer sentiment that values self-confidence, self-expression, and a positive attitude towards aging. As a result, aging care products have become a significant segment within the cosmetics industry, reflecting the industry's adaptability to changing consumer preferences and societal values.

The popularity of aging care products is further driven by the demographic composition of aging societies like Japan and Korea, where more than half of the female population is aged 50 or above. This demographic trend has created a substantial consumer base for these products. Moreover, the shift towards embracing aging as a positive transformation is not limited to a specific region; it is a global phenomenon. Consumers worldwide are increasingly seeking products that support graceful aging, promote self-assuredness, and celebrate the unique beauty that comes with maturity (Ehlinger-Martin et al., 2016). As the cosmetics industry continues to respond to these evolving consumer preferences, the market for aging care products is expected to experience sustained growth, making it a focal point for both consumers and cosmetics companies alike.

This growing interest in aging care products is also influenced by advancements in cosmetic technology and research. Modern formulations are increasingly sophisticated, incorporating innovative ingredients and technologies that offer more than just superficial results. These advancements include breakthroughs in understanding the skin's aging process, leading to the development of products that can effectively target specific concerns like hydration, pigmentation, and collagen production. As a result, aging care cosmetics are not only about maintaining a youthful appearance but also about promoting skin health and resilience over time. This scientific approach adds credibility and effectiveness to the products, making them more appealing to a consumer base that is both knowledgeable and discerning.

Furthermore, the marketing and branding of aging care products have evolved to reflect this shift in consumer attitudes. The narrative around these products has moved away from anti-aging rhetoric to a more positive and empowering message. Marketing campaigns now focus on celebrating the beauty of aging, featuring mature models and real-life testimonials that resonate with the target audience. This change in messaging has helped to destigmatize aging and position it as a natural and beautiful part of life. By embracing a more holistic and affirmative perspective on aging, the cosmetics industry is not only catering to the needs of mature consumers but also fostering a broader cultural shift towards acceptance and appreciation of the aging process. This approach aligns with a more inclusive and respectful portrayal of beauty, further strengthening the bond between consumers and brands.

2.7 Empowering Women's Wellness: The Rise of Femtech in Cosmetics

The cosmetics industry is witnessing a groundbreaking development with the emergence of femtech, a fusion of "female" and "technology." (Westwood, 2023). This innovative intersection is dedicated to addressing the distinctive health and wellness concerns that women face throughout their lives, including menstruation, marriage, pregnancy, breastfeeding, menopause, PMS, hormone balance, and skin issues, by leveraging cutting-edge technology and cosmetics expertise. Femtech in cosmetics represents a pioneering approach that prioritizes women's well-being and provides tailored solutions to enhance their overall quality of life.

Femtech's entrance into the cosmetics arena has introduced a range of products that go beyond traditional beauty considerations. These products are specifically formulated to alleviate the unique challenges women encounter due to hormonal fluctuations, skin sensitivities, and other physiological changes. For instance, cosmetics enriched with ingredients designed to soothe menstrual skin irritations or mitigate the effects of hormonal imbalances have gained popularity among women seeking effective and empathetic solutions. Additionally, femtech-driven cosmetics brands are committed to transparency, ensuring that consumers have access to detailed information about product ingredients and their potential impact on women's health. As the femtech market continues to evolve, it is poised for significant growth, driven by a rising awareness of women's wellness needs and an increasingly tech-savvy consumer base. This growth underscores the industry's responsiveness to the multifaceted aspects of women's lives and the ongoing commitment to empowering women through cosmetics.

The femtech movement extends far beyond cosmetics, encompassing a wide spectrum of technologies and services that cater to women's health and well-being. It aligns with broader societal trends of prioritizing women's empowerment, inclusivity, and health equity. The femtech market is projected to experience substantial expansion in the coming years, reflecting the growing recognition of women's unique concerns and the need for innovative, technology-driven solutions. As femtech continues to gain momentum, it is poised to make a lasting impact on the cosmetics industry, offering women a new era of cosmetics products that not only enhance beauty but also contribute to overall health and wellness.

This integration of femtech into the cosmetics industry also signals a shift towards more personalized and holistic approaches to beauty and wellness. The traditional one-size-fits-all model is giving way to products and services that are tailored to individual needs and life stages. This personalization is achieved through the use of advanced technologies such as AI and data analytics, which enable brands to better understand and address the specific concerns of their female consumers. For example, apps that track hormonal cycles can be linked to skincare routines, suggesting products that align with the user's menstrual cycle or menopausal stage. This level of customization not only enhances the effectiveness of the products but also fosters a deeper connection between the brand and the consumer, as it demonstrates a genuine understanding and consideration of women's unique health and beauty needs.

Moreover, the rise of femtech in cosmetics reflects a growing trend towards wellness and self-care, where beauty is perceived as an integral part of "a whole-system approach"(McMillan, 2022). This perspective challenges the conventional view of cosmetics as purely aesthetic and positions them as tools for promoting mental and physical well-being. Femtech products often include ingredients that are beneficial for stress relief, mood improvement, and other aspects of mental health, acknowledging the interconnected nature of physical appearance and inner wellness. As consumers become more aware of the holistic nature of health and beauty, the demand for products that cater to this understanding is likely to increase, positioning femtech as a significant and influential sector within the cosmetics industry. This evolution underscores the industry's ability to adapt to changing consumer priorities and paves the way for a more inclusive and health-focused approach to beauty and wellness.

2.8 The Era of Personal Brands: Rise of Individual-Created Cosmetics Brands

In recent years, a remarkable shift has taken place in the cosmetics industry, marked by the ascent of brands founded by individuals who are not traditional experts or industry insiders. This phenomenon represents a significant departure from the conventional model, where cosmetics brands were predominantly developed by skincare experts, makeup artists, or dermatologists. Instead, these emerging brands are often the brainchildren of individuals with diverse backgrounds, including media personalities, influencers, and even self-taught beauty enthusiasts. The rise of personal brands in cosmetics underscores the transformative power of personal narratives, unique perspectives, and authentic connections with consumers.

These individual-created cosmetics brands have harnessed the influence of social media and digital platforms to establish a direct and authentic relationship with their audience. Through platforms like Instagram, YouTube, and TikTok, founders share their personal beauty journeys, skincare routines, and makeup techniques. This transparency and relatability resonate with consumers who appreciate the genuine, unfiltered insights into beauty and self-care. Furthermore, these founders often leverage their personal stories and experiences to develop products that cater to specific beauty needs, effectively addressing the diverse and evolving demands of their followers.

One notable example is Tiffany Masterson, who gained recognition as a self-proclaimed "skinfluencer." Her journey in skincare led her to create Drunk Elephant, a skincare brand that resonated with consumers seeking simplicity and effectiveness. Similarly, brands like Fenty Beauty by Rihanna and Huda Beauty by Huda Kattan have disrupted the industry by championing inclusivity and diversity in cosmetics. This trend showcases the democratization of beauty, where anyone with a passion for cosmetics can become a driving force in shaping the industry. As consumers increasingly seek authenticity and relatability in the products they purchase, personal brands founded by individuals and manufactured by ODM (Original Design Manufacturing) are likely to remain a powerful and transformative force in the cosmetics landscape (Park et al., 2023).

The success of these personal brands also highlights the shifting dynamics of consumer trust and brand loyalty in the cosmetics industry. In an era where traditional advertising is often met with skepticism, consumers are increasingly drawn to brands with a relatable human face and story. They prefer to invest in products created by individuals they can connect with on a personal level, rather than faceless corporations. This connection is cultivated through ongoing engagement on social media, where founders frequently interact with their audience, solicit feedback, and create a sense of community around their brand (Hodge et al., 2015). This direct interaction not only builds trust but also allows these entrepreneurs to swiftly adapt to consumer needs and trends, giving them a competitive edge in a rapidly evolving market.

Additionally, the rise of personal brands is indicative of a broader trend towards customization and niche marketing in cosmetics. These brands often start by addressing specific gaps in the market or offering solutions to particular beauty challenges that are overlooked by larger companies. This niche focus allows them to cater to underserved segments of the market, such as specific skin types, underrepresented beauty standards, or unique aesthetic preferences. As a result, these brands contribute to a more diverse and inclusive beauty landscape, where consumers can find products that truly resonate with their individual needs and identities. This trend toward personalization and niche targeting is shaping the future of the cosmetics industry, making it more responsive, inclusive, and diverse.

2.9 *Inclusive Business Models: Expanding Cosmetics Markets to Lower-Income Groups*

In alignment with the Sustainable Development Goals (SDGs), the cosmetics industry is experiencing a noteworthy shift toward inclusive business models that aim to extend their reach to the bottom of the pyramid (BOP) or lower-income groups. This strategic approach recognizes the potential of previously underserved consumer segments and aligns with broader social and environmental sustainability objectives. One of the prominent manifestations of this shift is the rise of inclusive business models that prioritize accessibility and affordability. Brands are increasingly developing product lines tailored to the specific needs and budget constraints of lower-income consumers (Pathak & Nichter, 2021). These products are formulated to provide quality beauty and skincare solutions without the premium price tags typically associated with high-end cosmetics. By doing so, cosmetics companies not only tap into a new and potentially vast customer base but also contribute to the democratization of beauty, making quality products accessible to a more diverse audience.

Furthermore, some cosmetics companies are actively engaging with local communities and supporting sustainable sourcing practices. This includes partnerships with small-scale farmers and cooperatives, particularly in regions known for natural ingredient cultivation. By incorporating ethically sourced ingredients and fair-trade practices, these companies not only enhance the quality of their products but also foster economic empowerment and social development in the regions where they operate. The emphasis on inclusive business models reflects a broader commitment within the cosmetics industry to address social inequalities and environmental concerns while simultaneously expanding market reach and fostering sustainable growth.

This shift towards inclusivity also involves innovating distribution channels to reach lower-income consumers. Traditional retail models often fail to penetrate remote or underserved areas, limiting access to quality cosmetics for many. To overcome this barrier, companies are adopting alternative distribution strategies, such as partnering with local vendors, utilizing mobile commerce, and establishing micro-franchise models. These strategies enable cosmetics brands to make their products available in regions that were previously unreachable, ensuring that consumers in these areas have access to the same beauty and skincare options as those in more affluent communities. By diversifying their distribution networks, these companies are not only expanding their customer base but also playing a role in reducing economic disparities.

Moreover, the inclusive business model in the cosmetics industry often goes hand-in-hand with educational initiatives. Brands are investing in community education programs that inform consumers about skincare, hygiene, and beauty practices. These programs are particularly impactful in regions where access to such information is limited. Education empowers consumers to make informed choices about their beauty and wellness, ultimately leading to better health outcomes and increased consumer confidence. Through these educational initiatives, cosmetics companies are not only building brand loyalty but also contributing to the overall well-being and development of the communities they serve. This holistic approach to business demonstrates the industry's evolving ethos, where commercial success is increasingly intertwined with social responsibility and sustainable development.

2.10 Emphasis on Environmental Sustainability and Packaging Innovations

In the contemporary cosmetics landscape, environmental considerations and sustainable packaging have risen to the forefront of industry priorities. Consumers are becoming more conscious of the ecological impact of their beauty products, prompting cosmetics companies to explore innovative solutions for reducing their environmental footprint (Amberg & Fogarassy, 2019).

One noteworthy initiative in this regard is Loop, a pioneering system introduced to combat the issue of plastic waste. Loop's approach revolves around a circular economy model that reimagines the entire lifecycle of a product. Customers purchase products in durable and reusable containers, which are then returned, cleaned, and refilled once empty. This approach significantly reduces single-use plastic packaging, addressing a critical concern for both consumers and the environment. Notably, Loop has garnered support from influential cosmetics companies such as Shiseido and Ion, which have recognized the importance of participating in sustainable initiatives to meet the evolving expectations of eco-conscious consumers.

Beyond Loop, cosmetics companies are proactively investing in research and development to create more sustainable packaging options. This includes exploring biodegradable materials, minimizing excess packaging, and adopting eco-friendly printing techniques. By prioritizing sustainable packaging, companies aim to reduce their carbon footprint and contribute to the global effort to combat plastic pollution. This commitment aligns with the broader trend of environmental consciousness in the cosmetics industry, demonstrating a dedication to environmental stewardship while meeting consumer demand for eco-friendly beauty products (Morea et al., 2021).

Additionally, these environmental sustainability efforts extend to the sourcing and production processes of cosmetics. Many brands are now focusing on creating products with minimal environmental impact, which involves using sustainably sourced ingredients, reducing water usage in production, and implementing energy-efficient manufacturing practices (Bom et al., 2019). These changes are indicative of a shift towards a more holistic approach to sustainability, where every aspect of the product's lifecycle is considered. The use of renewable energy sources in production facilities and the reduction of greenhouse gas emissions are also key components of this strategy. By adopting these practices, cosmetics companies are not only reducing their ecological footprint but also setting a new standard for responsible production in the industry.

The emphasis on environmental sustainability has also given rise to collaborations and partnerships aimed at fostering innovation in sustainable practices. Cosmetics companies are joining forces with environmental organizations, research institutions, and other industries to develop new solutions for sustainable beauty. These collaborations are crucial in driving progress, as they combine diverse expertise and resources to tackle complex environmental challenges. For instance, partnerships aimed at developing new recycling technologies or finding alternative, eco-friendly raw materials can have a significant impact on the industry's sustainability efforts. This collaborative approach reflects a growing recognition within the cosmetics industry that addressing environmental challenges requires collective action and shared responsibility. As a result, these efforts not only contribute to the sustainability of individual brands but also pave the way for a more environmentally responsible future for the entire cosmetics industry.

3 Conclusion: Navigating the Future of Cosmetics Marketing

In conclusion, the cosmetics industry stands at a pivotal juncture, characterized by rapid transformation and shifting consumer dynamics. The trends outlined in this chapter underscore the industry's dynamic nature and the imperative for companies to remain agile in the face of evolving consumer values and expectations. As the era of digital transformation (DX) unfolds, staying attuned to these trends will be essential for crafting and executing successful cosmetics marketing strategies.

From the surge in demand for natural and organic cosmetics to the global spread of clean beauty, the industry is witnessing a redefinition of beauty standards rooted in purity, sustainability, and transparency. Clean beauty certification systems, led by pioneers like Credo Beauty and embraced by major retailers like Sephora, reflect a commitment to meeting the demands of discerning consumers who seek products aligned with their values. Meanwhile, the rise of male grooming, the phasing out of whitening cosmetics, and the exploration of alternative distribution channels all exemplify the industry's adaptability in catering to diverse consumer segments.

Moreover, as aging care products redefine the aging process as a positive transformation and femtech addresses women's unique concerns through technology, the industry is embracing inclusivity and innovation. Brands founded by non-experts and media personalities are reshaping the market, and businesses targeting lower-income groups align with Sustainable Development Goals (SDGs), promoting economic and social inclusivity. Environmental considerations and sustainable packaging, exemplified by initiatives like Loop, are becoming central to cosmetics companies' strategies, reflecting a commitment to environmental sustainability.

In this era of profound change and heightened consumer consciousness, cosmetics companies must embrace these trends as opportunities for growth and differentiation. By aligning their strategies with the evolving values and expectations of consumers, they can thrive in the competitive landscape of the cosmetics industry's digital transformation.

The future of cosmetics marketing will be shaped by the industry's ability to integrate digital innovations and maintain ethical and sustainable practices. The role of technology, particularly in areas like artificial intelligence, augmented reality, and data analytics, will continue to revolutionize how beauty products are marketed and experienced. Virtual try-on apps, personalized skincare recommendations powered by AI, and interactive online shopping experiences are just a few examples of how digital tools can enhance customer engagement and satisfaction. Embracing these technologies will be crucial for brands to stay relevant and connected with their tech-savvy consumer base.

Furthermore, the cosmetics industry continues to navigate the challenges and opportunities presented by social and environmental responsibility. As consumer awareness and expectations around sustainability grow, brands must commit to transparency, ethical sourcing, and reducing their environmental impact. This commitment extends beyond packaging and product formulations to encompass every aspect of the business, from supply chain management to corporate social responsibility initiatives. In doing so, cosmetics companies will not only contribute to a more sustainable and equitable world but also build deeper trust and loyalty among their customers.

Ultimately, the future success of the cosmetics industry will hinge on its ability to navigate these dynamic shifts with agility, innovation, and a profound understanding of evolving consumer needs and values. By placing inclusivity, sustainability, and technological advancement at the forefront, cosmetics brands have the opportunity to forge deep, meaningful connections with consumers, paving the way for a resilient and thriving future in the ever evolving world of beauty and personal care.

References

Amberg, N., & Fogarassy, C. (2019). Green consumer behavior in the cosmetics market. *Resources, 8*(3), 137.

Baird, M. L. (2021). 'Making Black More Beautiful': Black women and the cosmetics industry in the post-civil rights era. *Gender & History, 33*(2), 557–574.

Bom, S., Jorge, J., Ribeiro, H. M., & Marto, J. O. A. N. A. (2019). A step forward on sustainability in the cosmetics industry: A review. *Journal of Cleaner Production, 225*, 270–290.

Borja Guerrero, B., López Pecharromán, A., & Sánchez León, R. C. (2022). Trends in cosmetics: Product packaging at the point of sale. *Cosmetics, 9*(2), 27.

Choi, Y. H., Kim, S. E., & Lee, K. H. (2022). Changes in consumers' awareness and interest in cosmetic products during the pandemic. *Fashion and Textiles, 9*, 1–19.

Coelho, P. M., Corona, B., ten Klooster, R., & Worrell, E. (2020). Sustainability of reusable packaging–Current situation and trends. *Resources, Conservation & Recycling: X, 6*, 100037.

D'Amato, D., Veijonaho, S., & Toppinen, A. (2020). Towards sustainability? Forest-based circular bioeconomy business models in Finnish SMEs. *Forest Policy and Economics, 110*, 101848.

Del Saz-Rubio, M. M. (2019). The pragmatic-semiotic construction of male identities in contemporary advertising of male grooming products. *Discourse & Communication, 13*(2), 192–227.

Ehlinger-Martin, A., Cohen-Letessier, A., Taïeb, M., Azoulay, E., & du Crest, D. (2016). Women's attitudes to beauty, aging, and the place of cosmetic procedures: Insights from the QUEST Observatory. *Journal of Cosmetic Dermatology, 15*(1), 89–94.

Ferreira, M. S., Magalhães, M. C., Oliveira, R., Sousa-Lobo, J. M., & Almeida, I. F. (2021). Trends in the use of botanicals in anti-aging cosmetics. *Molecules, 26*(12), 3584.

Grappe, C. G., Lombart, C., Louis, D., & Durif, F. (2022). Clean labeling: Is it about the presence of benefits or the absence of detriments? Consumer response to personal care claims. *Journal of Retailing and Consumer Services, 65*, 102893.

Hodge, A. C., Romo, Z. G., Medina, I. G., & Fionda-Douglas, A. (2015). Consumer–brand relationships within the luxury cosmetic domain. *Journal of Brand Management, 22*(8), 631–657.

Jang, M. A., & Lee, J. M. (2021). Research on domestic and international industrial trends of functional cosmetics. *Journal of the Korean Applied Science and Technology, 38*(2), 618–627.

Jones, G. (2011). Globalization and beauty: A historical and firm perspective. *EurAmerica, 41*(4), 885–916.

Kumar, S. (2005). Exploratory analysis of global cosmetic industry: Major players, technology and market trends. *Technovation, 25*(11), 1263–1272.

Kumar, V., Ramachandran, D., & Kumar, B. (2021). Influence of new-age technologies on marketing: A research agenda. *Journal of Business Research, 125*, 864–877.

Liu, C. (2019). Men and their groomed body: Understanding personal grooming as both a discursive and embodied practice. *European Journal of Marketing, 53*(5), 1015–1034.

Łopaciuk, A., & Łoboda, M. (2013). Global beauty industry trends in the 21st century. In *Management, Knowledge and Learning International Conference* (pp. 19–21).

McDonald, J. A., Llanos, A. A., Morton, T., & Zota, A. R. (2022). The environmental injustice of beauty products: Toward clean and equitable beauty. *American Journal of Public Health, 112*(1), 50–53.

McMillan, C. (2022). Monitoring female fertility through 'Femtech': The need for a whole-system approach to regulation. *Medical Law Review, 30*(3), 410–433.

Morea, D., Fortunati, S., & Martiniello, L. (2021). Circular economy and corporate social responsibility: Towards an integrated strategic approach in the multinational cosmetics industry. *Journal of Cleaner Production, 315*, 128232.

Mu, J., & Zhang, J. Z. (2021). Seller marketing capability, brand reputation, and consumer journeys on e-commerce platforms. *Journal of the Academy of Marketing Science, 49*(5), 994–1020.

Ngoc, L. T. N., Tran, V. V., Moon, J. Y., Chae, M., Park, D., & Lee, Y. C. (2019). Recent trends of sunscreen cosmetic: An update review. *Cosmetics, 6*(4), 64.

Nguyen, J. K., Masub, N., & Jagdeo, J. (2020). Bioactive ingredients in Korean cosmeceuticals: Trends and research evidence. *Journal of Cosmetic Dermatology, 19*(7), 1555–1569.

Park, Y. W., Hong, P., & Shin, G. C. (2023). Rising and thriving in the post COVID-19 era: A case study of COSMAX, a leader of the Korean cosmetic industry. *Asia Pacific Business Review, 29*(4), 1105–1124.

Pathak, G., & Nichter, M. (2021). Cleanups, confidence, and cosmetics: Marketing beauty in India. *Journal of Consumer Culture, 21*(3), 411–431.

Rawlings, A. V. (2003). Trends in stratum corneum research and the management of dry skin conditions. *International Journal of Cosmetic Science, 25*(1–2), 63–95.

Redondo, G. L. M., Salas, M. F. R., Rojas, M. C., Corrales, D. G., Navarro, E. P., & Barquero, M. R. (2021). Characterization and comparison of quality management systems for cosmetic products in the world. *International Journal of Drug Regulatory Affairs, 9*(3), 47–56.

Shanbhag, S., Nayak, A., Narayan, R., & Nayak, U. Y. (2019). Anti-aging and sunscreens: Paradigm shift in cosmetics. *Advanced Pharmaceutical Bulletin, 9*(3), 348–359.

Siahaan, E. A., Pangestuti, R., Munandar, H., & Kim, S. K. (2017). Cosmeceuticals properties of sea cucumbers: Prospects and trends. *Cosmetics, 4*(3), 26.

Simay, A. E., Wei, Y., Gyulavári, T., Syahrivar, J., Gaczek, P., & Hofmeister-Tóth, Á. (2023). The e-WOM intention of artificial intelligence (AI) color cosmetics among Chinese social media influencers. *Asia Pacific Journal of Marketing and Logistics, 35*(7), 1569–1598.

Su, J., Zhang, Y., & Wu, X. (2023). How market pressures and organizational readiness drive digital marketing adoption strategies' evolution in small and medium enterprises. *Technological Forecasting and Social Change, 193*, 122655.

Underhill, P. (2009). *Why we buy: The science of shopping–updated and revised for the Internet, the global consumer, and beyond*. Simon and Schuster.

Vecino, X., Cruz, J. M., Moldes, A. B., & Rodrigues, L. R. (2017). Biosurfactants in cosmetic formulations: Trends and challenges. *Critical Reviews in Biotechnology, 37*(7), 911–923.

Westwood, H. L. (2023). Reinventing the beauty Myth? FemTech's cost to the consumer. In *FemTech: Intersectional Interventions in Women's Digital Health* (pp. 47–71). Singapore: Springer Nature Singapore.

SPRINGER NATURE

GPSR Compliance

The European Union's (EU) General Product Safety Regulation (GPSR) is a set of rules that requires consumer products to be safe and our obligations to ensure this.

If you have any concerns about our products, you can contact us on ProductSafety@springernature.com

In case Publisher is established outside the EU, the EU authorized representative is:

Springer Nature Customer Service Center GmbH
Europaplatz 3
69115 Heidelberg, Germany

The manufacturer's authorised representative in the EU is Springer Nature Customer Service Centre GmbH, Europaplatz 3, 69115 Heidelberg, Germany. If you have any concerns regarding our products, please contact ProductSafety@springernature.com

Printed and bound by CPI Group (UK) Ltd, Croydon, CR0 4YY
30/09/2026
02225300-0004